Erratic Wandering

Explorer's Hiking Guide to Astonishing Boulders in Maine, New Hampshire and Vermont

Jan & Christy Butler

"Do not go where the path may lead, go instead where there is not a path and leave a trail."

-Ralph Waldo Emerson-

"Erratic Wandering" Copyright © 2018 by Jan & Christy Butler

All rights reserved. No part of this book may be reproduced in any form or by any electronic or mechanical means including information storage and retrieval systems without permission in writing from the author.

Many outdoor activities by their very nature involve exposure to possible hazards and unknown or changing variables such as trail erosion, obstructions, variance of weather, etc. The authors have done their best to ensure that all the information contained in *Erratic Wandering* is as accurate as possible. They cannot accept responsibility for any loss, injury, or inconvenience sustained by readers as a result of information or advice contained in the book. Hikers need to be respectful of private property and go no further should posted signs be encountered.

In cases where the information presented appears to be in error, or where material has become dated and needs updating, please contact the author at: www.erraticwandering.com.

ISBN-13: 978-1540569875 (CreateSpace-Assigned)
ISBN-10: 154056987X
Printed by CreateSpace: www.createspace.com

Photography & Illustrations by Christy Butler

Cover Photo: **Mowgli Boulder** .N43°06' 00.1" W71°10' 29.9"
Split Rock Trail - Pawtuckaway State Park. Nottingham N.H.

Back Cover: **Elephant Head** N44°12' 52.1" W71°24' 28.4"
Route-302, Crawford Notch State Park. N.H.

Wally Rock (Painted Rock) N43°49'27.3"W69°50'51.3"

My undying love and admiration goes to **Jan Butler**, with her awesome patience, who shared so many WOW experiences and who through her eyes greatly enhanced the discoveries for the *Erratic Wandering* saga. How many times can you find Jan? Count them…. that is about one ice cream or coffee roll per photo.

If you're going to write a book, it is good to have the enthusiasm of a prolific author and hiker like **Russell Dunn** on your side. The advantage of previously creating ***Connecticut Waterfalls*** and ***Rockachusetts*** with Russell provided me the zest to create ***Erratic Wandering***. So many thanks Russ for the partnerships, friendship and the journey. Russell's latest title *"****Rambles to Remarkable Rocks****: An Explorer's Hiking Guide to Amazing Boulders of the Greater Capital Region, Catskills, & Shawangunks."*

One last thanks is to **Jim Boyle** who has gusto or zing for several impromptu forays into unknown New England jungles, with uncertain outcomes and to see each venture through to its finish. Also, thanks for buying the coffee after my suggestion is followed *"I forgot my Wallet!* ☺ "

New Hampshire

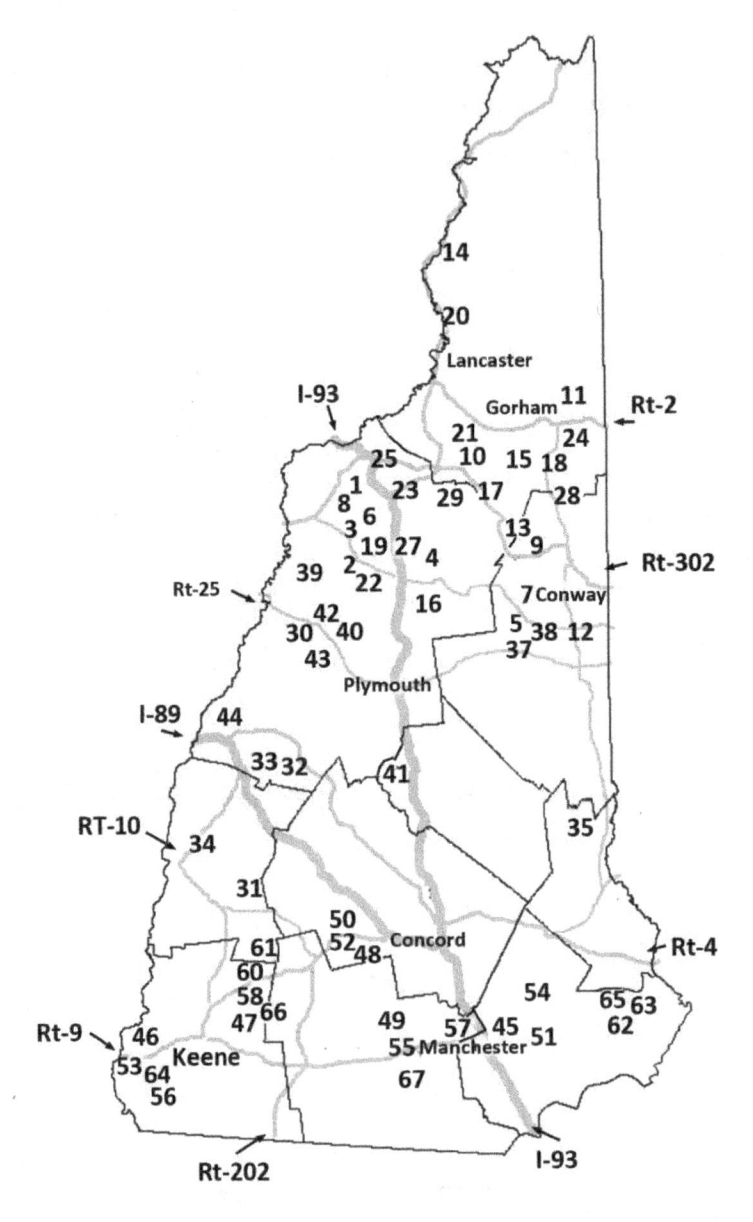

Map not to Scale - For reference only

New Hampshire - North - White Mountains

1. Admiral Dewey Profile: Artist's Bluff (Franconia Notch)
2. Agassiz Boulder Basin (North Woodstock)
3. Balanced Rock: Bells Cascade (North Woodstock)
4. Big Rock Boulder Campground (Lincoln)
5. Big Rock Caves: Mt. Mexico (Albany)
6. Bosie Rock: Franconia Notch (Franconia)
7. Boulder Trail (Albany)
8. Cannon Rock (Franconia Notch)
9. Cote Boulder, Cathedral & White Horse Ledge (North Conway)
10. Elephant Head Rock (Crawford Notch)
11. Fish Rock (Shelburne)
12. Foss Mountain Erratics: Upper Saco Valley Land Trust (Easton)
13. Frog Rock-Painted Rock (Glen)
14. Frog Rock-Painted Rock (Stratford)
15. Glen Boulder (Pinkham Notch)
16. Goodrich Boulder & Davis Boulders (Waterville Valley)
17. Hart's Ledge Boulders (Bartlett)
18. Imp Profile Rock: Imp Mountain (Beans Purchase)
19. Indian Head Profile: Mt Pemigewasset (Lincoln)
20. Jeremy's Boulders: Fay Allin Farm (Lancaster)
21. Martha Washington Profile (Crawfords Purchase)
22. Mummies The (North Woodstock)
23. Old Lady Watcher Profile (Franconia Notch)
24. Old Man Of the Valley (Shelburne)
25. Pine Hill Trails Summit & Teapot Boulder (Littleton)
26. Rest Area Boulder (Woodstock)
27. The Flume Glacial Boulders (Lincoln)
28. Washington Profile Boulder (Jackson)
29. Willey's House Boulders (Crawford Notch)

New Hampshire – Central

30. Baker River Rock (Wentworth)
31. Balance Rock: Pillsbury State Park (Washington)
32. Balance Rock: Ragged Mountain (Andover)
33. Cooks Conservation Property Trails (New London)
34. Elephant Rock (Newport)
35. Franklin Piece Lake Boulder (Antrim)

36. Little Brother Profile (Milton)
37. Madison Boulder (Madison)
38. Ordination Rock (Tamworth)
39. Papoose Rock – Holts Ledge: (Lyme Center)
40. Pound Rocks (Rumney)
41. Rest Stop Boulder: Interstate I-93, Exit-22 South (Tilton)
42. Rumney Boulders (Rumney)
43. Sculptured Rocks (Groton)
44. Tipping Rock (Lebanon)

New Hampshire - Southern

45. Butterfield Boulder (Windham)
46. Chesterfield Gorge (Chesterfield)
47. East Side Trails: Harris Center (Hancock)
48. Erratic: Old Concord Rd (Henniker)
49. Frog Rock (New Boston)
50. House Rock (Hillsborough)
51. Indian Rock (Windham)
52. Keystone Bridges: (Keene, Gilsum, Stoddard, Hillsborough,Keene)
53. Madame Sherri's Castle (Chesterfield)
54. Pawtuckaway Park (Nottingham)
54a. *Area 51*
54b. *Natural Area*
54c. *North Marsh*
54d. *Round Pond*
54e. *Split Rock Trail*
55. Pulpit Rock-Indian Rock (Bedford)
56. Revolutionary Rock (Richmond)
57. Rock Rimmon a.k.a. Rock Raymond (Manchester)
58. Rye Pond (South Stoddard)
59. Simonds Rock a.k.a.Pennichuck Rock (Merrimack)
60. Stoddard Power line Boulders (Stoddard)
61. Stoddard Rocks: Highland Lake Conservation (Stoddard)
62. The Rinks Boulder (Exeter)
63. Thompson Farm Boulder (Durham)
64. Tippin Rock (Swanzey)
65. Vincent Rock a.k.a. Big Rock (Epping)
66. Willards Pond Balance Rock (Antrim)
67. Wolf Rock (Mason)

Tipping Rocks - Shirley Hill – Goffstown: N42°59' 18.1" W71° 34' 07.9"

(Top Photo) Once a center piece on the lavish and sprawling grounds of the Shirley Hill House Resort (1870 -1938), the rocks were a main attraction atop of Shirley Hill with its panoramic view and a cool breeze for guests to languish about. The resort was demolished after extensive damage from the 1938 hurricane.

(Bottom Photo) Only the rocks remain along with their spectacular view, the pavilions, picnic tables, and the resort vacationers are all gone without a trace.

Located on private property – no directions provided.

Vermont

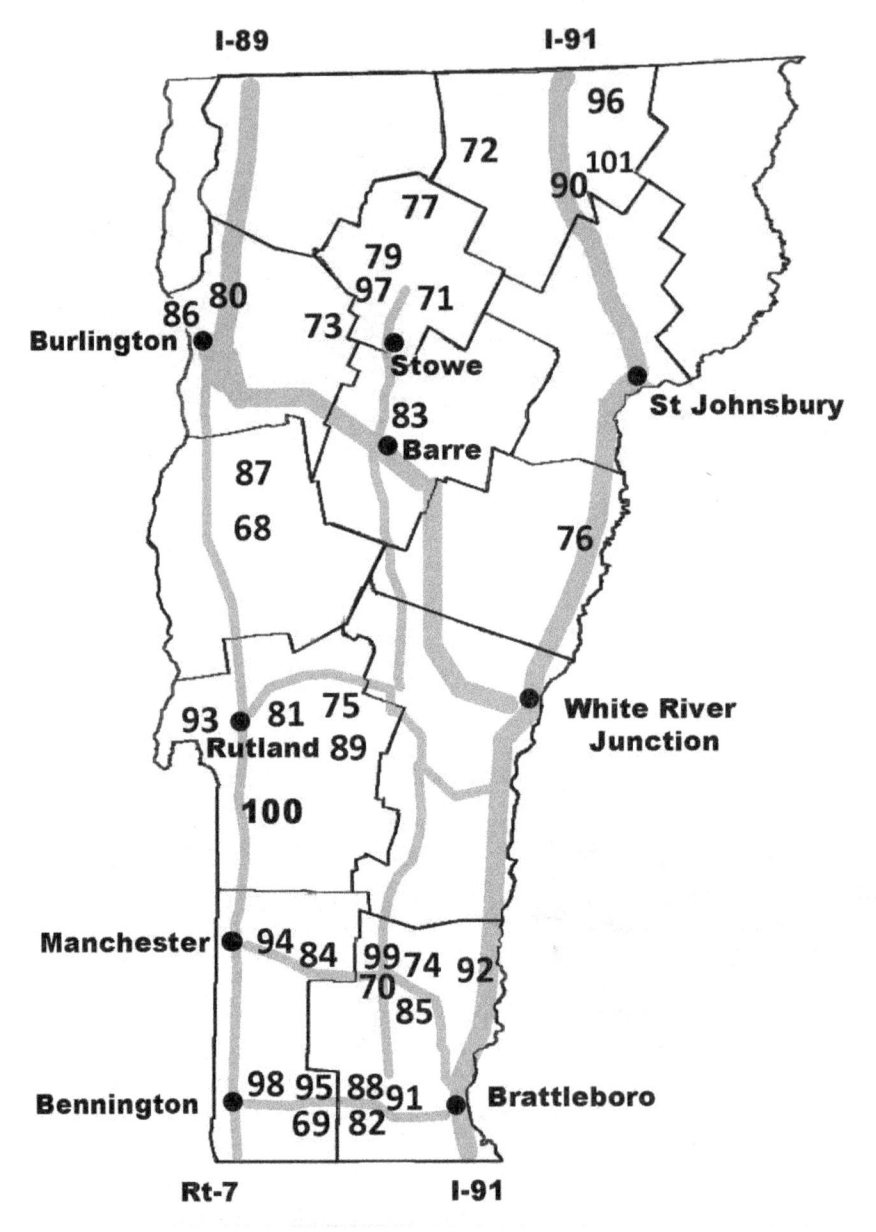

I-89   I-91

96
72
101
77   90
79
97   71
80
86   73
Burlington
Stowe
83
Barre
87
68
76
93 81 75
Rutland 89
100
94 84 99 74 92
Manchester   70
85
98 95 88 91
Bennington   69 82   Brattleboro

St Johnsbury

White River Junction

Rt-7   I-91

MAP Not to Scale – For Reference Only

Vermont

68. Abbey Pond Boulders (Middlebury)
69. American Legion Balance Rock (Readsboro)
70. Balance Rock (Jamaica)
71. Balance Rock: Mt Elmore (Lake Elmore)
72. Balance Rock (Westfield)
73. Cantilever Rock: Mt. Mansfield (Underhill)
74. Creature Boulders (Grafton)
75. DEKD Boulders: Appalachian Trail (Killington)
76. Devils Den - Wright's Mountain: (Bradford)
77. Devils Gulch: Long Trail (Eden)
78. Devil's Rock: Lake Willoughby (Westmore)
79. Dog Head Rock (Johnson)
80. Ethan Allan Park Boulders (Burlington)
81. Green Mountain Lodge Ruins (Killington)
82. Green Mountain Giant (Whitingham)
83. Hope Cemetery (Barre)
84. Indian Head-Painted Rock (Windham)
85. Jamaica Ball Field (Jamaica)
86. Lone Rock Point (Burlington)
87. Lord's Prayer Rock a.k.a Bristol Rock (Bristol)
88. Medburyville Bouldrs (West Wilmington)
89. Mouse Rock-Painted Rock (Killington)
90. Mt Hor Boulders-Willoughby State Forest: (Sutton)
91. Perched Rock Brickhouse Road (Whitingham)
92. Petroglyphs: Bellows Falls-Town of Rockingham
93. Pine Hill Park Glacial Erratic (Rutland)
94. Power Line Boulders (Windham)
95. Searsburg Boulders (Searsburg
96. Sentinel Rock (Westmore)
97. Smuggler's Notch Vermont
98. Split Rock: Appalachian Trail (Woodford)
99. Target Rock (Grafton)
100. White Cliffs Ice Beds - Cairns (Wallingford)
101. Willoughby Lake *The Boulders* (Westmore)

Maine

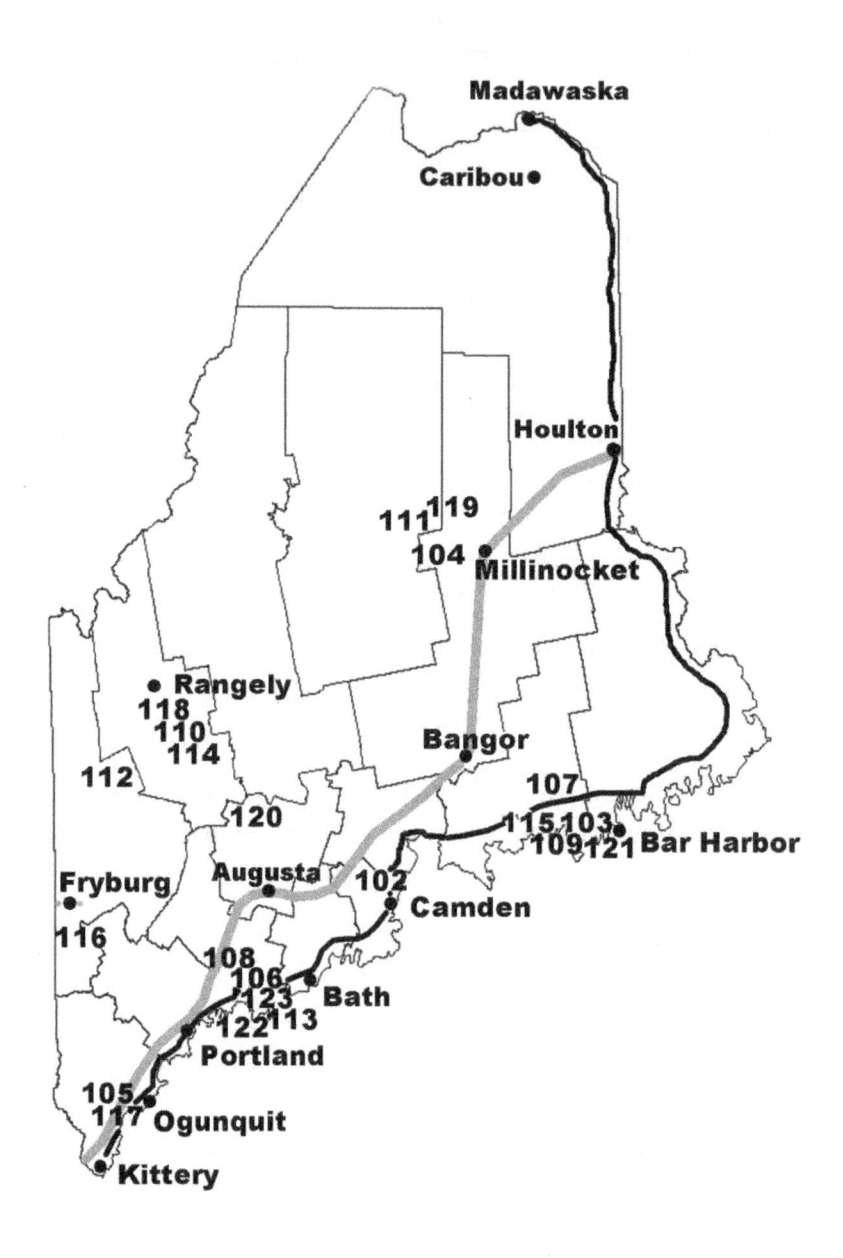

MAP Not to Scale – For Reference Only

Maine

102. Balance Rock: Fernald's Neck Preserve (Lincolnville-Camden)
103. Balance Rock: Shore Walk (Bar Harbor)
104. Balance Rock Upper Jo-Mary Lake: (Millinocket)
105. Balance Rock: Orris Falls Conservation (South Berwick)
106. Big Green Thing-Painted (Brunswick)
107. Big Rock: Little Webb Pond: (Waltham)
108. Bradbury Mountain Boulders (Pownal)
109. Bubble Rock: Acadia National Park (Mt Desert Island)
110. Daggett Rock (Phillips)
111. Debsconeag Wilderness- Ice Cave
112. Devil's Den (Andover)
113. Flag Rock-Painted Rock (Phippsburg)
114. Gnome Rock House-Painted Rock (Avon)
115. Jack-O-Lantern Rock-Painted Rock (North Ellsworth)
116. Jockey's Cap (Fryeburg)
117. Kenyon Hill Preserve (South Berwick)
118. Piazza Rock Appalachian Trail (Sandy River Plantation)
119. Pockwockamus Rock-Painted Rock (Baxter State Park)
120. Snapper Rock- Sanders Hill (Rome)
121. The Beehive; Acadia National Park (Bar Harbor)
122. The Pebble: Curtis Farm (Brunswick)
123. Wally Rock-Painted Rock (Phippsburg)

Permanent Stone Pick-up Truck - N44° 22' 34.69" W72° 29' 43.56"

In tribute to the fatigued, overgrown, abandoned, rusty old truck genre readily seen through-out Vermont's back fields and roads. Vermont sculptor and stonemason Chris Miller in 2012 completed a 18 ton crafted curiosity; it sits upon his property situated on a back country road in Calais for people to discover.

Visit Chris Miller Studio for more information on his Design Process for Wood and Stone Sculpture or Stone Wall, Terraces and Patios.

E-mail: chris@chrismillerstudio.com *or* http://chrismillerstudio.com

I really cannot imagine a mile thick sheet of ice! However, as the story goes, evidently the glacier plowed the boulders, rubble and mountain remnants southwards; upon receding, it lifted the icy blade and dropped a fair share of glacial erratic's across northern New England. Indubitably, you will find and hopefully enjoy many other boulders that are not presented here, which is terrific, for that is what we want this book to achieve, for you to get out and explore.

New England's *"urban wildernesses"* are four season destinations that require you to think safely and ecologically. Becoming completely lost or blundering through a mucky bog can be completely avoided. A compass and GPS devise are also great items to keep your adventure safe and happy, learn how to use them before you venture out. Ask and tell people what your plans are and familiarize yourself to the area through topographical maps, Google Earth and other search engine results. In addition, readers are reminded to stay alert in "urban" settings where a matrix of unmarked paths are constantly being created by "someone." This can add to overall confusion, especially with your first visit to a new location—another reason why GPS coordinates prove so invaluable.

Practice environmental etiquette; Carry in and Carry Out all your trash, no fires or camping allowed other than in designated areas. Plan and prepare for all your outings with good hiking boots and proper clothing, bring water, some energy or emergency foods, matches, flashlight and a first aid kit stashed into a fanny pack are good considerations.

The selection of titles or names for many of these boulders can vary. Boulderer's have more often than not, provided me with multiple, colorful and sometime humorous labels, often to the same boulder with many moniker's usually relating to a particular boulder challenge or its various climbing routes. For my sanity, I have labeled all GPS coordinates numerically and usually with some sort of a name. Some names are created and attached in the moment; others are used with historical distinction or were positivity identified via the status quo of answers to questions.

Hikers today are increasingly using GPS-related programs and devices for navigation. Unlike roads and trails that can be altered, repositioned or destroyed, GPS coordinates are not subject to the whims of humans or the alteration of nature. Therefore, GPS latitude and longitude coordinates have validity that will remain unchanged.

Global Positioning System (GPS) coordinates presented in this book are given in *Degrees-Minutes-Seconds* using a map Datum-*WGS 84*. Which particular format utilized is not as important, but conversion to additional formats may need to be performed depending on the application or devise you use or prefer. Matching a device for various formats are often found under settings, simply set your preference to degree-decimals or degrees, minutes, seconds etc.

A dedicated hand-held GPS device is probably your best or most reliable GPS receiver; GPS devices such as automotive, camera or cell phones often do not have the sensitivity for deep forested, mountainous terrain or battery longevity. As a tool, GPS devices function differently for off-road than turn for turn with city street addresses. There will be no step by step turns for trails or bushwhacking terrain towards a destination. Off-road GPS definitely will show your present location to your destination only. Also, specialized topographical maps can be uploaded to dedicated GPS devices which will show the terrain off road and not a blank screen after the road ends. One can construct a route within mapping applications, but maps from kiosks or web sites will be your guide.

We encourage readers to utilize the GPS coordinates we have provided as a way of reconnoitering locations prior to making an actual visit. This can be done through mapping applications such as Google Earth, Google Maps or other topographical mapping applications and devices. In doing so, you will find that having an increased understanding of the type of terrain you'll be encountering can help in preparation for a hike, provide insight to time expectations, identify other points of interest nearby, and overall create a safer experience through awareness.

In most of the photographs shown, a human presence has been included, this is done intentionally. A person standing within a photograph or next to a boulder provides you a sense scale and its dimension. Without one, there is no way to form conclusions or valid estimates about the rock's size dimensions.

One last and extremely important observation, in the spring into summer, a very good bug repellant or even a meshed head-net may be required. Also, think ticks! Body checks after a hike could save you from sickness by removing ticks before they embed into your skin. If any tick is found implanted, use a safe removal tool or procedure, watch the site, if it produces a rash or you start to feel ill with fever, body ache or flu like symptoms seek medical attention.

New Hampshire - Northern

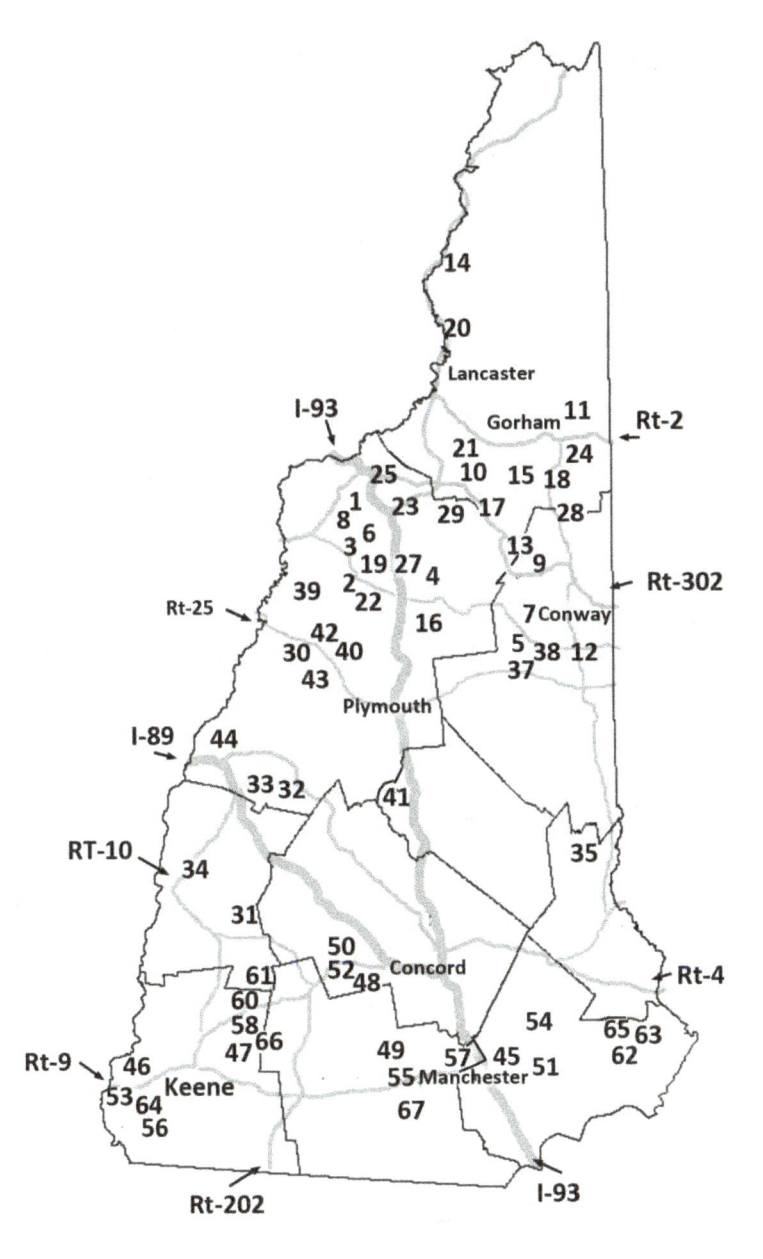

Map not to Scale - For reference only

New Hampshire - Northern

1. Admiral Dewey Profile: Artist's Bluff (Franconia Notch)
2. Agassiz Boulder Basin (North Woodstock)
3. Balanced Rock: Bells Cascade (North Woodstock)
4. Big Rock Boulder Campground (Lincoln)
5. Big Rock Caves: Mt. Mexico (Albany)
6. Bosie Rock: Franconia Notch (Franconia)
7. Boulder Trail (Albany)
8. Cannon Rock (Franconia Notch)
9. Cote Boulder, Cathedral & White Horse Ledge (North Conway)
10. Elephant Head Rock (Crawford Notch)
11. Fish Rock (Shelburne)
12. Foss Mountain Erratic's: Upper Saco Valley Land Trust (Easton)
13. Frog Rock-Painted Rock (Glen)
14. Frog Rock-Painted Rock (Stratford)
15. Glen Boulder (Pinkham Notch)
16. Goodrich Boulder & Davis Boulders (Waterville Valley)
17. Hart's Ledge Boulders (Bartlett)
18. Imp Profile Rock: Imp Mountain (Beans Purchase)
19. Indian Head Profile: Mt Pemigewasset (Lincoln)
20. Jeremy's Boulders: Fay Allin Farm (Lancaster)
21. Martha Washington Profile (Crawfords Purchase)
22. Mummies The (North Woodstock)
23. Old Lady Watcher Profile (Franconia Notch)
24. Old Man of the Valley (Shelburne)
25. Pine Hill Trails Summit & Teapot Boulder (Littleton)
26. Rest Area Boulder (Woodstock)
27. The Flume Glacial Boulders (Lincoln)
28. Washington Profile Boulder (Jackson)
29. Willey's House Boulders (Crawford Notch)

1. Admiral Dewey Profile:

Admiral Dewey Profile – Franconia Notch, NH

Location: Artist's Bluff. Franconia Notch (Grafton County)
Delorme Atlas & Gazetteer-New Hampshire: p.43, D-11
Parking GPS: N44° 10' 41.08" W71° 41' 48"
Destination GPS: N44° 10' 44.50" W71° 41' 38.38" (View Point)
Wow Factor: 6 **Accessibility:** Roadside viewing, short walk 0.1 mile

Information: The profile is named for resemblance to the U.S. Admiral George Dewey who visited here in the early 1800's. It is found on Artist's Bluff western end and can be best seen from the southern road side on Route-18 (Profile Road) near Echo Lake parking area. Looking at the bluff, the profile will be located on the left end with a very prominent chin, nose, eye-brow and forehead. (Note the arrow.) The 1.5 mile loop trail to the summit, has usually been called the "Bald Mountain-Artist's Bluff Path," but in 2011 it was renamed the "Veterans Trail" in honor of New Hampshire's military veterans, if not for all veterans in general.

Directions: Traveling in Franconia Notch on Interstate I-93, use Exit-34C, Route-18, for Echo Lake Beach-Peabody Slopes-Canon Mountain. Heading west on Route-18 you will find the Echo Lake parking area the quickest and most convenient, however sometimes is manned by attendants collecting a fee. From this parking area walking back 0.1 mile towards Exit-34C, this will bring you to a good viewing spot and just across the road is the trail head if you desire to climb Artist's Bluff.

2. Agassiz Boulder Basin

Agassiz Boulder Basin – Indian Leap- North Woodstock, NH

Location: Woodstock (Grafton County)
Delorme Atlas & Gazetteer-New Hampshire: p.43, I-11
Parking GPS: N44° 1' 44.20" W71° 43' 3.20"
Destination GPS: N44° 1' 43" W71°43' 4.00"
Wow Factor: 6 Accessibility: Easy short walk 0.1 mile

Information: *Jean Louis Rodolphe Agassiz* a.k.a. Louis Agassiz was a pioneering Harvard geologist. The gorge is named after him for Louis Agassiz was the first to propose that continental glaciers and not the forces of floods is what polished the bedrock and carried the enormous boulders to distant places. The gorge has small waterfalls, circular potholes and is considered one of the premier swimming areas. The Agassiz Basin is also known as Indian Leap, legend suggest that young Native American braves leaped across the gorge from a distinctly pedestal rock as a test of their courage.

Recent changes of ownership have altered the Agassiz Boulders for parking and hiking. The previous landmark Govoni's Italian Restaurant has been totally removed and replaced by a barrier of boulders along with the posting of "Private Property" signs. In addition, the two bridges above and below *Indian Leap Rock* have been removed and require one to rock hop to cross Mount Moosilauke Brook. Crossing is safest upstream and not during high water. The gorge is steep and rocks can be slippery. While parking and visitation does not seem to be prohibited, access is by the eastern parking area still allows viewing of *Indian Leap* Rock and access to the swimming hole.

Old Postcard of "Indian Leap" Agassiz Boulder Basin

Directions: At the intersection of Rt-112 and Rt-3 in the center of North Woodstock, follow Rt-112 west for 1.6 miles. Parking on left.

3. Balanced Rock: Bells Cascade

Balance Rock – North Woodstock, NH

Location: North Woodstock (Grafton County)
Delorme Atlas & Gazetteer-New Hampshire: p.43, I 11
Parking GPS: N44° 02' 04.6" W71° 41' 57.9"
Destination GPS: N44° 02' 29.6" W71° 42' 19.7"   **Wow Factor:** 7
Accessibility: Moderate hiking 1.0 mile on access road, last 100 yards

being difficult with off trail bushwhacking downstream to rock location.
Contact: Pemigewasset Ranger Station 71 White Mountain Drive Campton, NH 03223 (603) 536-6100 https://www.fs.usda.gov/whitemountain
White Mountain Visitor Center I-93, Exit 32 200 Kancamagus Highway North Woodstock, NH (603) 745-3816

Information: In the late 19th and early 20th century, Bells Cascade along with its Balanced Rock, were popular hiking destinations and the subject of postcards in the late 1800's and early 1900's. This vintage tourist location used to be heavily visited, but like other destinations has slipped away into obscurity. Bells Cascade pours down over a series of several ledges, with churning pools and small waterfalls before flowing pass the perched Balanced Rock. Access can be perilous with slick mossy covered wet boulders along with steep humus embankments making footings a concern for safety and to maintain a limited environmental impact.

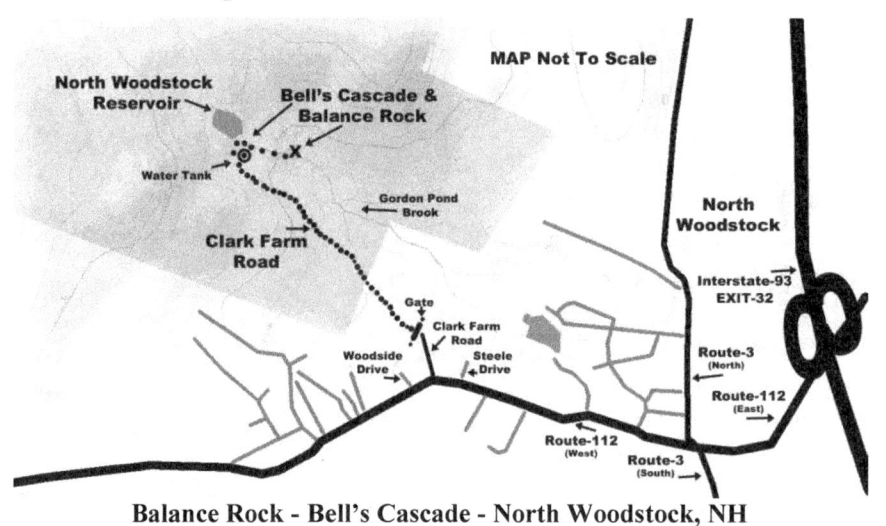

Postcard sent in July 1907

Balance Rock - Bell's Cascade - North Woodstock, NH

Directions: From the junction of Route-3 and Route-112 in North Woodstock, follow Route-112 west for 0.6 mile to the Clark Farm Road on your right. The gated access road to the North Woodstock Reservoir, water tower and the top of Bells Cascades is at the end of Clark Farm Road. There are some posted road restrictions by the U.S. Forestry Service to prevent damage to the road. No Motor Vehicles beyond the gate and Do Not Block Gate. Otherwise, non-motorized use appears to be welcome. We were permitted to park near this gate without blocking it; the area is posted by the land owner and may not be feasible all the time. Alternative parking may require one to park down towards Route-112 at the beginning of Clark Farm Road and walk up the extra 0.1 mile to the access road.

4. Big Rock Campground Boulder

Big Rock Boulder – Lincoln, NH

Location: Lincoln. (Grafton County)
Delorme Atlas & Gazetteer-New Hampshire: p.43, I-14
Parking GPS: N44° 2' 49.18" W71° 33' 34.19"
Destination GPS: N44° 2' 52.30" W71° 33' 34.50"
Wow Factor: 8 **Accessibility:** Short walk 0.1 mile.
Contact Info: Big Rock Campground. White Mountain National Forest. Route 112 Lincoln NH 03251 (603) 745-3816
White Mountain National Forest. 71 White Mountain Drive. Campton NH 03223 (603)536-6100 www.fs.usda.gov/whitemountain

Information: This large 20-foot glacial erratic is somewhat the center piece for the "Big Rock" campground located off the Kancamagus Highway. This seasonal campground is normally mid-May to mid- October; all sites are first-come, first-served basis. Recreational activities, camping or trailhead parking may require local fees or permits and are available as annual, weekly or daily passes. We visited during off season and just visited the rock without disturbing anyone.

Directions: From Exit-32, at the interchange of Interstate I-93 and Route-112 in North Woodstock, follow Route-112 east through the center Lincoln, pass the Loon Mountain Ski Resort and into White Mountain National Forest better known as the *Kancamagnus Highway* for 7.4 miles. The gated entry to the campground will be on your left. In addition, two miles before the campground is the Lincoln Woods Visitor and Information Center with facilities.

5. Big Rock Caves – Mt Mexico

Big Rock Caves - (interior looking out) – Albany, NH

Location: Albany (Carroll County)
Delorme Atlas & Gazetteer-New Hampshire: p.41, B-5
Parking GPS: N43° 54' 30.40" W71° 20' 29.40"
Destination GPS: N43° 55' 36.30" W71° 19' 18.00"
Wow Factor: 10 **Accessibility:** Moderate Hike 4..2 miles RT
Contact: Saco Ranger District 33 Kancamagus Highway Conway, NH 03818 (603) 447-5448

Information: Definition for a *cave*; *"is a hollow place in the ground, specifically a natural underground space large enough for a human to enter."* However, one will find that the *Big Rock Caves* are not underground, but entirely above ground. Of interest for me, is this humongous erratic, in some manner, split into sections that came to rest against each other creating several "shelter caves" found on this eastern hillside location. For this particular style, these are the largest of these slab-boulder caves that I have found in New England. There are a couple more smaller and less dynamic caves as you walk around this remarkable boulder.

Mt. Mexico located in the Sandwich Range of the White Mountains has a relatively low 2,000-foot, wooded summit with no mentionable vistas. Access to the *Big Rock Caves* begins at the trailhead on Route-113A, you will begin on the Cabin Trail and initially you feel like you are walking up someone's driveway. Continue for 0.3 mile and where the Cabin Trail bears left, you bear right onto the *Big Rock Trail* hike1.0 mile up onto the summit and then descending 0.4 mile down the other side to the *Big Rock Caves*. The trail utilizes blue rectangular markings; hiking up the slope is easy to moderate, with returning back from the Big Rock Caves being slightly steeper. To return from the Big Rock Caves retrace your approach or continue down the Big Rock Trail 0.1 mile to the Whiting Brook trail. From here you can turn left and rejoin the Cabin Trail to return back to the trailhead or take a right and keep bearing right to use the Bickford Trail. I have not hiked either loop.

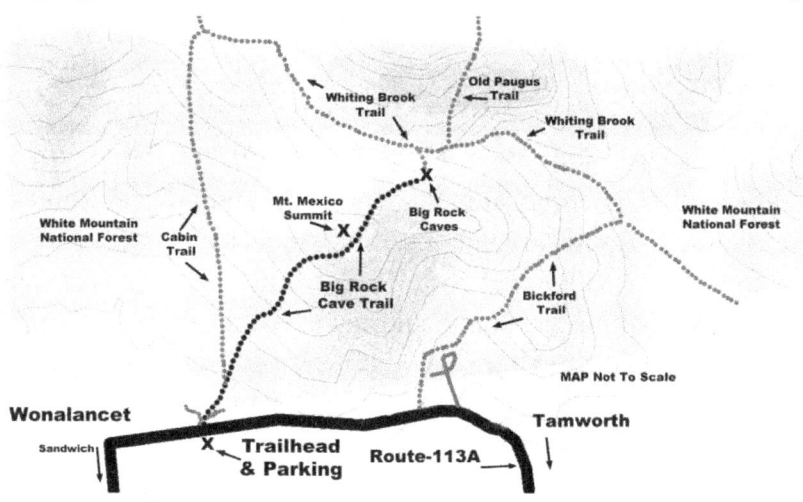

Big Rock Caves Map – Albany, H

Big Rock Cave (front) - Mt Mexico - Albany NH

Big Rock Caves (side) - Mt Mexico - Albany, NH

Directions: In Chocorua, at the junction of Route-16 and Route-113, travel west on Route-113 for 3.0 miles into Tamworth. Turn right onto Route-113A and travel north for 6.3 miles towards Wonalancet. The trailhead will be seen on the north side of the road with roadside parking across the street for several cars, if you pass the trailhead the road will have a sharp 90° bend and head south, you have gone too far, return 0.4 mile for the trailhead.

6. Boise Rock

Boise Rock – Franconia Notch, NH

Location: Franconia Notch (Grafton County)
Delorme Atlas & Gazetteer-New Hampshire: p.43, E-11
Parking GPS: N44° 09' 08.9" W71° 40' 41.7"
Destination GPS: N44° 09' 09.9" W71° 40' 41.2"
Wow Factor: 6 **Accessibility:** Roadside attraction viewing, 100yards.

Information: Located within Franconia Notch State Park Boise Rock is a long term historical landmark as well as a unique glacial erratic. Below is the folk lore story of how the rock became known as Boise Rock. There are no parking fees.

"Thomas Boise, a noted teamster of this region was sledding through the Notch in mid-winter, soon after the first road was built. Overtaken by a fierce snowstorm, he was unable to continue on. Realizing he must take drastic action to survive, he killed and skinned his horse. Crawling under the overhang of this rock, he wrapped himself in the hide and spent the night. Men sent out the next day to search for him found Tom still alive but encased in the frozen hide that had to be cut away with axes in order to release him."

Directions: Access to *Boise Rock* exit is from **Interstate I-93 north bound only,** south bound traffic will need to travel south to Exit-34A and use the Route-3 Flume Gorge and Park Visitor Center interchange to reverse direction back onto I-93 North. Once north bound on I-93 travel 3.25 miles and exit at the Boise Rock attraction.

7. Boulder Trail

BT-10 – Cracked Boulder- Albany, NH

Location: Albany (Carroll County)
Delorme Atlas & Gazetteer-New Hampshire: p.45, J- 8
Parking GPS: N44° 0' 17.90" W71° 14' 21.10"
Destination GPS: As listed below.
Accessibility: Moderate 3.0 mile loop trail, well-marked. Seasonal fee,
Contact: Saco Ranger District 33 Kancamagus Highway Conway, NH 03818 (603) 447-5448 www.fs.usda.gov

Information: Appropriately named, the *Boulder Loop Trail* is a 3.0 mile loop with its trailhead located near the Albany Covered Bridge on Passaconaway Road. Being a loop hike, the trail will provide a host of interesting boulders and ledges that will offer great views regardless which way you proceed. Many seem to prefer a counter-clockwise direction citing the uphill climb is shorter or is less steep. From the beginning and within in the first 0.2 mile to where the trail will split, some impressive boulders are located on the trail or within a short distance from it. The boulder fields appear to be on the lower elevations below the cliffs. This hike is a popular family hike requiring a time allotment of 2–3 hours and is best used between May and October. Dogs are allowed, but are required to be leashed.

Directions: In Conway at the junction of Route-16 and Route-112 (Kancamagus Highway), follow Route-112 for 6.2 miles; turn right for the Albany Covered Bridge. Crossing the bridge is usually seasonal and if is closed park and walk across for the trailhead.

BT—3 – Shelter Rock – Albany, NH

BT-1: N44° 0' 19.40" W71° 14' 17.50" (Split Rock) *WOW-6*
As with many such rocks in New England, this rock having been cleaved–in–half, with the remaining segments lying in place.

BT-2: N44° 0' 18.20" W71° 14' 15.80" (Loaf Boulder) *WOW-7*
An elongated rock with the appearance of a loaf of bread where the end section has been sliced off.

BT-3: N44° 0' 20.10" W71° 14' 15.90" (Shelter Rock) *WOW-7*
Large rock with end overhang, suitable to build an enclosed lean-to shelter.

BT-4: N44° 0' 20.10" W71° 14' 15.50" (Pebble Boulder) *WOW-6*
A massive boulder formation, not overly impressive, but still remarkable.

BT-5: N44° 0' 20.10" W71° 14' 16.90" (The Walls) *WOW-7*
A sheer cliff facing 25-30-feet in height, along with a large boulder 14-feet high which runs parallel for 100-feet creating a rift valley between them.

BT-6: N44° 0' 18.70" W71° 14' 13.90" (The Marble) *WOW-6*
Roundish large boulder 16 feet in height located on trail.

BT-7: N44° 0' 18.20" W71° 14' 13.20" (Bear's Den) *WOW-7*
Two large boulders, with the larger 16-feet taller and leaning atop a smaller boulder creating a passageway or shelter cave.

BT-8: N44° 0' 18.10" W71° 14' 9.60" (Campground Rock) *WOW-6*
Large squarest 14-16-foot boulder, located just above campground area.

BT-9: N44° 0' 17.60" W71° 14' 8.40" (Profile Rock) *WOW-7*
A large chuck of rock with its left end having a prominent stoic face profile.

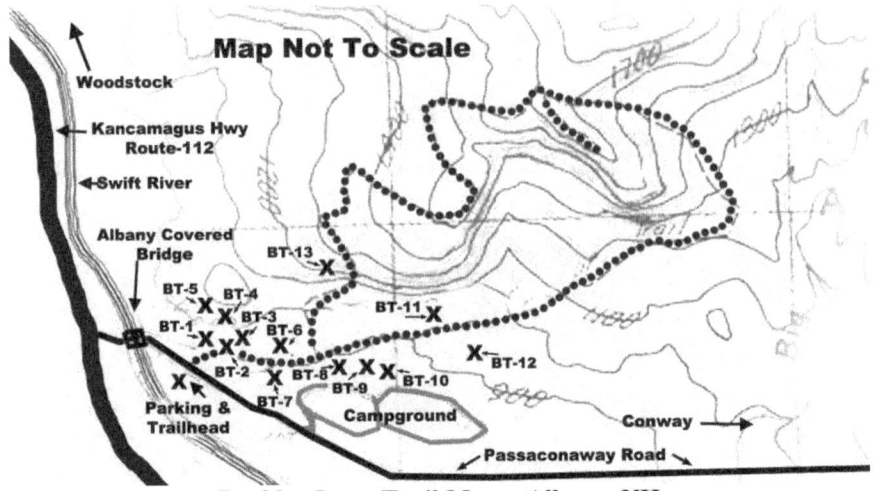

Boulder Loop Trail Map – Albany, NH

BT-9 – Profile Rock – Albany, NH

BT-10: N44° 0' 18.00" W71° 14' 6.80" (Cracked Boulder) *WOW-9*
An immense cracked boulder, 25-30-feet in height, with a lemon squeeze passageway the length and between the two half's. (Near the campground.)

BT-11: N44° 0' 19.50" W71° 14' 7.30" (Twin Rocks) *WOW-6*
A smallish split rock with both halves relatively the same size.

BT-12: N44° 0' 18.30" W71° 14' 4.60" (Peaked Rock) *WOW-7*
Slightly east off trail, peaked pinnacle boulder 12-14 feet in height.

BT-13: N44° 0' 22.30" W71° 14' 12.70" (Big Drop) *WOW-8*
Impressive vertical rock facing, 45-feet in height, located on the trail.

8. Cannon Rock

Cannon Rock – Franconia Notch, NH

Location: Franconia Notch (Grafton County)
Delorme Atlas & Gazetteer-New Hampshire: p.43, E-11
Parking GPS: N44° 10' 3.29" W71° 40' 57.95"(Old Man of Mountain)
Destination GPS: N44° 9' 30.29" W71° 41' 32.02"
Wow Factor: 6 **Accessibility:** Roadside viewing. (Binoculars required)
Contact: Franconia Notch State Park 260 Tramway Drive. Franconia/Lincoln, NH 03580 Phone: 603-823-8800

Information: Perched upon a ridge is a remarkable rock profile that resembles that of an old 32 pounder naval cannon. It was the early visitors to Franconia Notch who provided the moniker for what we know as Cannon Mountain. The stone formation consists of a large flat erratic serving as its carriage along with another 11-foot long erratic serving as its stone barrel. Binoculars will enhance any viewing situation, in addition fog or clouds can obscure its viewing. My unofficial viewing location for *Cannon Rock* is a roadside pull-off on the northbound on I-93. GPS: N44° 10' 3.30" W71° 40' 52.90"

Cannon Mountain has a rich history; in 1938, the 265 acre Cannon Mountain Ski Area along with the original Aerial Tramway went into service. The Tramway operated for 42 years until it was replaced with the current aerial tramway in May, 1980. As a major tourist attraction, in the summer you can ride the tramway to the summit and hike to the cannon rock formation position if you have that desire.

The infamous "Old Man of the Mountain" did reside upon one of Cannon Mountain cliffs. This beloved icon of New Hampshire was found on New Hampshire license plates, state emblems, road signs, coins and stamps until its demise on May 3, 2003. Presently, there is a conceptual viewing area which allows one to artificially visualize how the "Old Man" would have looked. The *Old Man Historic Site* is located on the northern end of Profile Lake and is accessed off Interstate I-93 at Exit-34B; use this same exit for access for the Cannon Mountain Tramway.

Cannon Rock – Postcard early 1900's – Franconia Notch, NH

Like the Cannon Mountains Ski Area, rock climbers were pioneering climbing routes on Cannon's cliff since the 1920's. Cannon's cliff with a vertical rise of 1,000-feet and more than a mile long is a premier rock and ice climbing location in the northeast.

Cannon Mountain Cliff – Franconia Notch, NH

9. Cote Boulder- Cathedral Ledge

Cote Boulder – Cathedral Ledge – North Conway, NH

Location: North Conway (Carroll County)
Delorme Atlas & Gazetteer-New Hampshire: p.45, I-9
Parking GPS: N44° 3' 51.15" W71° 9' 51.20" (Cote Boulder)
Destination GPS: N44° 3' 51.90" W71° 9' 52.80" Cote Boulder)
Wow Factor: 10 **Accessibility:** Easy 0.1 mile from Cathedral Ledge Road.
Contact: Echo Lake State Park 68 Echo Lake Road North Conway, NH 03818 Phone: 603-356-2672 www.nhstateparks.org

Information: Cote Boulder is a colossal stand-alone boulder that sits 50 yards from Cathedral Ledge Road at the base of Cathedral ledge. While not labeled you might pass it by on the way to Mordor Wall or Thin-Air-Face of Cathedral Ledge. In actuality, Cathedral Ledge along with White Horse Ledge is the big draw here for their sheer cliff faces, dramatic vistas and is noted for ice or rock climbing. Everything is encompassed within Echo Lake State Park and all are exquisite natural wonders being top destinations in the White Mountains. Echo Lake is a pristine body of water, has a beach and hiking trail around its perimeter, White Horse Ledge and Cathedral Ledge are epicenter's for tradition climbers, both are easily accessible and has a little something for every climber, regardless of ability. While White Horse Ledge is 1425-feet and Cathedral Ledge is 1125-feet high; Cathedral Ledge has a paved access road to its top and provides an observation point over-looking North Conway with a stunning panorama vista. The road is gated for winter.

White Horse Ledge from Echo Lake Beach – North Conway, NH

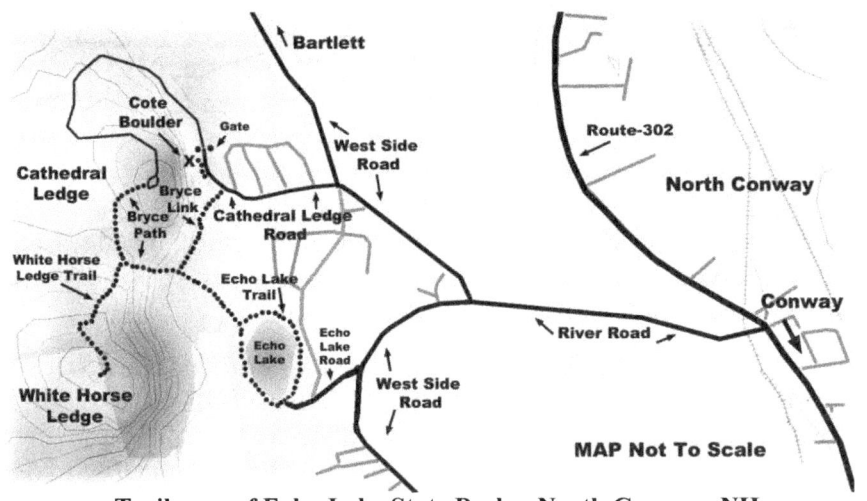

Trail map of Echo Lake State Park – North Conway, NH

Directions: To Cote Boulder; from Route-302 approximately 0.2 mile north of North Conway center, at the intersection with Pine Street and River Street, turn onto River Street heading west, downhill and under the Conway Scenic Railway Bridge. Continue for 1.0 mile, over the Saco River, where you will junction with West Side Road. Taking a left will go south on West Side Road and to the Echo Lake State Park. Go straight and continue north on West Side Road, within 0.5 mile you will turn left onto Cathedral Ledge Road. Within 0.5 mile and after a sweeping right turn, but before the seasonal gate you'll be in the vicinity to Cote Boulder off to the left. Parking on can be tight, a seasonal self- parking fee may apply.

10. Elephant Head Rock

Elephant Head Rock – Carroll, NH

Location: Carroll, Crawford Notch (Coos County)
Delorme Atlas & Gazetteer-New Hampshire: p.44, C-4
Parking GPS: N44° 12' 52" W71° 24' 28" (view point)
Destination GPS: N44° 12' 48.6" W71° 24' 22.4" (top)
Wow Factor: 8 Accessibility: Roadside viewing, moderate hike 0.3 mile.

Information: On Route-302 east at the entry to Crawford Notch State Park, the *Elephant's Head* is readily seen. There appears to be no arguments that it does looks like an elephant, its head and trunk emerging from the trees and with a uniquely placed spot of quartz providing a perfect eye. There is a 0.25 mile hike that can be taken to the top of the Elephant's Head, it is a bit steep, but is very short and provides remarkable views of Crawford Notch area. Rock climbers like to scale and repel down its trunk.

Directions: In Twin Mountain, at the junction of Route-3 and Route-302 (the only traffic light around.) take Route-302 east for .8.5 miles; just pass Crawford Depot Station on the right and the small Saco Lake on the left, park at the trail-head parking lot on the right. The Webster-Jackson trail is across the road, follow that in for 0.1 mile where a side trail to the Elephant Head summit will be apparent.

11. Fish Rock

Fish Rock – Shelburne, NH

Location: Shelburne (Coos County)
Delorme Atlas & Gazetteer-New Hampshire: p.49, H-11
Parking GPS: N44°24' 19.29" W71° 6' 2.22"
Destination GPS: N44° 24' 19.1" W71° 6' 2.1"
Wow Factor: 6 Accessibility: Roadside viewing

Information: Although not a totality natural creation, this is worth checking out. The *Stone Fish* is still located in Shelburne and originally had companions of a stone turtle and stone alligator nearby. They were created by George Emory around 1900 for the estate of William Kronigberg Aston whose property was located on what is now Village Road. Unfortunately, in 1927 the turtle and alligator stones were used as fill for a washed out bridge. George Emory's clever use of small stones to elongate the length of the fish body at the same time created a surface having a faux texture of fish scales. Only the eyes have a manufactured look, circular cut, cement and there is an appearance that perhaps an old beer bottles were incorporated into the eye as a translucent pupil.

Directions: In Gorham Route-16 and Route-2, head east 3.0 miles, located 0.5 mile past the Appalachian Trail and Mt Moriah trailhead parking, *Fish Rock* can be seen along Route-2, on the south side of the road, probably 50 feet from the road shoulder near the tree line. The stone is readily seen unless covered by snow or leaves.

12. Foss Mountain Erratics

Foss Mountain Erratic's – Easton, NH

Location: Eaton (Carroll County)
Delorme Atlas & Gazetteer-New Hampshire: p.41, D-12
Parking GPS: N43° 53' 6.20" W71° 2' 16.47"
Destination GPS: N43° 52' 56.5" W71° 02' 28.6" (summit)
Destination GPS: N43° 52' 55.1" W7°1 02' 24.5" (erratic down slope)
Wow Factor: 6 **Accessibility:** Easy to moderate slope, Short 1.0 mile RT.
Contact: Contact: Eaton Conservation Commission Evans Memorial Building PO Box 8883 Brownfield Road Eaton, NH 03832
Phone: (603) 447-2840 eatonth@roadrunner.com

Information: On March 1, 2011, the Upper Saco Valley Land Trust transferred ownership of the 99 acre Foss Mountain Project property to the Town of Eaton. Foss Mountain is a unique mountain with an elevation of only 1647-feet, yet with its barren rock summit provides spectacular 360° panorama views of surrounding mountains and lakes. Its slope from the eastern side from the Foss Mountain parking area is relatively short and easy. Some small roundish erratic's dot the summit or the surrounding landscape and there are blueberry's for the picking on the summit when in season.

Probably the only concern is to watch where you step and where you pick blueberries. There are a few rules which will be found on the kiosks or repeated along the trail about staying on trail and where one may pick the blueberries. Foss Mountain features a long, open ridge, which is home to a low bush blueberry farm. This endeavor in the lower parcels includes private and town-owned land on Foss Mountain, but at the summit, blueberry picking is allowed for private use and consumption. Along with the organic practices, staying on the trails is highly encouraged to reduce environmental impact for plants. There has been a new trail recently developed starting from the summer parking area on Foss Mountain Road, the older trail had erosion issues and was much steeper. Dogs are allowed.

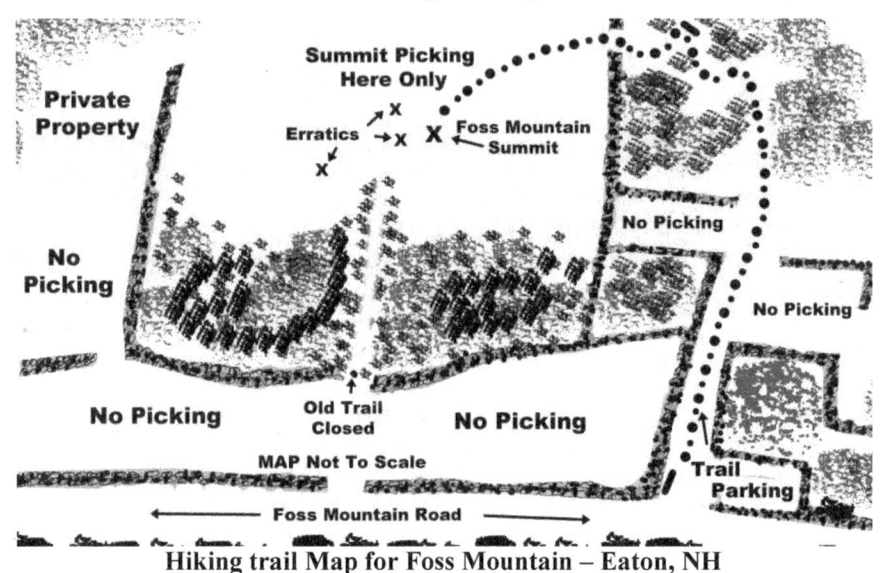

Hiking trail Map for Foss Mountain – Eaton, NH

Directions: In Conway, at the junction of Route-302 and Route-153, follow Route-153 south for 5.0 miles towards Eaton Center. Prior to Eaton Center, at Crystal Lake, turn left onto Brownfield Road and head east for 1.0 mile; turn right onto Stewart Road heading south for 2.0 miles. Turn right onto Foss Mountain Road and continue south for 1.3 miles. A kiosk and a dirt parking area for several cars will be on your right. Foss Mountain Road is passable from May through October, trucks or SUV's may be better suited for the muddy conditions of spring or snow and icy weather of winter.

13. Frog Rock

Frog Rock – Glen, NH

Location: Glen (Carroll County)
Delorme Atlas & Gazetteer-New Hampshire: p.45, G-8
Parking GPS: N44° 5' 12.10" W71° 12' 33.30"
Destination GPS: N44° 5' 12.10" W71° 12' 33.30"
Wow Factor: 6 **Accessibility:** Roadside – Private residence.

Information: While this rock is on the smaller size and that of the typical "Frog" genre, its recent upgrade in paint quality, along with some accessory touches of frog family cousins, toads and a sign for "Mom" makes it a little more whimsical. In addition, some planted ornamental grass; hostas and a white stone gravel bed, indicates this artistry will probably be well maintained for some time.

Directions: From the junction of Route-16 and Route-302 in Glen, follow Route-302 west for 2.5 miles. The Frog sits on the front lawn, some 25 feet back, on your right, just about 0.5 mile past the Covered Bridge B&B and Gift Shop just next to and over the Saco River.

14. Frog Rock

Frog Rock – Northumberland, NH

Location: Northumberland (Coos County)
Delorme Atlas & Gazetteer-New Hampshire: p.46, H-3
Parking GPS: N44° 33' 16.86" W71° 34' 39.99"
Destination GPS: N44° 33' 17.25" W71° 34' 39.80"
Wow Factor: 6 **Accessibility:** Roadside viewing - private residence.

Information: At first, this boxy rock's eyes reminded me of the "*Lighting McQueen*" animated character from the movie *Cars*, but it is a frog and a happy one at that. Painted with a brilliant shade of green and contrasted with yellow and black outlines for the legs, it is an enjoyable colorful break from the roadside monotony if your headed north in upstate New Hampshire. Keep an eye out for it and smile back.

Directions: In the center of Lancaster at the junction of Route-2 and Route-3 (a.k.a. Daniel Webster Highway) head north on Route-3 for 4.4 miles. The big Frog will be on your right shortly after Saw Mill Road.

15. Glen Ellis Boulder

Glen Boulder – Pinkham Notch, NH

Location: Pinkham Notch (Coos County)
Delorme Atlas & Gazetteer-New Hampshire: p.44, B-7
Parking GPS: N44°14' 44.9" W71°15'12.8"
Destination GPS: N44°14' 17.4" W71°16' 26.4"
Wow Factor: 10 **Accessibility:** Difficult steep- vintage rocky worn trail.
Contact: White Mountain National Forest, Jackson, NH 03846 (603) 466-2727 https://www.fs.usda.gov/whitemountain

Information: The Glen Boulder is an outstanding large erratic that appears to sit precariously on a ridge off southern Mt Washington. From the scenic Glen Ellis Falls parking area, the boulder is easily seen sitting prominently on the Glen Boulder Trail 1.7 miles away. From the trailhead, the trail ascends steeply up a worn and rocky trail, in a short time you will break through the tree line and into sunny open rocky ledge which has many exceptional panoramic views. For Jan & I, this hike was strenuous, packing pounds of camera gear, trekking poles and survival food. However, many "younger" and fit individuals might find this a lessor or moderate rating as we were passed frequently. There is one location which will require a short 3-points-of-contact to climb and scramble over a ledge. A National Park parking pass or permit is required to be displayed on your vehicles dash while utilizing or visiting many of these scenic areas throughout the White Mountains. Self-pay envelopes are available at a kiosk in the Glen Ellis parking area.

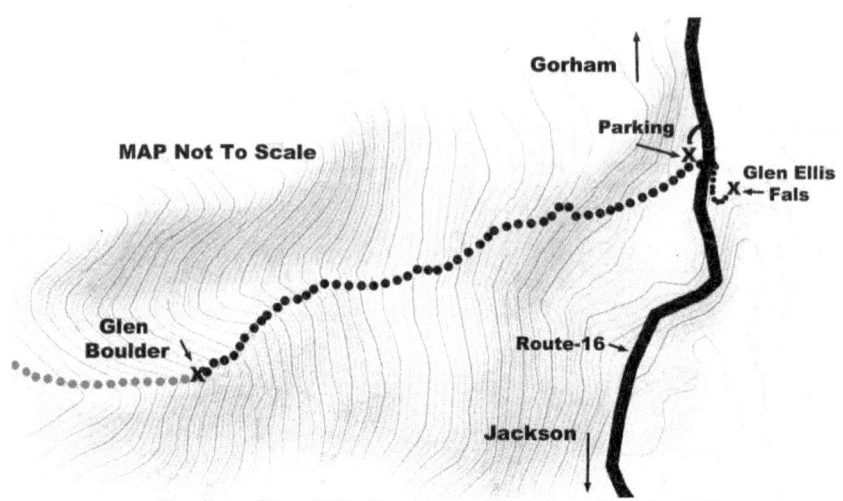

Trail to Glen Ellis Boulder – Pinkham Notch, NH

  As with many sites within the White Mountains, the pathways, stairs and tunnel to Glen Ellis Falls were constructed by the Civilian Conservation Corps during the 1930's, it's a short hike to this dynamic 65-foot waterfall, well worth the extra time. From the parking area, pass through the tunnel beneath Route-16, follow a short path and down some stone stairs that will bring down to the viewing area for this magnificent waterfall.

  Continuing north on Route-16, for 0.6 mile from the Glen Ellis Scenic Area, is the Pinkham Notch Visitors Center and Appalachian Mountain Club facilities. Here you'll find a busy hub of hikers questing for the summit of Mount Washington and beyond. Food and facilities can also be found here. In addition, another superb waterfall *Crystal Cascades* can also be found, from behind the information center follow the Tuckerman's Ravine trail for 0.3 mile. When you cross a wooden bridge, the falls overlook will be located less than 100 yards up on your right. GPS: N44° 15' 38" W71° 15' 25"

Directions: North of Conway and in Glen, at the junction of Route-302 and Route-16, follow Route-16 north for 11.0 miles. You will pass by the scenic town of Jackson and eventually leave all the development behind. Heading up-hill into Pinkham Notch the grandeur of the White Mountains Wildness area becomes apparent. As you crest the hill, the National Park Scenic Area of Glen Ellis Waterfall will be on your left. You'll find the Glen Boulder Trail in the southern end of the parking area.

16. Goodrich & Davis Boulders

DB-8 – Goodrich Boulder – Waterville Valley, NH

Location: Waterville Valley (Grafton County)
Delorme Atlas & Gazetteer-New Hampshire: p 40, A-2
Parking GPS: N43° 57' 57.40" W71° 30' 47.90"
Destination GPS: See list below.
Wow Factor: 8-10 **Accessibility:** Marked, moderate trail, 4.6 mile RT.

Information: Goodrich Rock, discovered in the late 1800,s by Arthur L. Goodrich, it is noted to be one of New Hampshire's largest glacial erratic's. Many think Goodrich Rock is the second largest glacial erratic in New Hampshire akin to the nearby Madison Boulder (see Chapter #37.) Whether its size is a true statement, it is certainly one of the tallest and most massive boulders to be found in Waterville Valley and the White Mountains. (e.g. Note cover of this book, the Mowgli Boulder in Pawtuckaway State Park.) While size matters, unique to Goodrich Rock is the massive ladder constructed for access to its top which provides a tremendous view of Mt. Tecumseh and the Waterville Valley ski slope.

But Wait, There's More! Prior to reaching the Goodrich Boulder, one has to navigate through the Davis Boulder Field, named for J.W. Davis, a summer resident of Waterville Valley who built the first trail here in the late 1890's. The Davis Boulders are in themselves impressive with the trail weaving through a large split rock and past many other astonishing or striking boulders, both large and small.

Hiking to Goodrich Rock which is located upon the lower eastern slopes of Mount Oceola is more of a pleasure than one would think. To access the Goodrich Rock Trail we started from the Depot large parking area off Tripoli Road and the West Branch Road junction. From the kiosk, follow the *Livermore Trail* for 0.3 mile, across a small bridge, to the *Greely Pond Trail* that will be on your left. Follow the *Greely Pond Trail* north for 0.9 mile. The first 1.2 miles is very easy to walk, wide and easily followed. Upon reaching the *Goodrich Rock Trail* junction on you left, the trail will narrows and quickly ascends steeply for 0.4 mile. When it levels off, the large entry boulder will be shortly encountered, then followed by the Davis Boulder (a.k.a Split Rock) which the trail travels through. Continue following the yellow blazes which you will notice painted on rocks or trees as you weave through the boulder field for 0.2 mile. The large *Ship Rock* DB-8 essentially means you are basically through the Davis Boulder Field. Continue following the yellow blaze trail for another 0.2 mile. You will encounter a couple of tedious rocky obstacles just prior to reaching the base of Goodrich Rock. To reach the ladder, it's one last steep scamper uphill until you reach the rear of Goodrich Rock. I will suggest three points of contact as you ascend and descend the ladder as the wooden rungs are smooth and worn.

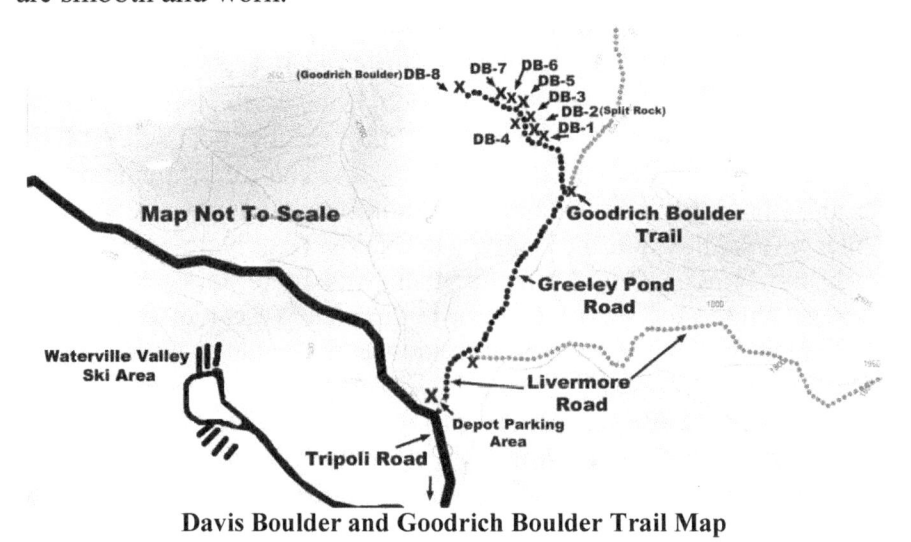

Davis Boulder and Goodrich Boulder Trail Map

DB-1: N43° 59' 3.00" W71° 30' 19.70" (Entry Boulder) *WOW-7*
An immense 20 feet x 25 feet boulder with an appearance of a crashed UFO, tilted and sitting right on the trail.

DB-2 Split Rock – Waterville Valley, NH

DB-2: N43° 59' 4.10" W71° 30' 20.30" (Split Rock) *WOW-8*
Split as if a third of rock was moved backwards creating a channel with a 90° turn at its center point. The trail passes through and is not as difficult as it looks to navigate through split and around the turn.

DB-3: N43° 59' 5.00" W71° 30' 21.10" (Twin Rock) *WOW-7*
Two 16 foot and 18 foot rocks similar in appearance until one examines the "smaller" boulders side length having a curved uniquely split rear section.

DB-5 – House Boulder (front) – Waterville Valley. NH

DB-4: N43° 59' 4.90" W71° 30' 21.40" (Table Rock) *WOW-7*
Across the trail from DB-3, a large squat boulder with flattish top has a small micro-cosmism of ferns, moss and brush growing atop.

DB-5: N43° 59' 5.90" W71° 30' 22.00" (House Boulder) *WOW-9*
A very impressive boulder with a large sloped over-hang in the lower front, a massive elongated body mass which tapers down from the front to its rear.

DB-6 - Boulder Pass – House Boulder (rear) – Waterville Valley, NH

DB-6: N43° 59' 6.40" W71° 30' 21.50" (Boulder Pass) *WOW-7*
An additional 18 foot boulder which may or may not be part of the original mass of DB-5, sits to its rear of DB-5 creating a narrowed passageway between the two which the trail will pass through. a.k.a *The Gate.*

DB-7: N43° 59' 9.10" W71° 30' 23.50" (Ship Rock) *WOW-8*
Rock climbers have christened it the "Old Wooden Ship." It also has a moniker of "Ocean Liner" or "Ship Rock." I think it has an appearance of a ship that has its bow run aground upon the rocky shores.

DB-7 Ship Boulder – Waterville Valley, NH

DB-8 - Goodrich Boulder (rear) – Waterville Valley, NH

DB-8: N43° 59' 14.1" W71° 30' 34.00" (Goodrich Boulder) *WOW-9*
While a phenomenal boulder with amazing height in the front, its mass and colossal size is slightly diminished from the slope of the mountain. From the front lower base a cathedral like recess has a stable flat slab of granite as a floor creating a natural patio. Wished I had brought my chair to sit a spell.

Directions: From Interstate I-93, take Exit-28 onto Routet-49, drive 10.0 miles northeast and turn left onto Tripoli Road. In 1.2 miles, bear right to avoid the ski area entrance and continue 0.5 mile down Tripoli Road. Turn right onto West Branch Road and immediately bear left into the Depot parking area. The parking area is very large, has rest rooms and is the trail head for the Livermore Road/Trail.

DB-3 Twin Rock - Side

17. Hart's Ledge Boulders

HL-1 – Sphinx Rock – Bartlett, NH

Location: Bartlett (Carroll County)
Delorme Atlas & Gazetteer-New Hampshire: p.44, H-5
Parking GPS: N44° 4' 56.50" W71° 19' 22.32"
Destination GPS: See list below.
Wow Factor: See list below. **Accessibility:** No trail marking – GPS only.

Information: Hart's Ledge is in the town of Bartlett, there are some old stereographic photographs that depict *Devil's Den* or *The Cathedral* being labeled Hart's Ledge as in North Conway. There are no signs to restrict parking, but upon entry, a sign was posted for *No Trespassing–Hunting or Fishing*. Unfortunately, no address or contact information was on the sign to verify or seek permission. From our parking area, access to the boulder area is via an old logging road. Enter into the woods, follow the road for 0.3 mile, heading west until you reach the first fork atop a steep hill section. Bear right and continue uphill to the HL-1 *Sphinx*. This being our first visit we stayed with this first boulder field and never reached Hart's Ledge. More to follow for I do believe a few large boulders further up toward the base of Harts Ledge reside.

HL 1: N44° 4' 59.50" W71° 19' 42.70" (Sphinx Rock) *WOW-9*
This rock has very small base circumference, yet still 1s a towering 20-feet tall. Its side profile reminds me of Egyptian royalty with a large swept back crown.

HL 2: N44° 5' 0.50" W71° 19' 41.80" (Hole-In-One) *WOW-8*
A trio of rocks with their juxtaposition forming a large hole or short tunnel at the center. Perplexing how these rocks end up in a configuration as these are.

HL 3: N44° 5' 0.80" W71° 19' 40.60" (Boot Rock) *WOW-6*
From the side, a shape of a boot, 18-feet tall at the heel and 10-feet at its toe.

HL 4: N44° 4' 58.00" W71° 19' 37.60" (Lone Rock) *WOW-6*
Large 14-foot boulder, located by its-self downhill from the Sphinx.

HL 5: N44° 4' 57.10" W71° 19' 42.80" (Biscuit Rock) *WOW-6*
A squat 12-feet tall and 18-feet long rock. Not overly impressive.

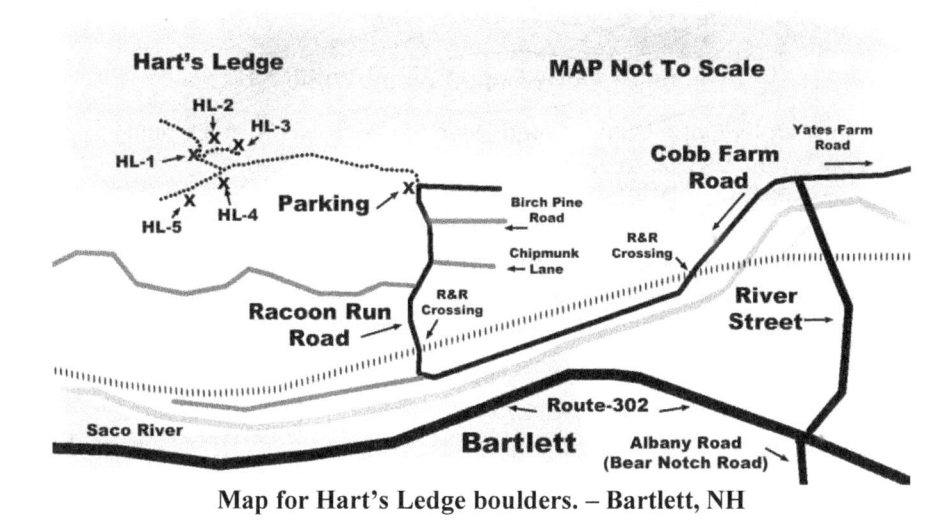

Map for Hart's Ledge boulders. – Bartlett, NH

Directions: In the town of Bartlett at the intersection of Route-302, Albany - Bear Notch Road and River Street, head north on River Street until it crosses the Saco River. Turn left onto Cobb Farm Road and travel 2.0 miles. You will be traveling next to the Saco River, shortly after you'll pass over the 1st railroad crossing, the road will turn sharply north becoming Raccoon Run Road. Pass over the 2nd railroad crossing and continue to the top of the hill where Raccoon Run turns sharply east. The sandy apron on the left at the top is where to park; from here a very old dirt road enters into the woodlands.

18. Imp Profile Rock

The Imp – Dolly Copp Campground, NH

Location: Dolly Copp Campground. Martins Location (Coos County)
Delorme Atlas & Gazetteer-New Hampshire: p.49, K-8
Parking GPS: N44°19'40.41" W71°13'11.00" (viewing location site #117)
Destination GPS: N44° 19'16.77" W71°11'30.08" (summit Imp Mt.)
Wow Factor: 7 **Accessibility:** Drive to Viewing point.
Contact: White Mountains National Forest; Androscoggin Ranger District 300 Glen Road. Gorham, NH 03581 (603) 466-2713   www.fs.usda.gov

Information: During the 1850's in the Glen Valley and Gorham the railroad and improved roadways were increasing the tourist travel to the White Mountains. This profile reportedly was first named by White Mountain legend Dolly Copp who claimed that it looked like an Imp. Among the summer tourists it became known as *"Dolly Copp's Imp"* and that it was also viewed best from her doorway. I do not know which came first, the naming of Imp Mountain or the Imp profile, but what remains true is that the Imp Profile is still seen best from the vicinity of original cabin site within the Dolly Copp Campground, look east to see the Imp profile which faces south. Since the profile is good distance away, using a camera with a telephoto lens or binoculars to enhance the viewing experience.

Directions: In Gorham, at the junction of Route-2 and Route-16. travel south 4.5 miles on Route-16. Turn right onto Dolly Copp Road (seasonally gated), travel 0.5 mile to campground entry. From May to October, see ranger for entry, information or directions.

19. Indian Head Profile

Indian Head Profile - Lincoln, NH

Location: Lincoln (Grafton County)
Delorme Atlas & Gazetteer-New Hampshire: p. 43, G-11
Parking GPS: N44° 5' 4.21" W71°41' 3.13"(Indian Head Resort)
Parking GPS: N44° 5'51.55" W71°40' 53.62" (Flume Parking)
Destination GPS: N 44° 5' 52.64" W71°41' 58.09"(Pemigewasset summit)
Wow Factor: 8 **Accessibility:** Roadside Viewing.

Information: According to legend, this mountain top profile is the profile of Chief Pemigewasset;

"Chief Pemigewasset is said to have used the top of the famous Indian Head profile as a lookout for hostile bands of Algonquins who might be traveling up the valley. At that time, the profile as it is seen today was not there, for it was hidden by a growth of tree in the Lincoln forest. A fire swept through the woods one day and after the fire, the profile of Indian Head could be seen, as through old Chief Pemigewasset himself had come to life again."

"History of the New Hampshire Albenaki" by Bruce D Hearld PhD

Indeed, nearly as iconic as the Old Man in the Mountain, but the Indian Head still remains there for the viewing. It can readily be viewed along Route-3 just north of Lincoln just prior to entering the Franconic State Park.

Although the best viewing site remains at the Indian Head Resort, with a history dating back to 1913, the resort has grown from a small campground to a destination in the White Mountains Nation Park area. Binoculars will assist in the viewing experience. Originally, the Indian Head Resort built a tall wooden tower on the west side of Route-3 which provided a commanding view of the Indian Head profile for tourists. Later the wooden tower was replaced by a 100-foot steel tower and in the 1950's that tower was moved across Route-3. Visit their gift shop for New Hampshire memorabilia.

There are two trails which allow you to hike up to the summit of Mount Pemigewasset, the Indian Head Trail (1.7 miles) and the Mount Pemigewasset Trail (1.8 miles). Both trails will converge just below the summit. The Mount Pemigewasset Trail is preferable because it has easy parking and available restrooms at The Flume Visitor Center. Note: Cars can't be left here overnight!

From the northern end of the Flume parking lot, follow the bike path north, shortly you find the sign for the Mount Pemigewasset Trail on the left, the trail is blazed with blue trail markings. Heading west, the trail will pass beneath Route 3 and Interstate 93 before beginning to gently ascend the slope of Mount Pemigewasset. The trail climbs steadily and moderate, with many switchbacks up the slope, when the two trails join, only 0.1 mile remains until you are on the summit.

Directions: For Mt. Pemigewasset Trail: Travel north from North Woodstock on Interstate I-93, for 4.0 miles. Take Exit-34A for the Flume and Park information Visitors Center, continue north on Route-3, in 0.5 mile you will reach the turn-off for the Flume parking area Warning! Cars can't be left here overnight. Leashed dogs are allowed.

Indian Head Trail: Travel north from North Woodstock on Interstate I-93 for 2.0 miles and take Exit-33. Travel north on Route-3 for 0.8 mile, on your left will be a gravel road leads to the trailhead for Mt Pemiqewasset. There is a sign "Trailhead Parking" but can only read from the south lane The Indian Head Resort will be on your right in an addition 0.2 mile.

20. Jeremy's Boulders

Jeremy's Boulders - Lancaster

Location Lancaster (Coos County)
Delorme Atlas & Gazetteer-New Hampshire: p. 47, E-13
Parking GPS: N44° 28 '30.19" W71° 36' 47.31"
Destination GPS: N44° 28' 30.89" W71° 36' 46.93"
Wow Factor: 8 **Accessibility:** Roadside viewing only – private property

Information: Located in a roadside hayfield just west of Lancaster, is a masterful piece of stonework that reminds me of solstice creation you would see at Stonehenge. True to the nature of the New Hampshire farmland, rocks and boulder have always plagued the farmer's efforts; notice the occurrence of stone walls throughout New England. On the Fay Allin Farm, rocks and boulders continued to be no exception for today's contemporary farmland work. Speaking with Fay Allin, who spoke of the large boulders still being a hindrance to the machinery during the cultivation of their land for crops. Fay spoke of her son Jeremy who evidently had plans, from my understanding and with having a delicate touch on the controls of a front loader; he placed these large boulders in impossible positions as if to defy gravity.

Directions: In Lancaster, at the junction of Route-3 and Route-135, follow Route-135 for 2.5 miles west. On your right are the boulders.

21. Martha Washington Profile

Martha Washington Profile - Crawford's Purchase, NH

Location: Ammonoosuc Upper Falls (Coos County)
Delorme Atlas & Gazetteer-New Hampshire: p.44, B-4
Parking GPS: N44°15' 59.1" W71°24' 58.6"
Destination GPS: N44° 15' 57.8" W71°24' 57.2" (view point from bridge)
Wow Factor: 7 **Accessibility:** Roadside, short walk to the bridge to view.

Information: Standing on the small bridge that crosses the Ammonoosuc River and looking down stream, the right side of the rocky gorge has 3 stony outcrops. Martha's Washington's profile is clearly seen in the 2nd outcropping 50 yards downstream. In addition, just past Martha's profile, the *Chimp* or *Gorilla* profile juts out. While not sanctioned, swimming does seem to be an attraction here, "*Running the Wall*" with fancy dives or lofty cannonballs. **The Chimp >**

Directions: West of the *Mount Washington Hotel* on Route-302, turn onto Base Station Road at the Fabyan's Station. Travel 2.3 miles east on your right there will be a dirt pull off with a kiosk for the Upper Ammonoosuc River Falls. At the small bridge crossing over the Ammonoosuc River above the waterfall; look downstream to the right to see these profiles. Continuing to the end of Base Station Road brings you to the Mt. Washington Cog Railway. Always an excitement of the Cog engines clambering up and down the track.

22. The Mummies

The Mummies – North Woodstock, NH

Location: North Woodstock (Grafton County)
Delorme Atlas & Gazetteer-New Hampshire: p.43, J-11
Parking GPS: N44° 1' 36.56" W71° 41' 6.24" (Public parking along Rt-3.)
Destination GPS: N44° 1' 35.43" W71° 41' 9.63"
Wow Factor: 8 Accessibility: Roadside short walk – limited access.

Information: The *Mummies* are a large section of rock in Moosilauke Brook that river erosion has created and looks like several embalmed mummies lying side-by-side. This is a vintage tourist oddity which today seems hardly known. Access is hampered due to private property. You can find public parking along this section of roadway.

Directions: Moosilauke Brook runs behind several private residences namely the Three Rivers House off Three River Drive (19 Daniel Webster Hwy.) From the junction of Route-3 and Route-112 in North Woodstock, travel south 0.3 mile to the bridge that crosses over the Moosilauke Brook. Do not cross the bridge, but descend down the eastern shoreline walking 0.1 mile north, back towards North Woodstock. Normally this is dry, but rocky and not too bad, although in spring one can find the waters swollen making access in this manner more difficult.

Old Lady of the Mountain

Old Lady Watcher – Franconia Notch, NH

Location: Franconia Notch (Grafton County)
Delorme Atlas & Gazetteer-New Hampshire: p.43, E-11
Parking GPS: N44° 9' 39.80" W71°40' 37.00" (Viewing location)
Destination GPS: N44° 10' 17.82"W71° 40' 37.68"(The Watcher location)
Wow Factor: 5 **Accessibility:** Roadside viewing. Look northeast from southern Profile Lake parking area.

Information: The *Old Lady of the Mountain* in Franconia Notch is not as famous as her counterpart, the *Old Man of the Mountain*. This natural rock profile is on the eastern side of Eagle Cliff and is equally prominent. She is also called "*The Watcher*" as she is facing east and has her head bent as if watching for strangers. A safe and clear viewing area is from the parking area at the south end of Profile Lake A pair of binoculars will enhance the viewing experience as the image above is photographed with a 450 mm telephoto lens.

Directions: The viewing and parking area is only accessible off I-93 south. The unnumbered exit is 0.8 mile south of I-93 Exit-34B; the unnumbered exit is labeled *"Trail Head Parking"* for the bike path and lower Profile Lake. If you miss this turn, you will have to continue south to Exit-34A and use the Route-3 Flume Gorge and Park Visitor Center interchange to reverse direction back onto I-93 north to Exit-34B and reverse direction again heading south. Of course if you are walking or bicycling the recreation trail this would a good stop to consider.

24. Old Man of the Valley

Old Man of the Valley – Shelburne, NH

Location: Shelburne (Coos County)
Delorme Atlas & Gazetteer-New Hampshire: p49, H-12
Parking GPS: N44° 23' 4.5" W71° 1' 19.8"
Destination GPS: N44° 23' 5.4" W71° 1' 25.00"
Wow Factor: 7 **Accessibility:** Easy walk 0.1 mile unmarked path to site.

Information: This one profile you have the chance to examine up close. For me, the rock has an Inca or Aztec carving feel to it. Readily accessible, yet still a hidden treasure, not visited nearly as much as you might expect.

Old Man of the Valley – Shelburne, NH

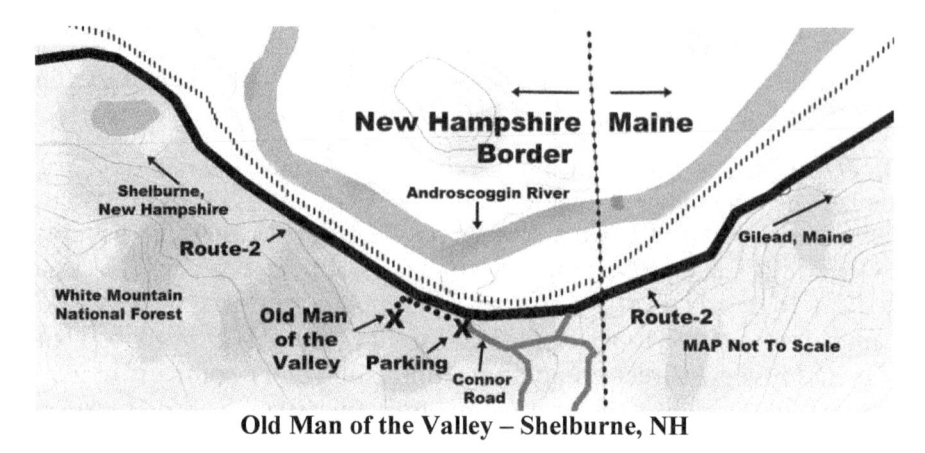

Directions: The *Old Man of the Valley* is just off Route-2 near the Maine Border. In Gorham, from the junction of Route-16 and Route-2, follow Rt-2 east for 8.8 miles. Look for a parking sign on the south side of the road. If you cross the state line and enter into Maine you need to go back 0.3 miles. From the parking area, walk west back on Route-2, to just before the start of the guardrail. On your left a woodland path can be found, the *Old Man of the Valley* is less than a hundred yards into the woods from the road.

25. Pine Hill Trails

Summit Boulder – Littleton, NH

Location: Littleton (Grafton County)
Delorme Atlas & Gazetteer-New Hampshire: p.49, H-12
Parking GPS: N44° 18' 37.21" W71° 46' 12.67"
Destination GPS: N44° 18' 51.3" W71° 46' 3.6"
Wow Factor: 5 **Accessibility:** Easy hike loop, 1.0 mile.
Contact: Littleton Conservation Commission 125 Main Street
Littleton, NH 03561

Information: The Pine Hill Trail is a short, an easy hike, of course we were interested in the glacial erratic's. The trail was well marked and the trail maintained very well. From the start, the trail begins mildly uphill; soon it crosses over a dirt road and continues to the summit and the "Summit Boulder." The summit boulder was the largest erratic we found, not very tall 8 feet to 10-feet, but 20-feet long and with a flat top it was easy to climb onto its top. The Teapot Rock actually being smaller is found on the downhill side from the summit. Again, not an overly significant rock, you will need to look closely to see how its amusing moniker was arrived and has endured. Continuing around the loop clockwise, you will pass *Two Sock* junction and return to the parking area by either turning left onto a cross-over trail or the dirt road you crossed earlier. Pine Hill was an easy and enjoyable walk during the fall foliage.

Directions: In Littleton at the junction of Route-116 and Junction Route-302, head west on main street for 0.1 mile, turn right onto

Jackson Street, which from the start will be the 3rd street on the right. Continue to follow Jackson Street 0.2 mile unitl it junctions with Oakhill Avenue, cross directly over onto Pine Hill Road and into Remich Park. There will be a paved parking lot for a dozen cars. The Pine Hill Trail begins near the north end of the parking area.

26. Rest Area Boulder

Rest Area Boulder – North Woodstock, NH

Location: North Woodstock (Grafton County)
Delorme Atlas & Gazetteer-New Hampshire: p.43, I-11
Destination GPS: N44° 2' 54.08" W71° 41' 14.35" (Tuttle Brook Parking)
Wow Factor: 4 **Accessibility:** Easy – limited access.
Contact: Clark's Trading Post Route-3 110 Daniel Webster Highway PO Box 1 Lincoln, NH 03251 603-745-8913 info@clarkstradingpost.com

Information: Situated in the Tuttle Brook Picnic Area, this is a large slab of rock 14-feet tall, 50-feet in length and is located directly across the street from the well-known Clark's Trading Post. It is posted as: *"private carry in/ carry-out area for use of guests at Clark's Trading Post."* A single table sits atop of this rock and presents a unique location to enjoy the coming and goings of this very busy establishment during the summer months.

Directions: Take I-93 to Exit 33, south on Route-3 for one mile, the picnic area is on the right, Clarks Trading Post will be on your left.

27. Flume Boulders

Flume Boulder #1 – Lincoln, NH

Location: North Woodstock (Grafton County)
Delorme Atlas & Gazetteer-New Hampshire: p.43, G-11
Parking GPS: N44° 5' 48.39" W71° 40' 51.24"
Destination GPS: Individual GPS locations below.
Wow Factor: 7 **Accessibility:** Easy hike, fee for access.
Contact: Franconia Notch State Park 9 Franconia Notch Parkway Franconia, NH 03580 (603) 823-8800 www.nhstateparks.org

Information: The Flume is another vintage tourist landmark that was discovered accidently in 1808 by 93 year-old "Aunt" Jess Guernsey while fishing. The Flume has an 800 foot natural chasm with walls of granite that rise to a height of 70 feet to 90 feet and are 12 feet to 20 feet apart. In addition, waterfalls, glacial erratic's, covered bridges and other iconic White Mountain scenery are accessible by a network of manicured trails. There is a fee for entry, open from May to October. The Flume chasm walk-way is removed during winter months. The astonishing glacial erratic's listed here are located on the return hiking trail from the Sentinel Pine Bridge and Pool back to the Visitor's Center main entry.

Flume Blder #1: N44° 5' 57.61" W71°40' 42.80" *WOW 8*
A massive 25 foot boulder with small shelter cave in front. (See above photo)

Flume Blder #2: N44° 6' 3.28" W71°40' 43.54"
No description provided.

Flume Blder #3: N44° 6' 4.13" W71°40' 42.88" *WOW- 8*
An astonishing and massive 20 foot, 300 ton boulder. (See photo below)

Flume Blder: #4 N44° 6' 4.43" W71°40' 42.68" *WOW- 8*
A large 20 foot perched boulder.

Flume Blder #5: N44° 6' 5.90" W71°40' 41.80" *WOW - 7*
A 16 foot perched boulder with small shelter cave in front.

Flume Boulder #3 – Lincoln, NH

Directions: Travel north on Interstate I-93 from Exit-32 in North Woodstock for 4.0 miles. Take exit-34A for the Flume and Park information, continue north on Route-3 for 0.5 mile to the turn-off for the Flume parking area.

Flume Bolder #5 – Lincoln, NH

28. Washington Profile Rock

Washington Profile Rock – Jackson, NH

Location: Jackson (Carroll County)
Delorme Atlas & Gazetteer-New Hampshire: p.45, F-9
Parking GPS: N44° 8' 22.3" W71° 9' 30.89"
Destination GPS: N44° 8' 22.9" W71° 9' 31.2"
Wow Factor: 7 **Accessibility:** Roadside on private property.

Information: The George Washington profile rock is a vintage New Hampshire tourist stop. Some of its popularity stems from that the rock profile is easily seen from ground level and being located at road side. The likeness of the profile does seem to be that of George Washington while others suggest its Alfred Hitchcock the film director. This area has seen a gradual process of transformation with new residential home development. The road maps over many years have morphed and developed from just Tin Mountain Road and now includes Switchback Drive or Thom Mountain Road and Profile Drive along with many other side drives. At this time no posted parking or trespassing signs were noted. Please maintain a common respect for the owner's property and the surrounding residences.

Washington Profile Rock – circa 1920's – Jackson, NH

Directions: From Route-16 entering into Jackson, cross through the covered bridge, from here travel 0.5 mile into the center of Jackson. At the junction of Route-16A and 16B, on your right is a secondary paved road, *Switchback Way,* a.k.a *Thom Mountain Road.* Follow the road uphill; twisting and turning for 1.4 miles, *Tin Mountain Road* will merge in from your left while Thom Mountain Road continues another 0.5 mile to the Profile Rock on your left. This last segment of Thom Mountain Road is also known as *Profile Drive*. A small unimproved pull off was being used for parking; however this might be someone's private property and parking may become restrictive if visitors become a nuisance.

29. Willey's House Boulders

Willey's House Boulders – Crawford Notch, NH

Location: Crawford Notch State Park (Carroll County)
Delorme Atlas & Gazetteer-New Hampshire: p.44, F-4
Parking GPS: N44° 10' 57.12" W71° 23' 58.44"
Destination GPS: N44° 10' 55.46" W71° 23' 59.08"
Wow Factor: 5 **Accessibility:** Easy, short 0.1 mile uphill path to site.
Information: The *Willey Boulders* are said to have saved the Willey House from destruction on August 28, 1826 when a massive landslide came down Mount Willey. These boulders were located just above the house causing the landslide to split into two debris flows that were diverted around the house. The house was said to be untouched, but all seven members of the family and two hired men perished in the slide while trying to escape to a safer area. The Willey House is one of the few buildings within the Crawford Notch State Park. A stop here allows one to stretch their legs, rest rooms and ice cream. Within the park there are many natural points of interest, waterfalls, vistas, and trail heads to the many ridges and mountains. Watch for kiosks at trailheads usually with a map and trail information. Both the National Parks along with the State of New Hampshire parks have informative Interrupter's at Visitor's Centers or Ranger Stations. .

Directions: From Fabyan Station or Bretton Woods, head east on Route-302 for 6.7 miles. The Willey House will be on your right noted by their distinctive New Hampshire style log cabins.

New Hampshire – Central

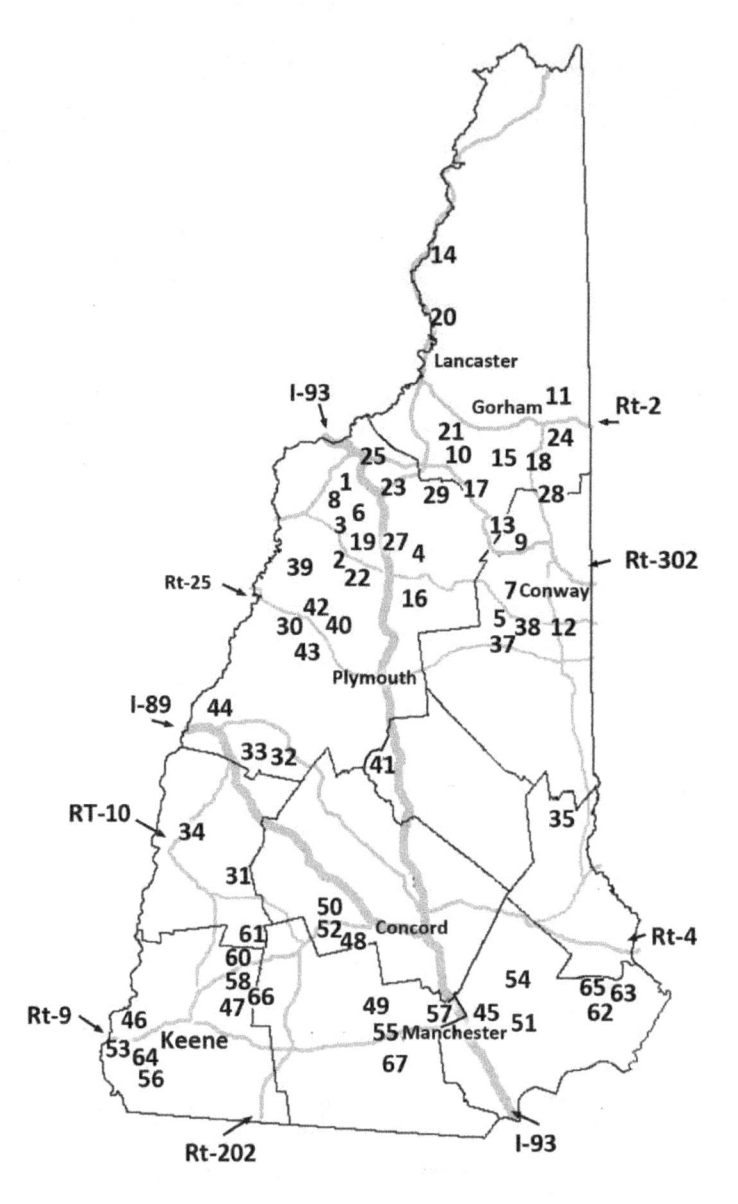

MAP Not To Scale – For Reference Only

New Hampshire – Central

30. Baker River Rock (Wentworth)
31. Balance Rock: Pillsbury State Park (Washington)
32. Balance Rock: Ragged Mountain (Andover)
33. Cooks Conservation Property Trails (New London)
34. Elephant Rock (Newport)
35. Franklin Piece Lake Boulder (Antrim)
36. Little Brother Profile (Milton)
37. Madison Boulder (Madison)
38. Ordination Rock (Tamworth)
39. Papoose Rock: Holts Ledge (Lyme Center)
40. Pound Rocks (Rumney)
41. Rest Stop Boulder: Interstate I-93, Exit 22 South (Tilton)
42. Rumney Boulders (Rumney)
43. Sculpture Rocks (Groton)
44. Tipping Rock (Lebanon)

30. Baker River Rock

Baker River Boulder – Wentworth, NH

Location: Wentworth (Grafton County)
Delorme Atlas & Gazetteer-New Hampshire: p.48, D-4
Parking GPS: N43° 52' 6.77" W71° 54' 36.80"(Point-A) (Riverside Park)
Parking GPS: N43° 52' 4.78" W71° 54' 32.80"(Point-B) (Covered Bridge)
Destination GPS: N43° 52' 5.70" W71° 54' 34.10"
Wow Factor: 8 **Accessibility:** No trail, River side short rock-hop.

Information: New England riverside townships often congregated on both sides of rivers such as Wentworth Village. The Baker River is a fine example of New England heritage; where running water was power, provided recreation and other interests for the growth of the community life. Our impromptu drive by at this location and being drawn into old New England covered bridges, water cascades, a jumble of rocks and one Hugh titan of a boulder came as a surprise.

The erratic is large and sits next to a poured foundation what could have been some sort of gate house or other mills that traditionally commercialized river sites. (E.g. Grist, Tannery, Textile, lumber mills.) The whole river segment on a sunny day is outstanding with multiple cascades or swimming pools. The aerial view from the foot bridge is an excellent location the see this. From the Riverside Park embankment (Point-A) is another good perspective for photography and is easier or safer to reach.

Seeking information on the river boulder or historical buildings in Wentworth was meager and sparse. However, a bridge has crossed here since the late 1700's and has been a vital part of linking Wentworth Village. Built by the United Construction Company and the American Bridge Company was installed 1909. The original truss bridge was recently condemned, removed and replaced in September 2016. A cost-effect replacement was The John Goffe's Mill Covered Bridge, rescued and re-cycled from demolition of the Wayfarer Inn's and Conference Center location in Bedford, New Hampshire.

Baker River Bridge - Gate House - Hugh Boulder. – Wentworth, NH 1920

Directions: At the junction of Route-25E and Route-25 head south on Route-25 (Mt Moosilauke Highway) as if going to Rumney. Heading south, within 0.3 mile at the Baker River Bridge, as you travel across, look east up-stream and you will see a covered Bridge and Hugh boulder. Access to a view Point-A can be found by turning into Riverside Park, just before crossing the bridge and drive to the riverside. Or just pass the bridge, on your left, enter onto East Side Road, and follow for 0.1 mile to Point-B. There may or may not be parking right at this entry/exit which has become a pedestrian only foot bridge. Bushwhacking down this embankment will not be user friendly; you will need to surmount bramble, logs, and old foundations to reach the rock this from this point. Otherwise, up on the overhead perch the aerial view from the covered bridge is much easier and very satisfying.

31. Balance Rock – Pillsbury State Park

Balance Rock – Pillsbury State Park – Washington, NH

Location: Washington (Sullivan County)
Delorme Atlas & Gazetteer-New Hampshire: p26, D-2
Parking GPS: N43° 13' 56.47" W72° 6' 12.98"
Destination GPS: N43° 14' 41.40" W72° 6' 31.60"
Wow Factor: 8 **Accessibility:** Moderate 1.2 mile hike, entry fee.
Contact: Pillsbury State Park_100 Pillsbury State Park Rd Washington, NH 03280 603-863-2860; Division of Parks and Recreation 172 Pembroke Road Concord, NH 03301 (603) 271-3556 nhparks@dred.nh.gov

Information: Pillsbury State Park in Washington, New Hampshire became a state park in 1952, and includes 2,400 acres of land donated to the state as far back as 1920. The park's total acreage now protects over 5,000 acres of heavily wooded forest with beautiful lakes, ponds, and streams. A variety of flora and fauna exit here from Moose to waterfowl, such as Loons. Admission and camping fees may apply, a variety of National and Seasonal passes along with discounts for students and seniors may also apply for day use.

Stepping off for Balance Rock starts just north of the campground parking area on the Five Summers Trail, precede pass the gate and shortly you will bear left onto the Balance Rock trail. The Balance Rock Trail is marked with yellow markers and moderately sloped; continue the ascent for 1.0 mile.

You will reach a small glacial erratic with a terrific view of the North Pond below. From this point you will arrive at the Balance Rock in less than 0.1 mile.

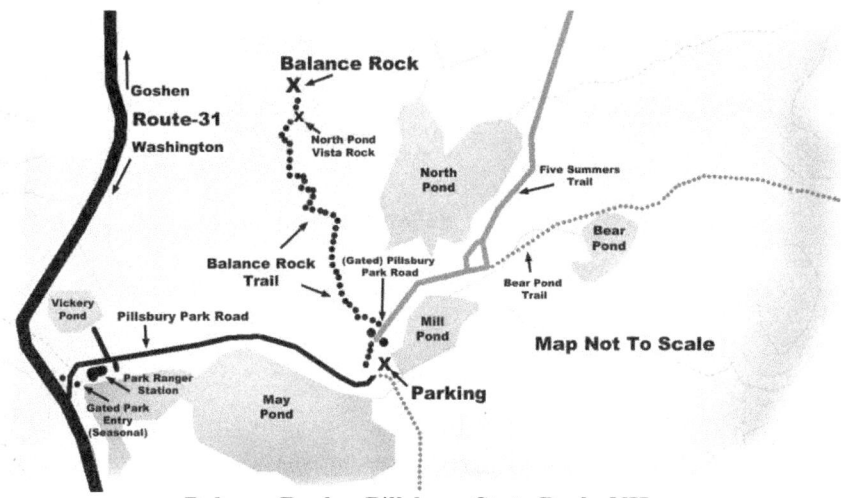

Balance Rock – Pillsbury State Park, NH

Directions: From Route-9 in Hillsborough, take Route-31 north for 13.5 miles. After the Town of Washington, Pillsbury State Park is on the right within 4.5 miles; the main gate is usually seasonally open from May to October. Stop into the Ranger Station after you enter. Travel to the end of the road to Mill pond and the camping site.

North Pond Vista Rock – Pillsbury State Park – Washington, NH

32. Balance Rock – Ragged Mountain

Balance Rock - Ragged Mountain - Andover, NH

Location: Andover (Merrimack County)
Delorme Atlas & Gazetteer-New Hampshire: p35, G-8
Parking GPS: N43° 26' 17.70" W71° 49' 38.60"
Spur-Trail Cut-off: N43° 27' 54.80" W71° 49' 56.30"
Destination GPS: N43° 27' 52.30" W71° 49' 52.90"
Wow Factor: 8 **Accessibility:** Moderate to Strenuous Trail-5 mile RT.
Contact: Sunapee-Ragged-Kearsarge Greenway Coalition Box 1684, New London, NH 03257 **e-mail:** srkgc@srkg.com

Information: Starting from the Proctor Academy in Andover, the Ragged Mountain Trail for the *Balance Rock* is part of the larger 75-mile Mt. Sunapee, Ragged Mountain and Mt. Kearsarge Greenway Trail system (SRKG). The SRKG is an all-volunteer organization with a mission to create and maintain a circle of trail corridors and conserved lands providing access to the mountains, lakes, vistas and historical sites of the central New Hampshire, Lake Sunapee Region. The SRKG trails are for day hiking only and overnight camping is not permitted. A white trapezoid shape is the universal blaze for the SRK Greenway.

The southern access for Ragged Mountain's *Balance Rock* begins from behind the Field House of the Proctor Academy. From the back of the parking lot, follow the gravel access road uphill towards the tennis courts, very shortly or where the road starts to curve left, the SRKG trail will begin on your right which leads you into the woodlands. From here you can expect a well-marked trail that is moderate in length, but with several repetitive short steep sections which can be strenuous and tedious for the next 1.7 miles as you ascend to the Balance Rock spur trail. Later, the Balance Rock Spur trail will be on your right, marked with signs and will have yellow triangular blazes. After 0.2 mile will you arrive to this truly magnificent balanced rock, the rock sits on a rounded stone ridge and protrudes off and over away from the ledge on each end; another example to ponder: How did this get this way and survive the eons? The rounded ledge of rock can be slippery and you would have a severe tumble-down for several feet, be careful if you approach the rock in this manner.

I have read that continuing pass the Balance Rock a few tenths of a mile will bring to the ledge called the "Bulkhead." The view from here is indicated to be exquisite of Mount Kearsarge and the surrounding valley.

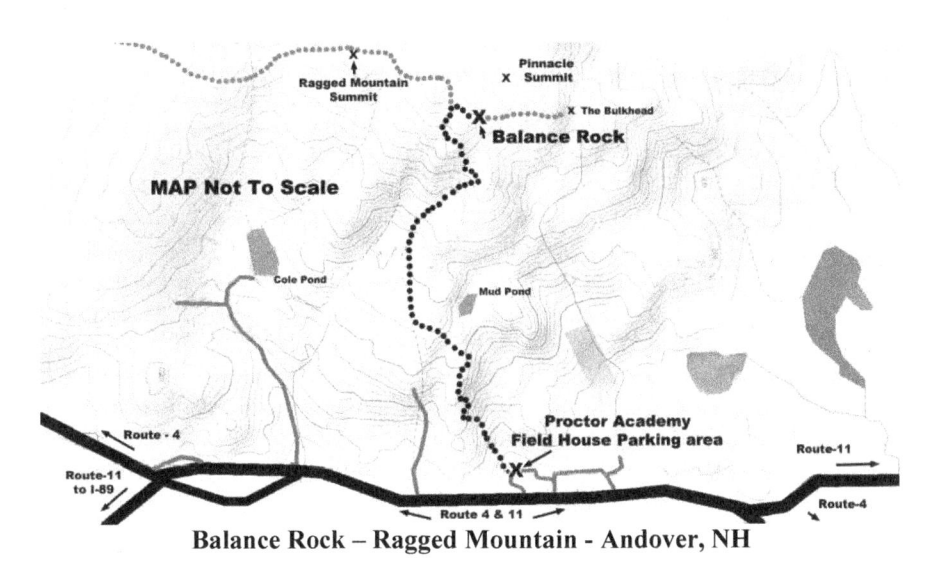

Balance Rock – Ragged Mountain - Andover, NH

Directions: From Interstate I-89 use Exit-11, Kings Hill Road, for New London. Follow Route-11 east for 7.5 miles until is junctions with Route-4. Continue east on Route-4/11as Main Street, for 1.6 miles towards Andover. The Proctor's Academy campus becomes apparent with large soccer fields on your right and with the entry to the Farrell Field House on your left directly across from the athletic fields. Follow Field House Lane all the way back to the parking area.

33. Cook Conservation Property

CK-6 – Spilt Rock B – New London, NH

Location: New London (Merrimack County)
Delorme Atlas & Gazetteer-New Hampshire: p34, H-6
Parking GPS: N43° 25' 59.20" W71° 55' 57.60"
Destination GPS: Following GPS listing – Elkins Erratic Loop Trail.
Wow Factor: varies below **Accessibility:** Moderate marked trail system.
Contact: The Ausbon Sargent Land Preservation Trust (ASLPT)
PO Box 2040, 71 Pleasant Street New London, NH 03257
(603) 526-6555 _info@ausbonsargent.org   https://ausbonsargent.org/

Information: The Cook Conservation Property Trails, ASLPT/New London Conservation Commission Trails on the Cook Easement is part of the land trust with the mission to preserve the rural landscape of the Mt. Kearsarge/Ragged/Lake Sunapee region. Presently with a body of 140 properties / 11,145 acres in their 12 town service area of Andover, Bradford, Danbury, Goshen, New London, Newbury, Springfield, Sunapee, Sutton, Warner, Webster, Wilmot, New Hampshire.

We were primarily interested in the 1.75 mile Elkins Erratic Loop Trail with the Blue Dot blazes. To note; a majority of this trail exists by the generosity of abutting neighbors allowing limited access to enjoy these erratic curiosities on their lands. Please respect their generosity by staying on marked trails along with carry in, carry out.

All trails are marked and using a color-coded Trail identification Color, a 1.5" dot placed at base of directional trapezoid. A pair of same colored dots indicates the start or finish of the trail. The dot closest to the trapezoid indicates the primary trail. We were primarily interested in the Elkins Erratic Loop Blue Trail. Some markings are easily seen others have faded or are on low rocks and can be missed if covered by leaves or snow.

The Cook easement is primarily a hiking area for the enjoyment of solitude and discovery. Therefore, there are no bicycling trails, vehicles of any kind, fires or camping, rock climbing, along with the emphasis of minimum environmental impact, carry trash in and out. Snow shoeing is suitable in the winter. A trail map and description of the Cook Easement can be found at the ASLPT website under "Connect with the Land-Trails" New London Cook #49.

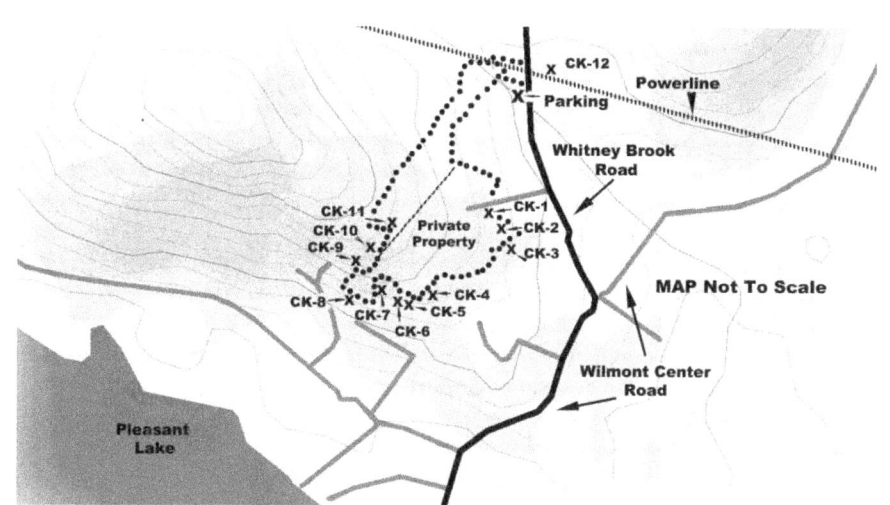

Cook Conservation Property – Elkins Erratic Trail – New London

Note: The above map is a guide of the Blue Dot - Elkens Erratic Trail only and does not indicate the additional trails within the Cook Conservation Property

CK-1: N43° 25' 46.00" W71° 55' 58.20" (Perched Rock) *WOW-4*
The top perched small rock and has that "How did natural forces create this?

CK-2: N43° 25' 45.10" W71° 55' 59.60" (Sitting Rock) *WOW -4*
Nice and easy location to sit a spell. Located on trail.

CK-3: N43° 25' 43.60" W71° 56' 0.30" (Kissing Rock) *WOW-4*
Small rock which is ideal to dispense an "Energy Kiss" as needed.

CK-4: N43° 25' 40.70" W71° 56' 7.30" (Big Top Rock) *WOW-6*
Good size rock perched at top of peak hill. The rock is located above a residential home.

CK-5: N43° 25' 41.50" W71° 56' 10.90" (Split Rock A) *WOW-6*
Good size rock with its right end split-off.

CK-6: N43° 25' 41.60" W71° 56' 10.40" (Split Rock B) *WOW-7*
Next to Split Rock A with more of a traditional center split.

CK-7 – Overhang Rock – New London, NH

CK-7: N43° 25' 42.30" W71° 56' 11.20" (Overhang Rock) *WOW-7*
Interesting rock pile with frontal overhang and a small shelter cave.

CK-8: N43° 25' 41.20" W71° 56' 13.50" (Big Boy Boulder) *WOW-8*
One of the largest and taller boulder on Elkins trail 18 feet in height.

CK-9: N43° 25' 42.40" W71° 56' 15.70" (Hill Top Rock) *WOW-5*
A good location where a refreshing cool breeze at the hill's top crest.

CK-10: N43° 25' 42.60" W71° 56' 11.70" (Table Rock) *WOW-4*
Flattish top to rock that needed to be named.

CK-11: N43° 25' 46.60" W71° 56' 10.10" (Puny Rock) *WOW-5*
Big, but not too big, chuck of rock, nothing overly significant.

CK-12: N43° 26' 1.50" W71° 55' 54.70" (Power line Rock) *WOW-8*
Large 14 foot boulder located on power line, not far from parking area
This boulder sits on private property boundary with a residence within 100 yards.

Directions: From Interstate I-89, use Exit-11; continue on Route-11 east toward Andover for 2.2 miles. Turn left on Elkins Road. Continue on Elkins Road past the dam of Pleasant Lake. At 0.8 miles you continue straight onto Wilmot Center Road. In 0.75 mile, turn left onto Whitney Brook Road. Travel 0.4 mile on Whitney Brook Road, a small roadside parking area is on the west side of the road near the Ausbon Sargent Cook Easement information kiosk.

CK-12 - Power Line Boulder – New London, NH

34. Elephant Rock

Elephant Rock – Newport, NH

Location: Newport (Sullivan County)
Delorme Atlas & Gazetteer-New Hampshire: p25, A-13
Parking GPS: N43° 19' 27.4" W72° 12' 22.6"
Destination GPS: N43° 19' 34.3" W72° 12' 11.2"
Wow Factor: 8 **Accessibility:** Moderate 0.75 mile mild uphill path to site.
Contact: Newport Historical Society. 20 Central Street. Newport, NH 03773 (603) 863-1294

Stereographic image of Elephant Rock - 1890's – Newport, NH

Information: Located at the summit of Pikes Hill, *Elephant Rock* has been a popular destination for over a century. An impressive boulder that does have a look of an elephant kneeling at rest. At 30 feet in length and 20 feet tall, standing atop the rock gave a commanding view over the town of Newport, until the reforestation of the woodlands enshrouded the hill top obscuring the view. Native Americans were also said to utilize its location to communicate to other distant landmarks.

The ATV trail accessible by Pike Hill Road will not be readily accessible by your average sedan. The beginning of Pike Hill Road is very suitable; however road size and condition will decrease to the point that a SUV or 4x4 definitely would be better suited. That said, my CR-V and dry road conditions allowed our access to the parking area unimpeded.

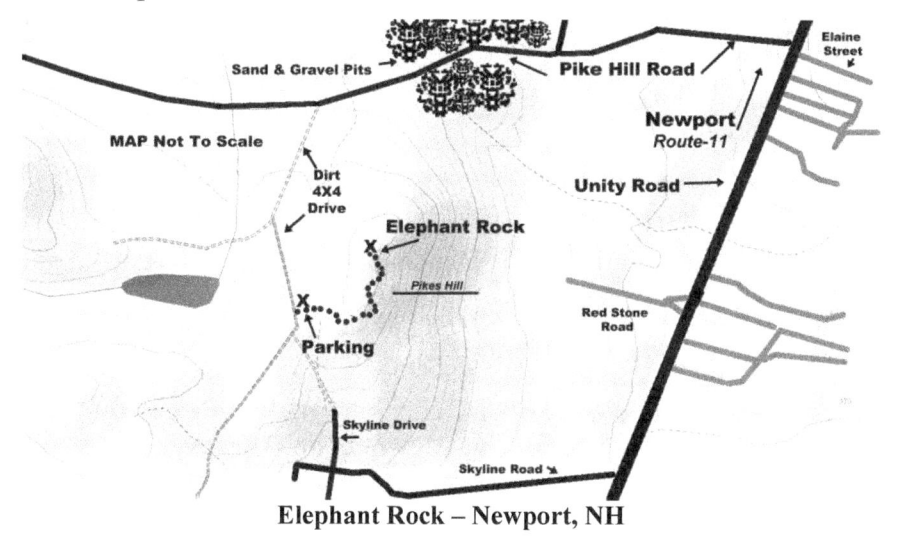

Elephant Rock – Newport, NH

Directions: In Newport at the junction of Route-10 and Route-11, follow Route-11west for 0.5 mile turning left onto E Unity Road. Drive 1.5 miles and turn right onto Pike Hill Road a hard packed dirt road. The first 0.5 mile is through a residential neighborhood and is well travel. Staying on Pike Hill road you will pass through Weed Sand & Gravel processing area and uphill into woodlands, in 0.6 mile the road will fork and become narrower and continue uphill. The next 0.3 mile becomes a less traveled and a narrower dirt road, at the fork bear left and travel 0.2 mile. On you left, heading down hill is an AVT trail which will lead one to Elephant Rock in 0.3 mile. Pull off the road the best one can, there is no noticeable parking area.

35. Franklin Pierce Lake Erratic

Franklin Pierce Lake Erratic – Antrim, NH

Location: Antrim (Hillsborough County)
Delorme Atlas & Gazetteer-New Hampshire: p 26 I-5
Parking GPS: N43° 6' 36.07" W71° 57' 5.74" (Public Boat Access)
Destination GPS: N43° 4' 46.25" W71°57'34.05"
Wow Factor: 5 **Accessibility:** Public lake - water access only.

Information: The majority of shoreline on Franklin Piece Lake a.k.a Jackman Reservoir is under private ownership. However, the public has legal access onto this navigable body of water; access is permitted and will allow one to canoe or kayak during summer and X-country ski or hike when the lake is frozen during winter. There is access from the public boat ramp on the northern end of the lake with parking. From the boat ramp it is about 2.5 miles to the southern island where the erratic sits. Watch and read any Franklin Pierce Lake Association postings for boating or regulations for lake usage.

Directions: In Hillsborough, at the interchange of Route-9 and where Route-31 turns north, follow Route-9 west for 0.5 mile, shortly after passing Ice House Road on your left, the next roadway on your left will go to the public boat ramp. Follow this road back for 0.2 mile, it will bear left sharply, continue 0.2 mile to the parking area.

36. Little Brother Profile

Little Brother Profile – Milton, NH

Location: Milton (Strafford County)
Delorme Atlas & Gazetteer-New Hampshire: p37, F-13
Parking GPS: N43° 29' 6.30" W70° 59' 40.90"
Destination GPS: N43° 29' 6.30" W70° 59' 40.90"
Wow Factor: 4 **Accessibility:** Roadside-25 yards.

Information: Interesting family likeness to original *Old Man of the Mountain*, however size is extremely different with profile being only 4-feet in height. Easy access allows close-up examination.

Directions: Rt-125, to Applebee Road, to Branch Hill Road, 425 yards up from junction 1/3 up hill, on left, in 30 feet.

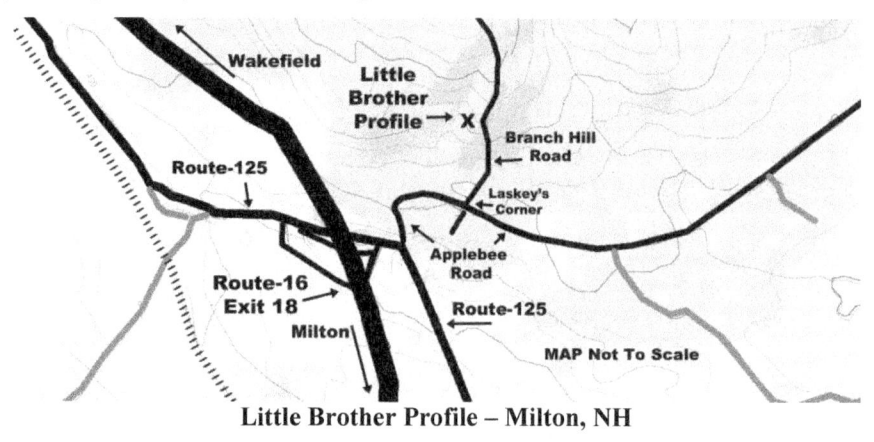

Little Brother Profile – Milton, NH

37. Madison Boulder

Madison Boulder – Madison, NH

Location: Madison (Carroll County)
Delorme Atlas & Gazetteer-New Hampshire: p41, B-9
Parking GPS: N43° 55' 53.88" W71° 10' 2.32"
Destination GPS: N43° 55' 52.19" W71°10' 4.01"
Wow Factor: 10 **Accessibility:** Easy, short 0.1 mile level path to site.
Contact: Madison Boulder Natural Area. 473 Boulder Road. Madison, NH 03849 (603) 227-8745

Information: "Largest" prominent free standing glacial erratic in New England, claimed to be one of the largest in North America if not the World! The phenomenal *Madison Boulder* measures 38 feet tall, 90 feet long, 40 feet wide and with an estimate weight upwards to 5,000 tons. Acquired by the state of New Hampshire in 1946, the park is always open for recreation unless closed or restricted by posting. During the off-season, the park is typically not staffed and comfort stations are not available. In 1970 Madison Boulder was designated a National Natural Landmark by the U.S. Department of the Interior; " is an outstanding illustration of the power of an ice sheet to pluck out very large blocks of fractured bedrock and move them substantial distances."

Directions: From junction of Route-16 and Route-113 in Albany, follow Route-113 south for 3.0 miles, on your right turn onto Boulder Road. Follow this road for 1.0 mile into the parking area.

38. Ordination Rock

Ordination Rock – Tamworth, NH

Location: Tamworth (Carroll County)
Delorme Atlas & Gazetteer-New Hampshire: p40, E-7
Parking GPS: N43° 51' 17.62" W71° 16' 47.34"
Destination GPS: N43° 51' 18.10" W71° 16' 47.53"
Wow Factor: 6 **Accessibility:** Roadside, stairs to top and memorial.

Information: On this rock after his graduation from Dartmouth College, Samuel Hidden was ordained as Tamworth's first minister on September 12, 1792. The town of Tamsworth in 1862 erected a monument on top of the rock in his memory. The monument is a white marble obelisk with a granite base, all four sides of the obelisk and base bear inscriptions. A sturdy stone staircase is on the east side of the rock which provides access to the monument. In addition, there is a large crack held in place by several embedded large steel clasps' to prevent further erosion.

Directions: From Route-113 in Tramworth center, head west on Cleveland Hill Road for 1.0 mile. Roadside parking is near the rock.

39. Papoose Rock – Holts Ledge

Papoose Rock – Lyme, NH

Location: Lyme Center (Grafton County)
Delorme Atlas & Gazetteer-New Hampshire: p38, G-2
Parking GPS: N43° 47' 28.80" W72° 6' 6.10"
Destination #1 GPS: N43° 46' 36.83" W72° 6' 17.11" (Holts Ledge)
Destination #2 GPS: N43° 46' 40.69" W72° 6' 18.29" (Ski-way Summit)
Destination #3 GPS: N43° 46' 54.50" W72° 6' 21.50" (Papoose Rock)
Wow Factor: 8 Accessibility: Moderate in distance and slope.
Contact: Dartmouth Skiway 39 Grafton Turnpike P.O. Box 161 Lyme Center, NH 03769 (603) 795-2143 dartmouth.skiway@dartmouth.edu

Information: Papoose Rock is a large glacial erratic, 20-foot in height with a very large over-hang on its top layer. I have no idea how it achieved its moniker, other than being located on the Papoose Ski Trail. However, which came first the rock's name or the trail?

To reach this boulder we followed the Appalachian Trail south for a moderate hike, uphill 1.7 miles to Holt's Ledge. Holt's Ledge is a cliff face on the south side of the Dartmouth Skiway. Along with a striking panoramic view, the ledge is a destination for rock and ice climbers. Upon reaching Holt's ledge, the return downhill trip is by way of the Dartmouth Skiway on the Papoose Trail. The ski area summit is located by walking northeast along the chain-link fence at Holt's ledge for 400-feet, until you come across a worn path which turns north for 0.1 mile and comes out onto the apex of the chair lift with several ski trails. The trails are grassy, wide and marked with signs that label or provide a level of difficulty for skiers. Looking downhill, *The Papoose trail* is the furthest to your left and labeled the easiest. Walking down the Papoose Trail for 0.2 mile, you will see the Papoose Rock on the right side. To return to the parking area, continue to walk down the Papoose Trail until you reach the roadway at the bottom, turn left and return to the parking area within 0.1 mile.

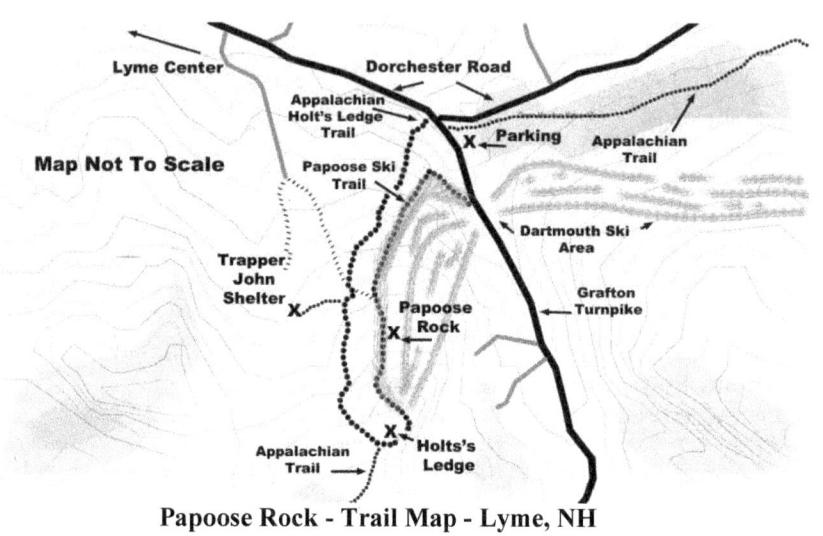

Papoose Rock - Trail Map - Lyme, NH

Directions: From Vermont, Interstate I-91 use Exit-14 Thetford, turn east onto Route-113 and travel 1.4 miles to the intersection of U.S. Route-5 in East Thetford. Turn right and head south for 100 yards, turn left across the Connecticut River Bridge into Lyme, N.H. Proceed 1.5 miles on East Thetford Road into Lyme, continue pass the north side of the Town Common, turn right at the fork at the white church and continue onto Dorchester Road. Drive 3.0 miles and bear right onto Grafton Turnpike towards the Dartmouth Skiway. Note: At this fork of Dorchester Road and the Grafton Turnpike, on the south side of the junction, is the trailhead that will go to the Holt's Ledge via the Appalachian Trail. Parking is 0.1 mile further down on your left towards the ski slope.

40. Pound Rocks

RP-5 – Pound Rocks – Rumney, NH

Location: Rumney (Grafton County)
Delorme Atlas & Gazetteer-New Hampshire: p39, F-9
Parking GPS: N43° 47' 55.72" W71° 47' 49.25"
Destination GPS: As listed below.
Wow Factor: 7-9 **Accessibility:** Roadside – No trail 100 yards or less.

Information: Judging by the chalk marks, climbers must enjoy these large and readily available boulders, especially when the Rumney Rocks, which are just down the road, are crowded with people and parking lots are jammed. It is important to be aware of the roadway, for traffic can be heavy with local residents- drivers concerned about the activities here from a safety stand point. Park well off the road and use caution when crossing.

RP-1: N43° 47' 55.40" W71° 47' 48.40" (Skip & Sandy) *WOW-7*
Roadside boulder, 16-feet in height.

RP-2: N43° 47' 55.83" W71° 47' 49.80" (EDCL Boulder) *WOW-8*
Tall 18-feet, roadside if not on or part the road. A utility pole stands in front.

RP-3: N43° 47' 55.86" W71° 47' 48.30" (Stone Wall Boulder) *WOW-8*
Large 16-feet boulder with attached plate "Old Town Pound erected in 1950."

RP-4: N43° 47' 56.30" W71° 47' 48.70" (Pound Crack) *WOW-9*
Large 25-feet in height boulder with over-hangs. Plaque attached: *"In Memory of Chris Hassig. Born May 26, 1955. Alpinist & Friend who perished climbing in Peru. Aug 25, 1985. He was in Heaven before he died." John Prine.*

RP-5: N43° 47' 56.90" W71° 47' 49.30" (Barn Door Boulder) *WOW-9*
Very roundish, 20-feet in height. Located **just slightly away from other rocks.**

RP-2 – Pound Rock – Rumney, NH

Directions: From Interstate I-93, take Exit-26 Plymouth-Rumney and follow Route-3A for 4.0 miles, Bear right at the West Plymouth traffic circle and follow Route-25 west for 3.3 miles into Rumney Depot. From Route 25, off on the right, follow Main Street 0.7 mile into Rumney, and turn right onto Quincy Road. Drive east 1.0 mile. The Pound Rocks are apparent and situated on both sides of the road.

41. Rest Stop Boulder

Rest Stop Boulder (rear) – Tilton, NH

Location: South Tilton (Belknap County)
Delorme Atlas & Gazetteer-New Hampshire: p35, F-13
Parking GPS: N43° 29' 29.59" W71° 35' 54.74"
Destination GPS: N43° 29' 27.70" W71° 35' 52.90"
Wow Factor: 8 **Accessibility:** Roadside – no trail 100 yards or less.

Information: Stopping while heading south just to stretch ones legs or if in search of a new out-of-the-way boulder to conquer, this erratic's location might be the one to check out. Approximately 28 feet tall and coupled with its unique location, this colossal boulder really surprised me and should not be a disappointment for anyone.

Rest Stop Boulder (side) – Tilton, NH

Directions: Traveling on Interstate I-93 south from Plymouth, approximately .08 mile pass Exit-22, turn into the tourist rest area and park towards the southern end of the parking area. Walk southwesterly into the woodland, within 100 yards; you will encounter this nice large rock cluster. If traveling north from Concord you will junction with Route-127 at Exit-22 traveling to re-enter onto I-93 going south for the rest area.

42. Rumney Rocks

RM-14 - Moat Boulder – Rumney, NH

Location: Rumney (Grafton County)
Delorme Atlas & Gazetteer-New Hampshire: p39, F-8
Parking GPS: N43° 48' 7.70" W71° 49' 48.33" (Parking Lot A)
Parking GPS: N43° 48' 6.61" W71° 50' 2.94" (Parking Lot B)
Destination GPS: See below Listings.
Wow Factor: 8-10 **Accessibility:** Moderate to difficult short trails.
Contact: White Mountain National Forest 71 White Mountain Drive Campton NH 03223 (603) 536-6100 Info and maps can be found; https://www.fs.fed.us

Information: While created over 300 million years ago, the cliffs, crags and boulders of Rattlesnake Mountain have become an increasingly reputable ice and rock-climbing destination. But, what do I know about this aspect of climbing? I can tell you, that both parking lots can fill up early or the unseen voices above the tree line along with the coming and goings of small groups of young men and women laden down with equipment create an enthusiasm and admiration for this sport.

Located in the southern most edge of the White Mountains National Forest, 36 acres have been address to ensure that Rumney Rocks remains accessible and sustainable for the climbing community. In partnership with the USFS and the Rumney Climbers Associations (RCA) the development of a management plan, has allowed upgrades in parking, access trails, waste control and sanitation. In response, environment impact issues also have been addressed such as cliff closures for nesting Peregrine Falcons and the monitoring and protection of Fragrant Ferns.

Up-to-date detailed information and maps of the many cliffs and trails can best found through the USFS website or through Google or other search engines. The Kiosk's provide regulations and an overview map. Both parking lots provide seasonal outhouse facilities. There is a parking fee through a self-payment system.

RM-5 – Two-Tier Boulder – Rumney, NH

While our main objectives were the many large boulders found on the lower slopes, there are many short trails which while not dead ended, will require the climbing skills and equipment to climb the cliffs and cobbles that this area has become noted for. Enjoy and explore.

Rumney Rocks Map – Rumney, NH

Parking Lot B Boulder Field.

These Parking Lot B boulders visited are within 100 yards of the parking area. While most of the climbers we saw here were bypassing these boulders with loftier goals among the cliffs above. There was some evidence of chalky foot or hand holds on some sections. I have to assume that *Blackjack Boulder's* might be a boulderer's favored destination.

RM-1: N43° 48' 7.00" W71° 50' 5.80" (Chunk Rock) *WOW-8*
Large 20-foot meatball boulder, visible from the parking area.

RM-2: N43° 48' 7.60" W71° 50' 5.90" (Pinnacle Rock) *WOW-7*
Good size rock sitting as if toppled over, located next to trail.

RM-3: N43° 48' 8.10" W71° 50' 7.20" (Perched Rock) *WOW-6*
Mini-van size boulder perched upon other smaller boulder cluster.

RM-4: N43° 48' 7.30" W71° 50' 4.40" (Middle Erratic) *WOW-7*
Not a remarkable 16-foot boulder.

RM-5: N43° 48' 7.50" W71° 50' 4.20" (Two-Tier Rock) *WOW-8*
From its uphill side, a 18-foot raised tier, the lower a tier 12-feet.

RM-6: N43° 48' 5.90" W71° 50' 7.00" (Twin Rock) *WOW-8*
A cluster of a half-dozen large boulders, 120-feet to 20 feet tall. Just a little further west from par Lot B.

RM-11 - Blackjack Boulder – Rumney, NH

Blackjack Boulder Field.

Access to the Blackjack Boulder area requires a short walk up Buffalo Road from either parking area. It is essential to note that parking along Buffalo Road is vigorously posted with no parking/tow zones. The main access trails can be located at either the main entry at utility pole #37 with a lesser used trail near pole #39.

Entry at Pole #37 GPS: N43° 48' 6.10" W71° 50' 29.20"
There is an additional entry at pole #39; we used it to exit from RM-14 Moat Boulder.

RM-7: N43° 48' 8.90" W71° 50' 30.50" (Entry Boulder) *WOW-8*
Two sides here, lower side has walk-in cave and the uphill side is all wall.

RM-8: N43° 48' 9.10" W71° 50' 29.70" (Tons of Fun) *WOW-8*
Large 16 foot boulder just above the entry boulder.

RM-9: N43° 48' 10.20" W71° 50' 28.90" (Cave Boulders) *WOW-8*
Over grown mossy cluster with many shelter caves found at different levels.

RM-10: N43° 48' 9.90" W71° 50' 32.50" (Umbrella Rock) *WOW-8*
Unique slanted boulder which appears to be climbed for its long lateral crack.

RM-11: N43° 48' 9.70" W71° 50' 32.80" (Blackjack Boulder)
Large and 30-feet tall and apparently the namesake of this boulder field.

SM-12 – Moby Dick Rock – Rumney, NH

RM-12: N43°48' 10.50" W71°50' 32.90" (Moby Dick) *WOW-8*
A cluster with two distinctive 14-feet up-right erratic's; left and right.

RM-13: N43°48'10.70" W71°50' 33.70" (Meeny-Moe Rocks) *WOW-7*
Two side by side boulders: left at 20-feet, slightly higher than the right.

RM-14: N43° 48' 11.10" W71° 50' 34.80" (Moat Boulder) *WOW-9*
Awesome gigantic boulder paired with a not as large bolder with top microcosm environment growth on its top.

Directions: From Fairlee Vermont off Interstate I-91 at Exit 15; Travel east 0.1 mile to Route-5, turn left heading north for 0.5 mile to the bridge over Connecticut River into Orford, New Hampshire. Turn south onto Rt-10, within 500-yards turn left onto Route 25A, travel east for 14.5 miles to Wentworth NH. Turn right onto Route-118/Route-25 heading easterly for 8.2 miles into Rumney. Turn left onto Main Street; heading north 0.7 miles, turn left on Buffalo Road, Rumney Rocks Climbing area is approximately 1.2 miles. The First parking area on your right, we address as *Parking Lot A* with another *Parking Lot B* on your right in an additional 0.2 miles. There is a parking fee self-service system in place at both locations.

From Interstate I-93 exit 26 in Plymouth, New Hampshire. Head west on Route-3A/Route-25 for 3.7 miles. At the traffic circle, follow Route 25 north towards Rumney for 3.4 miles turning right onto Main Street; heading north 0.7 miles, turn left on Buffalo Road, Rumney Rocks Climbing area is approximately 1.2 miles.

RM-10 - Umbrella Rock – Rumney, NH

43. Sculptured Rocks

Sculptured Rocks – Groton, NH

Location: Groton (Grafton County)
Delorme Atlas & Gazetteer-New Hampshire: p38, J-7
Parking GPS: N43° 42' 23.40" W71° 51' 24.20"
Destination GPS: N43° 42' 25.90" W71° 51' 19.20"
Wow Factor: 8 **Accessibility:** Roadside, off path slippery and hazardous.
Contact: N.H. Parks & Recreation P.O. Box 1856 251 Sculptured Rocks Road Groton, NH 03241 Phone (603)227-8745 www.nhstateparks.org

Information: Sculptured Rocks State Park is a 272-acre natural area in Groton, New Hampshire. The gorge is located on the Cockermouth River, which is the longest tributary leading into Newfound Lake. The main feature of the Sculptured Rocks, are a series of narrow, carved rocks that are astonishing smooth and uniquely shaped. The Cockermouth River carved this narrow and shapely gorge in bedrock as the last ice age drew to a close. Grains of sand suspended in the current, carved the walls of the canyon into curious shapes and created potholes in the bedrock. During the summer, the area is a very popular local swimming hole. This park is always open for recreation unless closed or restricted by posting. During the off-season the park is typically not staffed.

Directions: From the center of Groton, drive west on Groton Road for 2.7 miles, Groton Road turns into Sculptured Rocks Road. A dirt parking area will be on the left, entry and path are across the road.

44. Tipping Rock

Tipping Rock – Lebanon, NH

Location: Lebanon (Grafton County)
Delorme Atlas & Gazetteer-New Hampshire: p33, A-13
Parking GPS: N43° 38' 41.63" W72° 16' 26.90"
Destination GPS: N43° 39' 6.80" W72° 16' 7.20"
Wow Factor: 8 **Accessibility:** Moderate, some bushwhacking required.

Information: A conservation area presently owned by Dartmouth College is informally known as the Southern Bowl. The tract of land consists between 2,400 and 2,500 acres. Prior to the 1980's the area was being considered for commercial development by a real-estate developer for apartments, golf course and the like. Unlike so many other vintage hiking trail found throughout New Hampshire, this trail system is in developmental stages as recreation use increases. From my understanding, it is one of the newer conservation lands from the past few decades; end users include that of runners, hikers and mountain bikers along with x-country skiing and other winter activities. Many communities have been able unify tracts of conservation lands which have been reclaimed as reforested tracts of land. It appears that the Upper Valley Mountain Bike Association maintains the numerous mountain bike trails in the Southern Bowl area. We entered Nature's Walk through a southern entry off Pine Tree Cemetery Road. Our goal was to visit the *Tipping Rock* an iconic perched or balance rock that is a generational landmark.

Tipping Balance Rock – Lebanon, NH

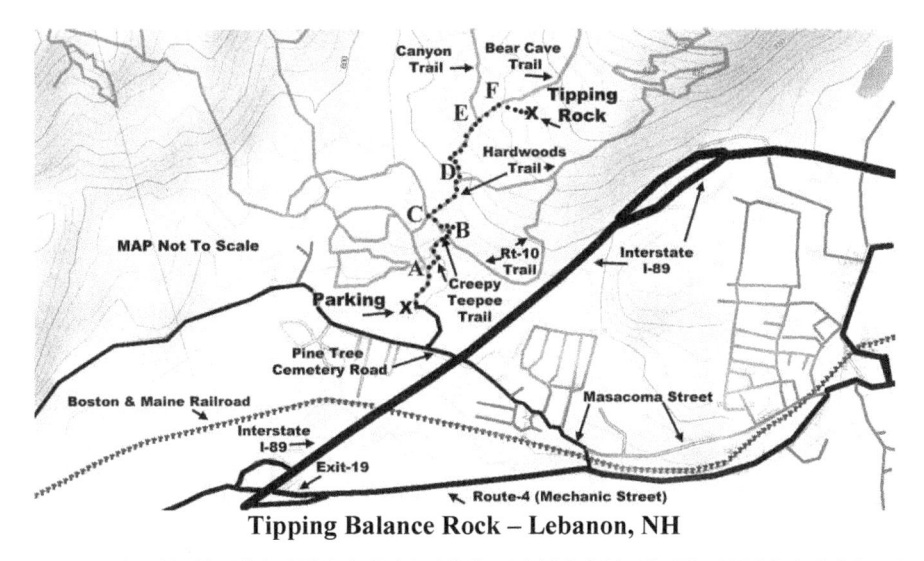

A: N43° 38' 48.7" W72° 16' 23.8" **B:** N43° 38' 52.5" W72° 16' 22.5"
C: N43° 38' 55.4" W72° 16' 22.4" **D:** N43° 39' 01.9" W72° 16' 15.8"
E: N43° 39' 05.5" W72° 16' 15.8" **F:** N43° 39' 06.4" W72° 16' 12.7"

Directions: From Interstate 89, exit-19, follow Route-4 (Mechanic Street) east for 0.7 mile, turn left onto Slayton Hill Road and pass beneath the Boston& Maine railway tracks. Turn left onto Mascoma Street, travel 0.5 mile, the street will become Pine Tree Cemetery Road and pass over I-89. Within 100 yards after passing over I-89, on your right is an unmarked dirt road which runs back to the Kiosk and trailhead into Nature's Walk southern entry point.

   From the kiosk, head north 0.1 mile, turn right onto *Creepy Teepee* trail (GPS: A) continue 0.1 mile and at (GPS: B) turn left staying on *Creepy Teepee* trail. In 100 yards at 4 corners, (GPS: C) bear sharply right onto *Hardwoods* trail. Heading north 0.2 mile, bear left onto *Canyon* trail (GPS: D) in 100 yards the *Canyon* trail will fork left (GPS: E), you will continue right up the *Bear Cave* trail. Heading north, 100 yards up the *Bear Cave* trail, you will turn sharply right,(GPS: F) into the woodlands between two small ridges into the woodlands. Bushwhacking easterly, *Tipping Rock* can be located within 100 yards. Note: There may be some orange logging ribbons attached to branches providing some clues for direction. Otherwise, destination GPS value just increased.

Vessel Rock – Gilsum

Vessel Rock 2017– Gilsum - N43° 1' 48.01" W72° 16' 31.80"

This prominent landmark located on Vessel Rock Road was originally named for its resemblance of a vessel under full sail. A major segment which represented the bow and the jib-boom of a vessel was altered by an earthquake in October 5, 1817. The the original school house (Top Photo) was constructed in 1850. As seen today, (Bottom Photo) occupied by the present resident in Gilsum.

"History of the Town of Gilsum, N.H. 1752-1879" by Silvanus Hayward."

Private Property – No directions

New Hampshire – Southern

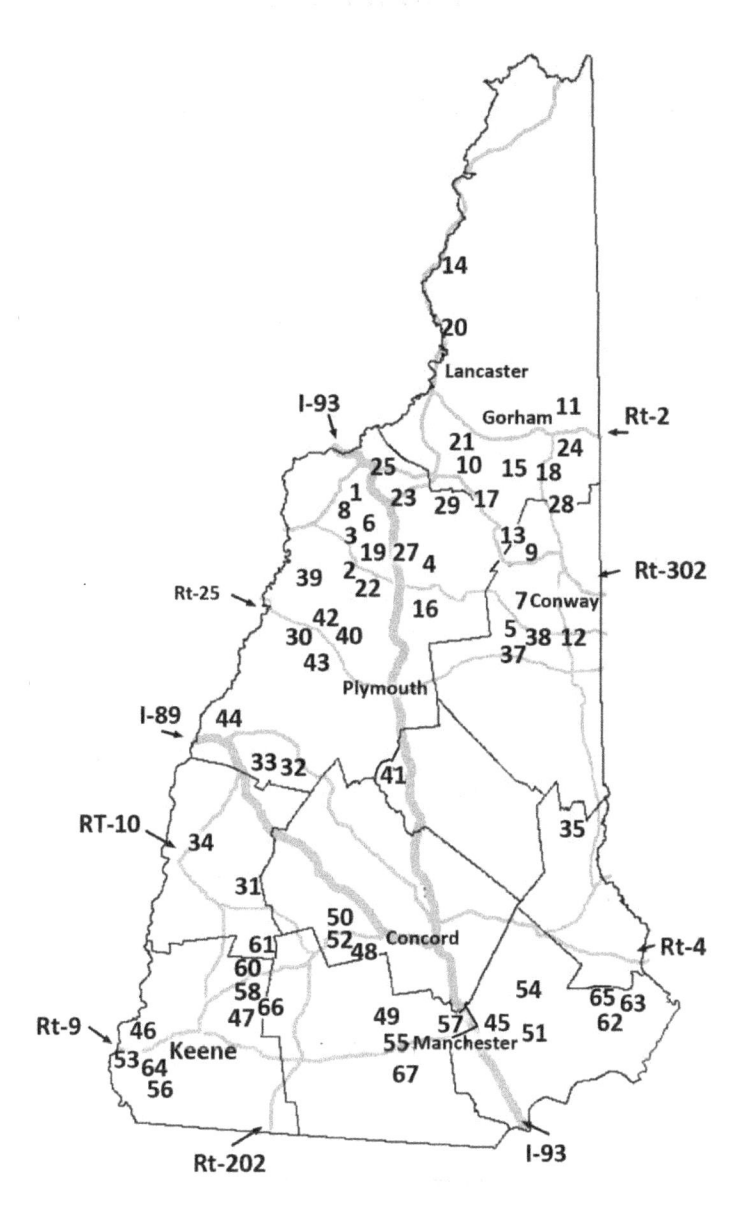

MAP Not To Scale - For Reference Only

New Hampshire – Southern

45. Butterfield Boulder (Windham)
46. Chesterfield Gorge (Chesterfield)
47. East Side Trails: Harris Center (Hancock)
48. Erratic: Old Concord Rd (Henniker)
49. Frog Rock (New Boston)
50. House Rock (Hillsborough)
51. Indian Rock (Windham)
52. Keystone Bridges: (Keene, Gilsum, Stoddard, Hillsborough,)
53. Madame Sherri's Castle (Chesterfield)
54. Pawtuckaway Park (Nottingham)

54a. *Area 51*
54b. *Natural Area*
54c. *North Marsh*
54d. *Round Pond*
54e. *Split Rock Trail*

55. Pulpit Rock –Indian Rock (Bedford)
56. Revolutionary Rock (Richmond)
57. Rock Rimmon a.k.a. Rock Raymond (Manchester)
58. Rye Pond (South Stoddard)
59. Simonds Rock a.k.a. Pennichuck Rock (Merrimack)
60. Stoddard Power Line Boulders (Stoddard)
61. Stoddard Rocks: Highland Lake Conservation (Stoddard)
62. The Rinks Boulder (Exeter)
63. Thompson Farm Boulder (Durham)
64. Tippin Rock (Swanzey)
65. Vincent Rock a.k.a. Big Rock (Epping)
66. Willards Pond Balance Rock (Antrim)
67. Wolf Rock (Mason)

45. Butterfield Boulder

Butterfield Boulder – North Windham, NH

Location: North Windham (Rockingham County)
Delorme Atlas & Gazetteer-New Hampshire: p22, G-6
Parking GPS: N42° 49' 3.85" W71° 18' 45.13"
Destination GPS: N42° 48' 51.45" W71° 18' 42.73"
Wow Factor: 8 **Accessibility:** Public Golf Course-limited viewing.
Contact: Windham Country Club One Country Club Road. Windham, NH 03087 (603) 434-2093 www.windhamcc.com

Information: "Butterfield's Rock is one of the natural curiosities and noted landmarks in the Town of Windham. Cited in boundary records for 300 years; *"under the date October 29, 1723,....land lying and being to the south west of the rock called Butterfield's rock;* "*...Windham was set off from Londonderry in 1742. There is an old path, still usable running through the woods from near Butterfield's rock."* This collection of images does show that trees may come and go, but the *Butterflied Boulder* just endures. Presently owned by the Windham Country Club, permission is required before a visitation, best for golf off season or poor golf weather days.

Butterfield Boulder, Windham Junction, N. H.

Butterfield Boulder – Notice the variants in the trees. – North Windham, NH

Directions: In New Hampshire, on Interstate Route-93 north, use Exit-3 to Route-111, Windham. Head west on Route-111 for 1.3 miles, turn right onto North Lowell Road. Continue north 1.1 miles until you turn left onto Londonderry Rd; head west for 0.5 mile, turn onto Country Club Road.

46. Chesterfield Gorge

Chesterfield Gorge State Park – Chesterfield, NH

Location: Chesterfield (Cheshire County)
Delorme Atlas & Gazetteer-New Hampshire: 19, D-9
Parking GPS: N42° 54' 51.49" W72° 24' 17.11"
Destination GPS: N42° 54' 59.50" W72° 24' 23.40"
Wow Factor: 4 **Accessibility:** Public access-0.8 mile loop trail.
Contact: Chesterfield Gorge Natural Area. 1823 Route-9, Chesterfield, NH 03443 Phone: 603-363-8373 www.nhstateparks.org

Information: Being labeled as a "Geological Park" with some sort of significant rifts with exposure of the rock formations and their geological history. e.g. *"This local bedrock is a type of igneous rock called a granodiorite...a granite with darker colored minerals in it. Geologists currently believe this rock formed in the crust as molten rock, during the Ordovician time period."* I thought wrong, what consisted of a few small 6-feet erratic's was a bust for our angle on its exploration. However, will not bash the park, for the day turned out very relaxing with enjoyment of the cascading stream and waterfall all within a very well maintained park, it was great! Just don't judge a book by its cover.

Directions: From the traffic circle in western Keene, travel Route-9 west for 6.2 miles. The Chesterfield Gorge State Wayside with a large paved parking area, ranger cabin, and kiosk will be readily found. A path from behind kiosk begins an elongated moderate trail, down one side of Wilde Brook Cascades and returns up on the opposite side. A newly well-constructed bridge is halfway enabling one to choose either side to hike.

47. East Side Trails

HC-2 – Split Rock – Harris Center – Hancock, NH

Location: Hancock (Cheshire County)
Delorme Atlas & Gazetteer-New Hampshire: p20, A-4
Parking GPS: N42° 58' 41.42" W72° 1' 13.85" (Harris Center)
Parking GPS: N42° 59' 04.11" W72° 0' 29.05" (Route-123 entry)
Destination GPS: Individual GPS locations below.
Wow Factor: 5 to 8 **Accessibility:** Marked trails – moderate conditions.
Contact: Information and trail maps can found posted on kiosk at Harris Center for Conservation Education, 83 King's Highway. Hancock, NH 03449 (603) 525-3394 www.harriscenter.org

Information: Beginning in 1928, Dr. L. Vernon Briggs purchased many parcels of property that grew into a 3,000-acre estate. Later, his granddaughter, Eleanor Briggs in 1966 started to re-purchase some of the land and in 1970 established the Harris Center for Conservation Education using her grandparent's house as its education center. Of interest is that the Harris Center for Conservation is named after her cat named *Harris*, who she felt *"represented certain wildness, humor, savvy and strong instinct, all elements needed for a successful environmental education center."*

Since then, the Harris Center along with a philosophical approach that *"bigger is better"* and the key is *"not who protects what, but what gets protected "* has played a role in over 34,500-acres of protected lands in the towns of Antrim, Dublin, Greenfield, Hancock, Harrisville, Nelson, Peterborough, and Stoddard.

Our hikes to the various boulders in "The East Side Trails" system began from the Harris Center parking lot on the Dandelyon Trail that connects with the blue blazed Boulder Trail, these boulders are readily encountered trail-side by this loop trail. Other erratic's will require an relatively easy jaunt off trail to discover hidden glacial erratic's that are scattered through-out this forest.

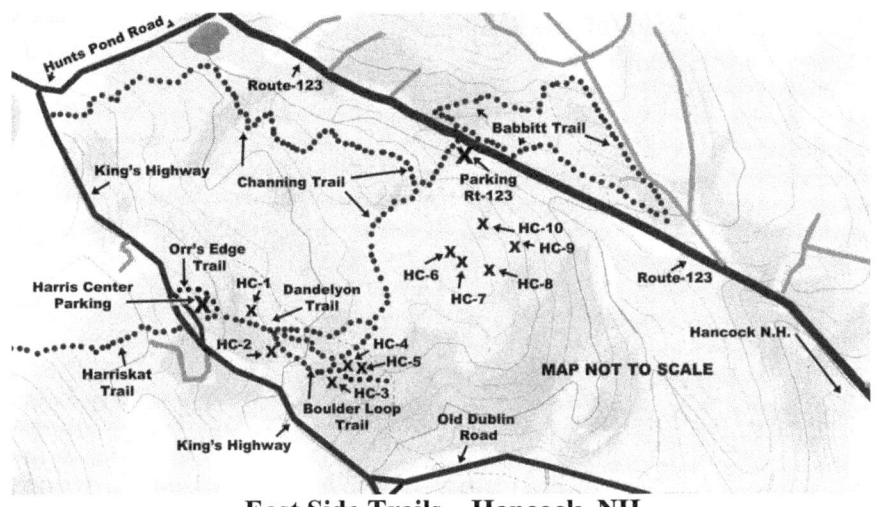

East Side Trails – Hancock, NH

HC-1: N42° 58' 39.78" W72° 1' 1.93" (Dandelyon Trail) *WOW-5*
Small unremarkable boulder cluster.

HC-2: N42° 58' 37.43" W72° 1' 0.37" (Split Rock) *WOW-8*
Almost a perfect walk-through split with two equal halves. Slightly off trail.

HC-3: N42° 58' 33.84" W72° 0' 54.43" (Overhang Rock) *WOW-8*
Unique balanced or perched 10 foot rock, with over-hang atop on stone tier.

HC-4: N42° 58' 33.76" W72° 0' 52.88" (Teepee Rock) *WOW-6*
Two rocks, angled creating a small triangular shelter cave on its end.

HC-5: N42° 58' 32.81" W72° 0' 52.49" (Rock Pile) *WOW-5*
Boulder field with several small 10 foot boulders strewn about.

HC-6: N42° 58' 49.00" W72° 0' 28.90" (Big Nose) *WOW-7*
Side profile of 12 foot rounded boulder with head and nose.

HC-7: N42° 58' 48.50" W72° 0' 27.30" (Twin Rock) *WOW-6*
Low slung split rock Two equally distributed 5-feet x 10-feet halves.

HC-8: N42° 58' 46.70" W72° 0' 23.50" (Moose Rock) *WOW-5*
Small 10-foot with sloping front – not overly a remarkable rock.

HC-9: N42° 58' 51.00" W72° 0' 20.80" (Fractured Rock)
Cluster of 10-foot fractured rocks among a boulder train of smaller rocks.

HC-10: N42° 58' 54.10"" W72° 0' 24.90" (Round Top)
Large 14-feet tall, roundish boulder, covered with lush moss and lichens.

HC-3 Balanced –Over-Hang Rock – Harris Center – Hancock, NH

Directions: From Keene, take Route-9 east past Munsonville. Turn right on Route-123 towards Hancock. Follow Route-123; 5.0 miles south to Hunt's Pond Road. Turn right on Hunt's Pond Road and follow the road west for about 0.4 mile, then turn left onto King's Highway. Follow King's Highway for 0.6 mile. The Harris Center will be on your left.

HC-6 - Big Nose – Hancock, NH

48. Old Concord Road Erratic

Old Concord Road Erratic – Henniker, NH

Location: Henniker (Merrimack)
Delorme Atlas & Gazetteer-New Hampshire: p27, F-9
Parking GPS: N43° 10' 54.24" W71° 47' 3.53"
Destination GPS: N43° 10' 54.24" W71° 47' 3.53"
Wow Factor: 5 **Accessibility:** Roadside

Information: So to say, we left no stone unturned! While this rock is probably known locally and even seems to have some boulderer's talc residue, it is apparent that being located on the roadway and sharing a boundary with private property, that activities here can only be limited. Yet, here we are looking at this tall, 18-feet boulder which for someone is their little patch of tranquility. Good for a drive-by evaluation, but no hikes here.

Directions: From Interstate I-89 in Hopkinton, take Exit-5 onto Route-9 heading west for 5.2 miles. At a cross-road with a flashing yellow light, on your left, turn onto Old Concord Road and continue left for 0.3 mile. The peaked rock will be roadside and on the left.

49. Frog Rock

Frog Rock – New Boston, NH

Location: New Boston (Hillsborough)
Delorme Atlas & Gazetteer-New Hampshire: p21, C-10
Parking GPS: N42° 55' 37.95" W71° 43' 25.21"
Destination GPS #1: N42° 55' 56.54" W71° 43' 23.55" (Frog Rock)
Destination GPS #2: N42° 55' 56.85" W71° 43' 22.08" (Teetering Rock)
Wow Factor: 7 **Accessibility:** 0.4 mile hike old road, then short path.

Information: During the mid to late 1800's several hotels in the New Boston vicinity were during the summer months tourist destinations. These "tourists" in those days developed a fond attraction to a large glacial erratic known for its unusual profile "Frog Rock." This 10-foot erratic has an uncanny resemblance to a frog squatting on a slab of stone out in the open. It was well photographed and subject to many postcard sentiments.

In 1974, Dr. Charles and Mrs. Frances Hildreth Townes donated several parcels (551 acres) of pasture land and forest. In 2004, another eight acres was donated in memory of their father Harold H. Wilkins Jr. by the Wilkins family. This last parcel of land also held the glacial erratic curiosities of "Frog Rock" and "Teetering Rock" Teetering Rock a 6-foot erratic, is located very near Frog Rock and was said to be rocked by a mere touch of one's hand. Today, Frog Rock has far fewer admirers and Teetering Rock doesn't. The open pastures and ledges have been hidden by forest re-growth with both of these locations are scarcely spoken or known about.

Both these historical landmarks are easily accessible by Frog Rock Road. Now abandon, the dirt road provides a 0.4 mile easy path to Frog Rock and Teetering Rock. The southern entry for Frog Rock Road is found off a corner on Francestown Turnpike, just prior to crossing over the town line for Mont Vernon, but still in New Boston. A small roadside pull-off can be found here to park also.

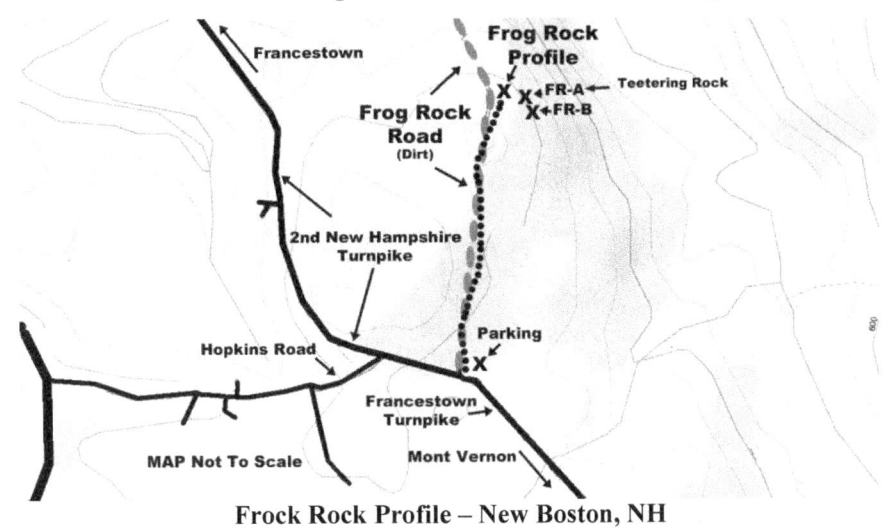

Frock Rock Profile – New Boston, NH

Frog Rock 1890's – New Boston, NH

Directions: In Milford, at the junction of Route-101A and Route-13, follow Route-13 north for 5.0 miles. Just north of Mt. Vernon turn left onto *Francestown Turpike* a.k.a. *2nd New Hampshire Turnpike*, continue north for 3.0 miles. Frog Rock Road will be off on your right, just after a sweeping left turn with warning caution signs and arrows. If you reach Hopkins Road on your left, turn back 0.1 mile.

50. House Rock

House Rock – Hillsborough, NH

Location: Hillsborough (Hillsborough)
Delorme Atlas & Gazetteer-New Hampshire: p26, E-6
Parking GPS: N43° 11' 29.22" W71° 55' 17.53"
Destination GPS: N43° 11' 28.90" W71° 55' 20.60"
Wow Factor: 9 **Accessibility:** 0.1 walk no path

Information: In the northeast corner of Hillsborough near the Farrar Marsh State Wildlife Management Area, a massive glacial erratic *House Rock* is located on its own 20-acre conservation parcel.

Folklore asserts that a family lost their home during a horrible fire in winter and needed shelter. The very unique feature of this boulder is the interior of fractured cervices and passageways, does allows one to walk around upright, finding survivable living shelter here is not that unbelievable. Today, the only survival instincts you might need here is a good mosquito repellant! Jan & I had a grand time exploring this rock; the only fear I had to dispel for Jan was that no grungy hermit was living inside.

Directions: In Hillsboro, traveling on Route-9/Route-202, exit onto Henniker Street, turn and head north for 0.1 mile and immediately turn left on Old Henniker Street for 0.3 mile and turn right onto Whitney Road for 0.2 mile and turn right again onto Bog Road. Travel north on Bog Road for 4.2 miles, Bog Road starts off residential and becomes more back dirt road, shortly after you pass Farrar Marsh State Wildlife Management area, the road will fork. Bear left onto Sand Knoll Road which is narrower and less maintained. Continue north for 0.5 mile, Kimball Road will be on the left; Sand Knoll Road will continue straight and becomes even less maintained. Fortunately from here, 100 yards up on the left, a single car pull-off can be found. House Rock is some 70 yards in from the road. Access on Bog Road is not always going to be suitable in a small sedan. All-wheel drive SUV's or a 4x4 vehicles may be better suited in spring thaw or after heavy rains.

51. Indian Rock

Indian Rock – Windham, NH

Location: Windham (Hillsborough)
Delorme Atlas & Gazetteer-New Hampshire: p22, G-7
Parking GPS: N42° 48' 29.40" W71° 16' 45.60"
Destination GPS: N42° 48' 29.40" W71° 16' 45.60"
Wow Factor: 4 **Accessibility:** 50 yard walk

Information: In early days the Native American tribe referred to as Indians of the Pawtucket Nation used to encamp on the shores of Cobbett's' Pond. In fact large settlements with open agricultural fields along with hunting and fishing at Pawtucket Falls appear to be well researched on their interaction prior to 1653 until the 1685 when the tribe departed for the settlement of Londonderry. Over time with the building of Cobbett's Pond Road and Route-111 many implements and tools of their culture have been unearth. The rock is a tribute to their remembrance; the worn grinding holes atop of *Indian Rock* memorialized their noble lifestyle. The plaque and rock have been spared eradication, but lays hidden in today's world.

"Over these rock strewn hills and through these woods the Indians roamed on their hunt for game, on these waters their canoes were launched in their quest for fish, nearby fields yielded their harvest of corn and on this rock it was ground in to meal."
This tablet erected by the Town of Windham, A.D. 1933."

Directions: In Windham on Interstate I-93, take Exit-3 entering onto Route-11, follow Route-11 west for 0.8 mile turning left onto Indian Rock Road, head east for 0.4 mile. On your left with no signs or markings, an old access road (across the street from Rocky Ridge Road) leads into the woodland strip. Indian Rock is the only rock on your right.

52. Keystone Bridges

KB-9 – Gleason Falls Road – Hillsborough, NH

Location: Varied by location
Parking GPS: Varied by location of bridge below.
Destination GPS: Varied by location of bridge below.
Wow Factor: 8 **Accessibility:** Roadside to short walk..

Information: Many of New England's keystone bridges still stand today in tribute to the stone masons and their craftsmanship. Since the 1840's, some earlier, these massive structures have withstood the elements of weather or raging flood waters. Constructed with a "dry mortar" technique meaning; without the use of mortar and cement; the characteristic masonry "arch" where a single "Keystone" or linchpin wedge, is placed at the apex of the arch which locks all the stones into position. While many blocks of stone were hand cut and crafted from quarries, true to New England resourcefulness, others found that glacial erratic remnants could be incorporated into their construction. Still standing, many are in daily use and still spanning the streams, rivers or chasms they were intended for.

KB-0: N42° 50' 48.90" W72° 11' 25.40" (Cheshire R&R –Troy)
One of the smaller Cheshire R&R Keystone Bridges spanning Shaker Brook. Adjacent to Route-12 and part of the Cheshire Rail Trail.

KB-1 - Webb Depot Road – Marlborough, NH

KB-1: N42° 52' 24.10" W72° 12' 46.90" (Webb Bridge –Marlborough)
Once carrying the Cheshire Railroad for over 100 years, the railway was an important commercial link between Keene, NH and Fitchburg, MA. New life has been found as being part of a Cheshire Rail Trail and pedestrian walkway. (Webb Bridge Road off Route-9.)

KB-1 - Route-101 Keystone Arch Bridge – Keene, NH

KB-2: N42° 54' 50.60" W72° 15' 10.80" (Cheshire R&R – Keene)
This Cheshire Railroad Stone Arch Bridge was built 1847, it is the largest of the (20) bridges built prior to 1850 with a 90-foot span across the Branch River. This stone arch bridge was placed on the National Register of Historic Places on August 14, 2012; it too has new life as part of the Cheshire Rail Trail and pedestrian walkway.

KB-3 - Keystone Bridge – Gilsum, NH

KB-3: N43° 2' 21.10" W72° 16' 14.10" (Surry Road – Gilsum)
Gilsum Stone arch bridge built 1863 over the over Ashuelot River on Old Route-10, rehabilitated in 1951 and still carrying traffic. Placed on National Register of Historic Places on August 31, 1989

KB-4: N43° 4' 27.30" W72° 2' 43.20" (Route-9 – Stoddard)
Built in 1852 spanning the Contoocook River River. Bypassed by Route-9 and open for pedestrians only. Very picturesque location.

KB-5 – Sawyer – Hillborough, NH

KB-5: N43° 6' 41.80" W71° 55' 7.70" (Sawyer Bridge- Hillsborough)
This 30-foot, double arch bridge was built over the North Branch River in 1867 and only removed from service in 1988. (Route-202/149)

KB-7 – Old Carr Bridge – Hillsborough, NH

KB-7: N43° 7' 49.00" W71° 56' 41.20" (Carr Bridge – Hillsborough)
Double arch bridge over the Beards Brook at the junction of the Beard and Jones Roads, a.k.a. the Old Carr Bridge, built by Captain Jonathan Carr in 1840 and allegedly was paid for with counterfeit money.

KB-8 Gleason Falls Bridge – Hillsborough, NH

KB-8: N43° 8' 36.90" W71° 57' 20.70" (Gleason Falls -Hillsborough)
Built 1830's this Keystone Stone arch bridge over Beards Brook on Beard Road. With a cascading waterfall you can only imagine the turrets of water that has passed beneath this stone arch bridge trying to dislodge or dispose of this bridge. (On Beard Road – Hillsborough)

KB-9: N43° 8' 41.90" W71° 57' 34.50" (Gleason Falls Road-Hillsborough)
Uniquely constructed with two different spans with two different span to arch aspect ratios. Unknown designer and date of construction remains

53. Madame Sherrie's Castle

Madame Sherrie's Castle - 2016 – Chesterfield, NH

Location: Chesterfield (Cheshire)
Delorme Atlas & Gazetteer: p18, H-7
Parking GPS: N42° 51' 53.46" W72° 31' 3.83"
Destination GPS: N42° 51' 52.20" W72° 31' 10.50"
Wow Factor: 7 **Accessibility:** 0.1 walk from parking area.

Information: Famous for its arched stone staircase in the middle of the forest, *Madame Sherri's Castle* is also legendary for its rumors of ghosts. Madame Antoinette Sherri was a costume designer, her plans were to build a castle here in the late 1920s, but she ran out of funds and the castle was left abandoned and incomplete. Still remaining are the staircase, foundation, some columns and a fireplace. Some say Madame Sherri's apparition has been seen on the staircase, called the *"Stairway to Heaven."* In addition, back in the day, Madame Sherri was noted for a few lavish parties with some modern day visitors describing the presence of haunting sounds or hearty laughter and eerie music within the silence of the woodlands.

Original staircase with railing and flower box posts – Chesterfield, NH

Truly the forest is here due to Ann Stokes who purchased the property shortly after Madame Sherri's death in 1965. Later, Ann Stokes donated the property to the Society for the Protection of New Hampshire Forest in February 1991. There is a network of popular hiking trails here. The kiosk has a map and more details to the combined efforts of Madame Sherri's 513 acre forest along with the Ann Stokes Loop trail. With interconnecting trails to scenic Indian Pond, the rocky Mine Ledges of Wantastiquet Mountain a.k.a. "Rattlesnake Mountain" and along with the 847 acre Wantastiquet State Forestland with parts of Chesterfield Cook Town Forest.

Direction: From the Brattleboro, VT and Chesterfield, N.H. border bridge crossing on the Connecticut River, head east on Route-9 for 0.1 mile, turning right onto Mountain Drive, head south for 0.1 mile and turn left onto Gulf Road. Follow Gulf Road southeast for 2.2 miles, on your right will be an improved dirt parking area with room for several cars. Beware, posted: *"PARKING Tickets. There is no parking on Gulf Road. Across Gulf Road there is overflow parking. Cross Gulf Road and go straight up the old road. In about 200 feet there is a right turn into a cleared area for overflow parking."* Behind the kiosk marks the beginning of the Wantastiquet Mountain Trail, begin here with the slight ascent and within a short distance a spur trail on your right will lead you to Sherri's Castle ruins.

54. Pawtuckaway State Park

PT-e Big & Tall – Round Pond – Pawtuckaway, NH

Location: Deerfield - Nottingham (Rockingham County)
Delorme Atlas & Gazetteer-New Hampshire: p29, H-9
Parking GPS: Listed per section explanation below.
Destination GPS: Individual locations below.
Wow Factor: 8, 9, 10's **Accessibility:** Varies to location.
Contact: Pawtuckaway State Park. 128 Mountain Road. Nottingham, NH 03290 (603) 895-3031 www.nhstateparks.org
http://www.nhstateparks.org/uploads/pdf/Pawtuckaway-Trail-Map.pdf

Information: Pawtuckaway State Park is situated in southern New Hampshire and consists of over 5,500 acres of a diverse landscape primarily in the town of Nottingham. The park offers many well marked and maintained hiking trails that provide access to hundreds of boulders that are easily classified as immense glacial erratics. This location must have been a magnet for colossal boulders. The Pawtuckaway Mountains are a small, rocky, circular range that forms the outline of an ancient volcanic ring. In addition to the many miles of documented trails and landmarks, new adventures await those who seek out the many "off trail" wonders. With excitement, one may explore unofficially named boulder fields such as: Round Pond, Magic Pond, Split Rock, Area-51, Blair Woods, Ridgeline Boulders, Natural and Boulder Trail all with striking and remarkable wonders which will leave you with more questions than answers.

Parking GPS: N43° 7' 13.23" W71° 09' 55.23" (Round Pond Road-East)

Directions: *Round Pond Road -East.* Nottingham/Deerfield Road.

From Route-4 /Route-202, take either Route-107 south out of Epsom or Route 43 south out of Northwood. From either direction in about 6 miles, Rt-43 and Rt-107 junctions in Deerfield. Travel south for 50 yards and immediately turn left onto Parade Road. Traveling southeast for 0.8 mile you will enter a small town common, Nottingham Road will enter on your right as Parade Road ends here. From the town common, continue southeast on Nottingham Road for 0.7 mile where the road will fork right. Bear right staying on Nottingham road for an additional 2.75 miles until you reach Round Pond Road on your right. The Welcome sign at this entry point comes with a multi warning that "Illegal parking will be towed at owner's expense and subject to an imposed fine." Follow Round Pond Road 0.3 mile to the end, to a parking area found off to your left, Round Pond Road continues down past this gated entry, walking down .75 miles you'll be at Round Pond. This entry is popular and can be difficult to park in during off season such as; winter, mud season and when all other entry points are closed for the season. This will provide access to Round Pond and Boulder Trail year around, but requires a 0.6 mile hike downhill and back.

Parking GPS: N43°6' 57.20" W71° 10' 41.90" (Round Pond)
Parking GPS: N43°7' 8.40" W71° 11' 18.10" (Round Pond-lower)

Directions: *Round Pond* Direct access to Round Pond is achievable when the Reservation Road gate if opened by the parks department. From where Routes-43/Route-107 junction in Deerfield, continue south for 3.5 miles, at the fork where Rt-43 bears right and Rt-107 bears left, follow Rt-107 left and south for an additional 0.6 mile, turn left onto Reservation Road. From here you will enter into Pawtuckaway State Park in approximately 1.5 miles, the dirt road is well maintained and you will shortly see North Mountain trail head and parking. Another 0.5 mile, on your left is the lower end of Round Pond Road; a maintained, dirt road, but narrower, if the gate is open, you can proceed to Tower Junction Road in 1.4 mile, the western end of the Boulder Field Trailhead in 2.0 miles and Round Pond parking and the other end of the Boulder Trail in 2.5 miles.

Parking GPS: N43°6' 03.48" W71° 11' 31.55" (Tower Road A)
Parking GPS: N43°6' 29.63" W71° 10' 49.25" (Tower Road B)

Directions: *Tower Road* Staying on Reservation Road to Tower Road will be found in 0.2 mile after passing the Round Pond Road turn-off. Turning left and on your right in 0.1 mile is a small pull-off (Tower Rd - Parking A) with a trail head for the Mountain Trail, South Mountain Trail and my bushwhack-short-cut through Area-51 over to the Split Rock Trail. In addition, continuing pass this small parking area and following Tower Road another 1.0 mile, is another small pull-off (Tower Rd - Parking B) just another access point to South Mountain and the Split Rock Trail via the Shaw Trail. Eventually driving pass parking area B on Tower Road, you will in another 0.5 mile reconnect with Round Pond Road.

PT-p – The Slab - Boulder Trail – Pawtuckaway, NH

PT-p - Split-Cave Rock – North Marsh - Pawtuckaway, NH

54a. Pawtuckaway: *Area 51*

PT-7 - Massive Rock A in Area 51 – Pawtuckaway, NH

Description: Area-51 is a large tract of marsh and woodland on the south-eastern side of South Mountain, flanked by the Mountain Trail to its west and the Split Rock Trail to its east. Access to Area-51 is really for those who enjoy the adventure of off-trail bushwhacking or seeking more solitude than some of the highly trafficked trails. This isolated location has many large boulders and is normally not as frequented by boulderer's as in more popular and easier accessible areas such as Round Pond or the Boulder Trail area. However, its negative aspects require navigation and direction to prevent the floundering into the boggy or marshy areas within its perimeters. A GPS devise or compass is highly recommended if you plan to visit this area.

Boulder Field – Area 51

PT-0: N43° 05' 50.0" W71° 10' 51.2" (Broken Rock) *WOW-5*
Erratic 12 feet to 14 feet tall with end cracked off.

PT-2: N43° 05' 51.1" W71° 10' 55.0" (Rock Group) *WOW-5*
Small 10 foot, roundish boulder atop small ridge line

PT-4: N43° 05' 58.6" W71° 10' 49.0" (Little Big Rock) *WOW-5*
Tall 12 foot pillar.

PT-5: N43° 05' 59.3" W71° 10' 48.9" (Bigger Rock) *WOW-6*
14 to 16 feet tall with small cluster of rocks around base.

PT-7: N43° 05' 57.6" W71° 10' 48.1" (Massive Rock A) *WOW-9*
Very large block, 16 x 30 x 25 feet

PT-8 - Massive Rock B in Area 51- Pawtuckaway, NH

PT-8: N43° 05' 59.4" W71° 10 43.5" (Massive Rock B) *WOW-9*
Very large Roundish 22' boulder, large vertical crack one side.

PT-9: N43° 06' 01.0" W71° 10' 41.9" (Small Group C) *WOW-5*
Slanted 8''- 10' main boulder with cluster with 3-4 small rocks

PT-10: N43° 06' 01.5" W71° 10' 40.0" (Cluster West) *WOW-7*
Very large boulder train 14' feet-by 20 feet, shelter caves, passageways

PT-11: N43° 06' 01.8" W71° 10' 39.2" (Cluster Center) *WOW-8*
Very large boulder train 16'- 22', shelter caves, passageways

PT-12: N43° 06' 01.8" W71°10' 40.6" (Cluster Center) *WOW- 7*
Very large boulder train 14'- 20', shelter caves, passageways

PT-13 - Ship Rock in Area 51 – Pawtuckaway, NH

PT-13: N43° 06' 03.5" W71° 10' 38.2" (Ship Rock) *WOW-8*
Very large boulder 20 feet to 30' eastern side adjacent to Cluster.

PT-14: N43° 06' 04.0" W71° 10' 38.2" (Cluster North) *WOW-9*
Large upended 20'x20'x 25' boulder

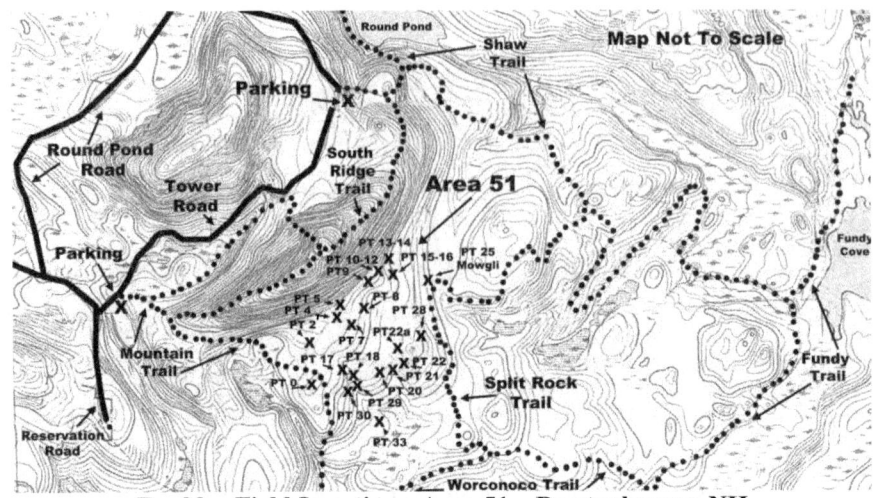

Boulder Field Location - Area 51 – Pawtuckaway, NH

PT-15: N43° 06' 03.5" W71° 10' 37.1" Cluster North *WOW-8*
Large roundish 20' boulder perched atop smaller rock.

PT-16: N43° 06' 02.1" W71° 10' 36.4" (Cluster lower East) *WOW-7*
Cluster 18' triangle shape boulder, leaning atop 16' boulder

PT-17: N43° 05' 49.1" W71° 10' 44.5" (South) *WOW-5*
Smooth oblong 10' boulder.

PT-18: N43° 05' 48.6" W71° 10' 41.6" (Odd Couple A) *WOW-6*
Medium sized Roundish 16' boulder.

PT-19: N43° 05' 48.6" W71° 10' 41.1" (Odd Couple B) *WOW-6*
Triangular 14 foot pinnacle.

PT-20: N43° 05' 47.6" W71° 10' 36.1" (Split Rock) *WOW-7*
Center split 14 foot, roundish boulder

PT-21: N43° 05' 48.0" W71° 10' 33.8" (Small Rock) *WOW-5*
Lumpish 12 foot boulder.

PT-22: N43° 05' 48.7" W71° 10' 30.3" (Perched Rock) *WOW-7*
Meatball 8 foot perched rock on rocky rift ledge.

PT-22a – Big Boy Boulder in Area 51 – Pawtuckaway, NH

PT-22a: N43° 05' 50.6" W71° 10' 30.4" (Big Boy Boulder) *WOW-9*
Very large 25'- 30' fractured roundish boulder with a Hi-Lo hillside position.

PT-27: N43° 05' 52.2" W71° 10' 25.3" (Boring Rock) *WOW-4*
Insignificant chunk 12' Triangular Boulder, we pasted, so it we document it.

PT-28: N43° 05' 47.2" W71° 10' 28.5" (Biscuit Rock) *WOW-6*
Smooth with horizontal mid-seam crack 14' boulder.

PT-29: N43° 05' 46.2" W71° 10' 44.0" (Puzzle Rock) *WOW-6*
Good size 16 feet 20 feet fractured Boulder, all the pieces are here, just needs to put together again.

PT-30: N43° 05' 45.9" W71° 10' 45.2" (Smiley Rock) *WOW-6*
Rounded 12' boulder with slanted horizontal mid-seam fracture.

PT-33: N43° 05' 40.6" W71° 10' 35.1" (Swamp Rock) *WOW-6*
Smooth in rear, fractured in front 16'-18' boulder. If you are here, you will be on a peninsular of hemlock and surround by a swamp on the lowest portion of Area-51. Unless low water or ice you best exit is the way you came in.

Area-51 –Segment of Southern Lower Swamp to avoid.

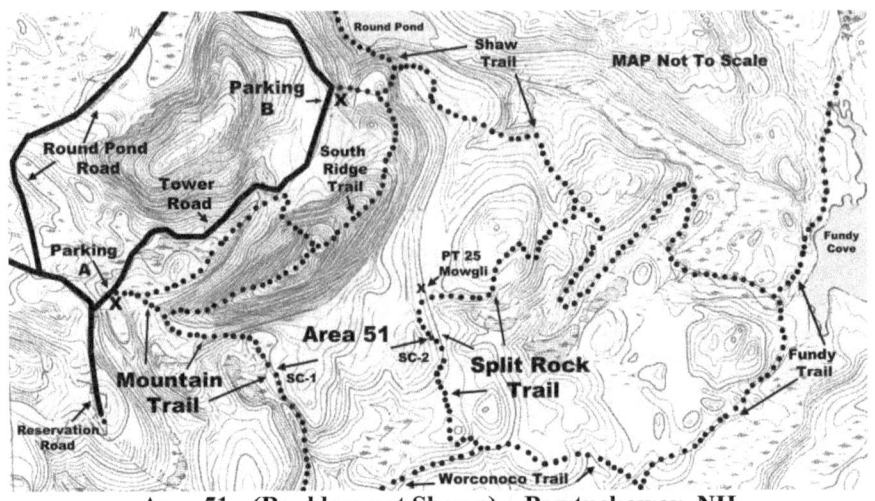

Area 51 - (Boulders not Shown) – Pawtuckaway, NH

Directions: From Tower Road Parking-A, follow the Mountain Trail south for approximately 0.7 mile. Positions SC-1 and SC-2 refer to points which between them span the Area-51 area. Referring to map position **SC-1, GPS: N43° 5' 50.15" W71° 10' 51.21"**, head east from here with a compass bearing 80 degrees northeast for 0.3 mile which will intersect with the Split Rock Trail at **SC-2, GPS: N43° 05' 53.8" W71° 10' 26.9"**. Actually, you do not have to be spot on like a Norton Bomb-Sight; you have some leeway or drift in encountering the Split-Rock Trail on the opposite side. While traversing this large Area 51 corridor starting too high might put you in a wet area: dropping too low one will encounter a large swampy area this is on its most southern perimeter. To the north the steepness of South Mountain aids in maintaining ones bearing's. In addition, one must be aware to encounter the Split Rock Trail without overshooting the trails location by walking over and beyond this smaller or less worn woodland path. A covering of snow, autumn leaves or rain can readily obscure the trail's pathway or its blazed trail's markings. Essentially, Area 51 is not difficult terrain, but it is essential to maintain awareness of your location to prevent you from making it difficult. Some Google Earth reconnoitering and using these GPS coordinates can help you greatly. Be careful not to become a 2nd lieutenant with a map.

54b. Pawtuckaway: *Natural Area*

PT-w - Yosemite Boulder - Natural Area – Pawtuckaway, NH

Location: Nottingham (Rockingham)
Delorme Atlas & Gazetteer-New Hampshire: p29, H-9
Parking GPS: N43° 7' 13.23" W71° 09' 55.23" (Round Pond Road-East)
Parking GPS: N43° 6' 57.20" W71° 10' 41.90" (Round Pond)
Parking GPS: N43° 7' 8.50" W71° 11' 18.20" (Round Pond-lower)
Destination GPS: Individual GPS locations below
Wow Factor: 8, 9, 10 **Accessibility:** Moderate trail.
Information: Early discovery of this small valley of immense erratic boulders was in 1878 under the prodding of then Governor Benjamin F. Prescott who was seeking bragging rights for geological wonders as other states were experiencing.

PT-q – Overlook Boulder – Boulder Trail – Pawtuckaway, NH

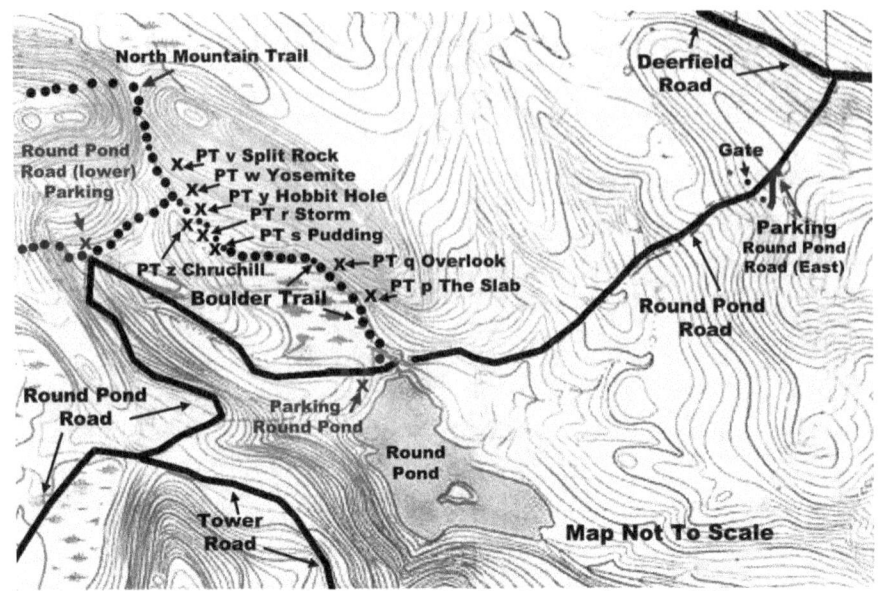

Natural Field – Boulder Trail – Pawtuckaway, NH

PT-p: N43° 07' 04.4" W71° 10' 44.8" (Boulder Trl Slab) *WOW-8*
Large 50' to 60' technical rope & repelling works here.

PT-q: N43° 07' 06.9" W71° 10' 49.3" (Boulder Trl Overlook) *WOW-8*
Jumble of boulders, top boulder with 8'-10' over-hang-shelf.

PT-r: N43° 07' 09.4" W71° 11' 03.7" (Storm Boulders) *WOW-8*
Very large and long 18x40x20 foot boulder.

PT-s: N43 07' 09.1" W71° 11' 02.4" (Pudding Boulder) *WOW-8*
Hugh 30' roundish Boulder, fractured remnants on side.

PT-v: N43° 07' 14.2" W71° 11' 09.5" (BIG Split Rock) *WOW-9*
Humongous set of (3) 30'- 35' boulders. furthest north in the boulder field.

PT-w: N43° 07' 12.5" W71° 11' 07.1" (Yosemite Boulder) *WOW-10*
Very Tall 30'-35' an immense Boulder.

PT-y: N43° 07' 10.4" W71° 11' 05.2" (The Zoo) *WOW-7*
Conglomerate of several 14'-16' Boulders a.k.a Hobbit Hole

PT-z: N43° 07' 08.9" W71° 11' 06.0" (Churchill Boulder) *WOW-9*
Large segmented with top to bottom crack. 40x60x40 foot Boulder
Historically called Churchill Boulder, a.k.a Split Bolder.

PT-z – Churchill Boulder – Natural Area – Pawtuckaway, NH

Historically, Churchill Boulder is a large erratic purportedly named after a "lunatic" by the same name, who eluded his searchers for a time by scaling its 35 to 40 foot height via a large vertical crack that divides the rock. For access and removal of Mr. Churchill, it is alleged that a nearby tree had to be felled to displace him from his perch atop of this massive boulder.

Originally, Churchill Boulder was thought to be the largest boulder in New Hampshire, although the 5,000 ton Madison Boulder further north has won that title.

Directions: Access this area via one the three parking areas already described this chapter. I prefer the parking directly at *Round Pond*, easy use of the *Boulder Trail*, which runs along the shoreline of North Marsh for 0.4 mile to reach the *Natural Boulder Field;* for time constraints, I do return the same route. This parking area is also perfect for the *North Marsh* section outlined below and is excellent for the *Round Pond* rocks also. Off-season when the gates are closed, access is really only from the *Round Pond Road East* parking area off the Deerfield Road. Anything is viable if it works for you.

PT-y - Zoo & Hobbit Hole Boulders (backside) – Pawtuckaway, NH

PT-h – Divided Rock – North Marsh – Pawtuckaway, NH

54c. Pawtuckaway: *North Marsh*

PT-h: N43° 06' 58.13" W71°10' 39.52" (Divided Rock) *WOW-8*
Tall 35 foot facing, with long 45° diagonal crack from bottom to top. Between Round Pond and North Marsh at the start of Boulder Trail.

PT-i: N43° 06' 58.3" W71° 10' 46.9" (North Marsh A) *WOW-8*
Large 20 feet tall, 40 foot length, runs perpendicular from edge of North Marsh.

PT-j: N43° 06' 58.6" W71° 10' 48.4" (Split Cave) *WOW-6*
Unique split half-moon segment rests upon another 10' boulder create small shelter cave. Located away from shore and above Swing Boulder.

PT-k: N43° 06' 59.1" W71° 10' 48.7" (Swing Boulder) *WOW-8*
Located on shoreline of North Marsh. it's a tall 25 foot hunched boulder. A rope swing has been tied of the adjacent tree for climbers to get down; it also works great for "Tarzan" just as a swing.

PT-k - Swing Boulder – North Marsh – Pawtuckaway, NH

54d. Pawtuckaway: *Round Pond*

PT-b - Balance Rock – Round Pond – Pawtuckaway, NH

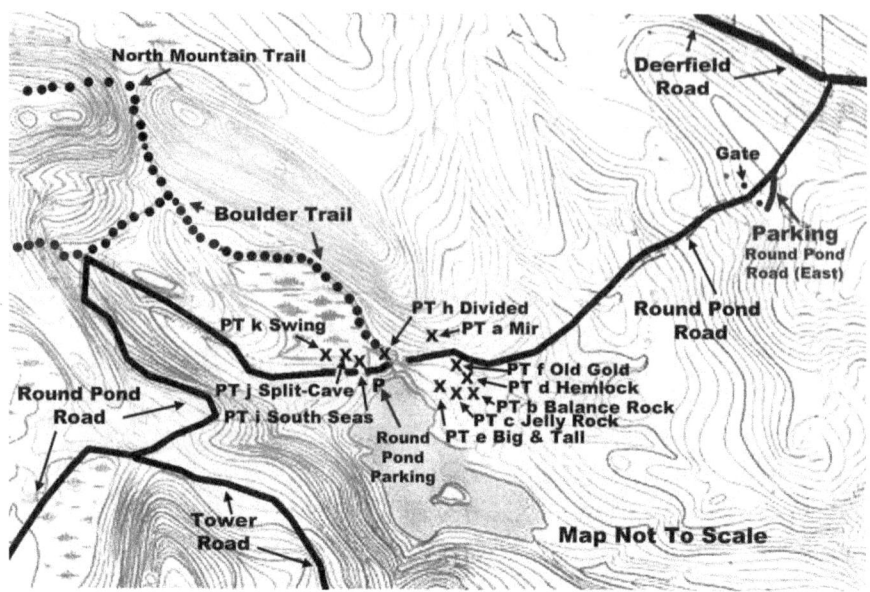

North Marsh & Round Pond – Pawtuckaway, NH

PT-a Mir Rock – Round Pond Road – Pawtuckaway, NH

PT-a: N43° 07' 00.7" W71° 10' 37.2" (Mir Rock) *WOW-8*
Large 25' tall boulder with 40' span, has a look of an open accordion. Located bottom of Round Pond Road, 200' before pond, east of road.

PT-b: N43° 06' 56.4" W71° 10' 34.0" (Balance Rock) *WOW-9*
Truly an awesome balanced 12' Boulder on lower rock pedestal. Located up and away 150' from shoreline atop of ridge and 200' Round Pond Road.

PT-c: N43° 06' 56.4" W71° 10' 34.0" (Jelly Rock) *WOW-7*
Popular with boulderer's, flat faced 16' split-rock with large crack bottom to top. Located above and away from Round Pound shoreline.

PT-d: N43° 06' 57.0" W71° 10' 35.1" (Hemlock aka Cream) *WOW-8*
Large 20' fractured rock, large chip on right side creates shelter cave. Closer towards the Round Pond Road from Balance or Jelly Rocks on the same level.

PT-e: N43° 06' 56.8" W71° 10' 35.7" (Big & Tall) *WOW-7*
Impressive 14' squat, dome shape boulder. Closer to Round Pond's shoreline, and slightly downhill below the Hemlock Boulder.

PT-f: N43° 06' 57.9" W71° 10' 35.6" (Old Gold) *WOW-6*
Small 14 foot boulder located somewhat away from the main hilltop boulders. Seems this boulder sees more usage when other boulders are crowed.

PT-g: N43° 06' 58.0" W71° 10' 36.1" (Perched Erratic) *WOW-7*
Being on hillside this 12 to 18 foot upright and perched boulder has Hi-Lo sides and is chocked in place by a smaller boulder in front. Located at bottom of Round Pond Road across on the opposite side from Mir Boulder, 100' into the woodland.

Information: The Round Pond Boulder Field sees frequent usage for rock climbing or just visitation for Balance Rock. Besides being known for its unique boulders, it's the easiest and nearest boulder field for the Round Pond parking area. Additionally, when the off-season gate closure occurs, access from the Round Pond Road East parking area is common. Most boulders are located atop the ridgeline on the hilltop 150-feet up from the Round Pond shoreline. While many of the bigger boulders are located in the Natural Boulder Field, this area's accessibility is far quicker and easier. Nearby the North Marsh Boulders are also very easy to access.

< PT-g - Perched Erratic - Round Pond

54e. Pawtuckaway: *Split Rock Trail*

PT-37 – Monolithic Rock – Split Rock Trail – Pawtuckaway, NH

Information: Besides the Natural Boulder Field having some of the most astonishing glacial erratics found in Pawtuckaway, the Split Rock Trail harbors a few more equally outstanding if not more phenomenal glacial erratic's! The cover photo of *Erratic Wandering* has *Mowgli Boulder*, a gigantic boulder and it's rather hard to believe that *Monolithic Rock*, another colossal boulder, was a contender for that honor. It was the Battle of the Titans with Mowgli Boulder winning.

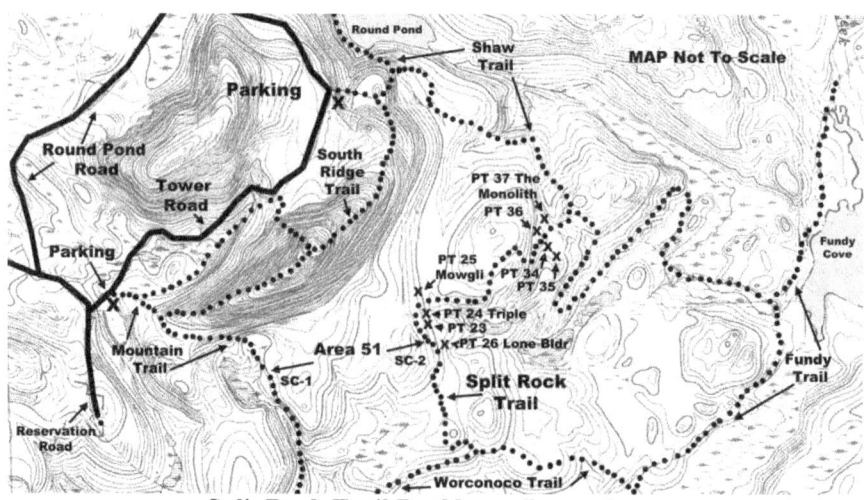

Split Rock Trail Boulders – Pawtuckaway

PT-23: N43° 05' 56.40" W71° 10' 28.3" (Big Erratic) *WOW-7*
Large 16' rock, across the Split Rock Trail and over on the crest of small slope, further downhill is the "Magic Pond" area which I not visited as yet.

PT-24: N43° 05' 57.4" W71° 10' 30.0" (Triple Rocks) *WOW-6*
A Trio of 12' boulders located right on the Split Rock Trail. Otherwise, not very remarkable compared to some of the big boys.

PT-25: N43° 06' 00.1" W71° 10' 29.9" (Mowgli Boulder) *WOW-10*
A very large 35' to 40' high, chunks laying aside of this mammoth suggesting its diameter was much larger at one time. Lays right on the Split Rock Trail.

PT-26: N43° 05' 53.2" W71° 10' 23.7" (Lone Boulder) *WOW-6*
Rather insignificant, rock top slanted top giving the erratic height ranging from 8'-14'. Located more westerly and just off the split Rock Trail

PT-34: N43° 06' 08.4" W71° 10' 01.6" (Hugh Rock) *WOW-9*
A good size boulder 18 feet high and with one largely slanted facing. Sits right along the Split Rock Trail and shortly before Monoliithic Boulder coming from Area-51 direction.

PT-35: N43° 06' 08.0" W71° 10' 01.5" (Runt Rock) *WOW-6*
Comparitively small 12' rock, just up the hillside from the Hugh Rock in the bushes.

PT-36: N43° 06' 09.4" W71° 10' 00.9" (No Name) *WOW-7*
We goofed here; we were over taken by the upcoming Monolithic Rock and forgot it. As we remember it was on the Split Rock Trail and good size.

PT-37: N43° 06' 10.8" W71° 09' 59.3" (Monolithic Rock) *WOW-10*
Amazing 35 foot block of rock, upended trapezoidal in shape with a wider base than top.

PT-34 – Hugh Rock – Split Rock Trail – Pawtuckaway, NH

Directions: To access Split Rock Trail; one can park at either area for parking as mentioned for Tower Road, I do prefer access by hiking in on the Mountain Trail, bushwhacking across Area-51 and onto the Split Rock Trail northward, through its boulder fields and continue back on the Shaw Trail, turning left and back onto Tower Road, than back down the road parking area A for a 4.5 mile loop.

55. Pulpit Rock – Indian Rock

Pulpit Rock – Bedford, NH

Location: Bedford (Hillsborough County)
Delorme Atlas & Gazetteer-New Hampshire: p21, B-13
Parking GPS: N42° 57' 20.89" W71° 36' 47.13"
Destination GPS: Individual GPS locations below.
Wow Factor: 7 **Accessibility:** Easy to Moderate marked woodland trails.
Contact: Bedford Land Trust c/o Cornerstone Association Management 53 Regional Drive; Suite 1 Concord, NH 03301 (603) 228-1231
info@BedfordLandTrust.org   www.bedfordlandtrust.org
Map; http://www.bedfordlandtrust.org/s/Pulpit-Rock-Trail-Map-rtx7.pdf

Information: A noted landmark in Bedford, a hand-colorized 1906 postcard states Devil's Pulpit as part of the Pulpit Farm, shown with stairways and railings. The caption then describes the walkways as being destroyed in a 1938 hurricane. Devils' Pulpit itself is a large boulder set upon the crest of a rocky ravine with a waterfall, sheer and rocky walls, with a depth of 40-feet. Pulpit Rock certainly has a large spacious flat top and a commanding view of the deep ravine down below. In addition, *Indian Rock* is accessible through a small maze of trails and located in the south portion of the Conservation area.

We parked in the northern entry off New Boston Road. From here the only trail Kennard Trail is easy, from here for the first 0.5 mile, the trail heads south in open hemlock and an occasional small rock outcrop following white blazes. When the *Blue* Trail, *Green* (Campbell Trail) and the *White* (Kennard Trail) junction is a small waterfall and pool off 100-feet on your right; from here continue to follow the white trail south 0.1 mile. You'll be at a kiosk that is right above the ravine and in front of *Pulpit Rock*. To *Indian Rock*, continue following white blazes, but you will now be on *Tufts Trail*, still with white blazes which runs higher, west and parallel to the Ravine a.k.a.the Gorge Trail for 0.6 mile. Along this trail we also marked PR-2, *Hippo Rock* and further along PR-3 a larger 14-feet glacial erratic. At the end of Tufts Trail, cross a small brook, on the other side you should see the *Red* Campbell Trail heads uphill north. For *Indian Rock* continue to follow the trail 0.1 mile south. For return, we followed the Red Trail back which morphed into the Green Trail crossing an old road, and rejoined the Kennard Trail, 0.6 miles, back north of the White Trail and back to the parking area in 0.5 miles.

PR-1: N42° 56' 55.50" W71° 36' 32.20" (Pulpit Rock) *WOW 7*
Part of a larger rock escarpment, Pulpit Rock sits separated by a deep ravine.

PR-2: N42 °56' 41.90" W71° 36' 18.90" (Hippo Rock) *WOW 5*
Off the Tufts Trails, a small 8 foot erratic with a shape of Hippo rising out of the brook onto the embankment.

PR-3: N42° 56' 42.00" W71° 36' 6.90" (Erratic) *WOW 5:*
14 foot erratic, located up from trail just prior to crossing over to the Ravine Trail

PR-4: N42° 56' 41.80" W71° 35' 58.10" (Indian Rock) *WOW 7*
14 foot gum drop shape with an interesting cavity in base with side opening.

Pulpit Rock – Indian Rock – Bedford, NH

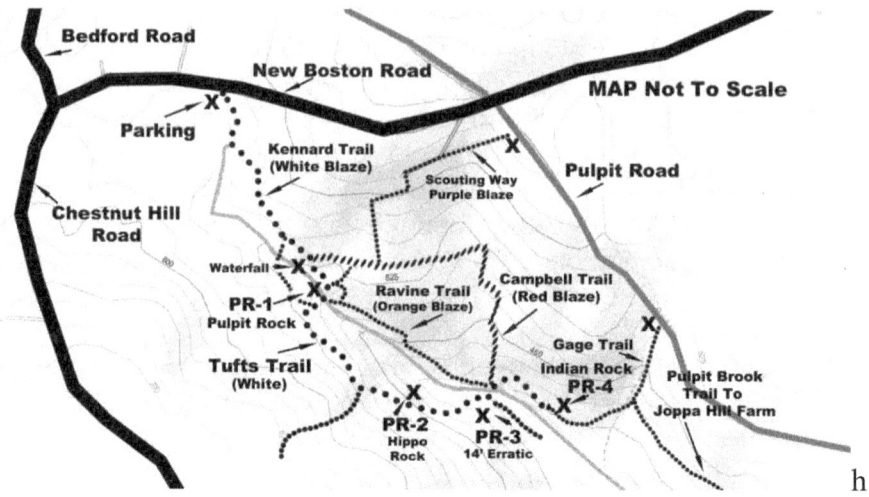

Indian Rock – Bedford, NH

Indian Rock

"There is a large rock that is situated on a thickly wood knoll which has since been cleared of underbrush and tree. The moss-covered boulder is fifteen feet high. It is nicely balanced on three flat ledge stones. On the south side of the rock is an opening enough to admit an ordinary person by stooping. The cavity widens on the inside. The walls of the miniature cave are fantastically grooved and hollowed out. It looks like the work of water. The pulpit brook flows only a few feet from the base of the hill on which the boulder

rests. On the inside of the cave is a stone seat, with arms at the sides and a hollow for a head rest. Legend says that the chair was a favorite place for the Indian medicine men to fast and listen to the voice of the Great Spirit. A number of years ago some men endeavored to overturn the boulder, but were unsuccessful."

Directions: In Bedford, at the junction of Route-114 and Route-101, follow Route-114 north for 0.7 mile, at the light, turn left onto New Boston Road. Head west on New Boston Road 5.7 miles; Esther Drive will be on your left, an additional 0.2 mile, the parking area for the Devil's Pulpit Conservation Area will be also on the left.

PR-2 –Hippo Rock – Bedford, NH

56. Revolutionary Rock

Revolutionary Rock – Richmond, NH

Location: Richmond (Cheshire County)
Delorme Atlas & Gazetteer-New Hampshire: p19, H-12
Parking GPS: N42° 47' 54" W72° 16' 7"
Destination GPS: N42° 47' 53.96" W72° 16' 5"
Wow Factor: 7 **Accessibility:** Easy 0.1 mile woodland stroll.

Information: In 1998 in tribute to the area's Revolutionary War Patriots, the Richmond Historical Society affixed to this large glacial erratic a plaque listing eight names of Richmond Patriots who fought in the Revolutionary War; **Moses Allen - James Balou - Jedeiah Buffum - Daniel Cass - Nicholas Cook - Oliver Hix - Gideon Man - John Martin.** Ponder if you would and think about their courage and feats to arise against a King of the British Empire, entrenched at such battles; *Bunkerhill, Bennington, Ticondergoga* these patriots with only the ideals being set forth in the new United State Constitution as inalienable rights and the freedoms that we have today.

Directions: Located on Route-32, just 0.2 mile north of the Fish Hatchery Road is Revolutionary Rock. A small, unimproved parking pull-in for 2 to 3 cars is evident on the road side. This large glacial erratic is located on the late George Fillian Tree Farm, is posted nearby and is on private land. Visitors are reminded that fires, camping, motorized vehicles, or rock climbing are not allowed at this memorial boulder.

57. Rock Rimmon - a.k.a Rock Raymond

Rock Rimmon – Manchester, NH

Location: Manchester (Hillsborough County)
Delorme Atlas & Gazetteer-New Hampshire: p68, H-12
Parking GPS: N42° 59' 55.20" W71° 29' 6.90"
Destination GPS: N42° 59' 54.89" W71° 29' 12.83"
Wow Factor: 7 **Accessibility:** Easy side of moderate 0.1 mile to top.

ROCK RIMMON, MANCHESTER, N. H.

Hand-tinted Postcard - Rock Rimmon – Manchester, NH

Information: There are many stories around the rocky landmark in Manchester both old and new.

The naming of said rock varies from early days known as *"Rock Raymond"* to a more updated label as *"Rock Rimmon"* In 1847 a lithograph, "View of Manchester NH from Rock *Raymond*," was created and colored by an artist named Uriah Smith, and published by Sharp, Peirce & Co. of Boston. From folk-lore, "an Indian maiden named *Raymond*, disappointed in a love affair with an Indian brave, threw herself from the top of this rock, and perished." However, a short 10 years later in 1857, it was becoming called Rock Rimmon and continues to be known by that name today.

"It is known far and wide as "Rock Raymond," a corruption of a well-known Scripture name. It is in itself a great curiosity. It is an outcropping of gneiss from the midst of a sandy plain, being an immense mass of that stone some three hundred feet in length, one hundred and fifty in width and some seventy or eighty feet in height....This rock is seen at a considerable distance up and down the valley of the Merrimack, and from its top is a splendid view of the city of Manchester and its neighborhood. It is a place of great resort in the summer, and the paths to it are kept well beaten, making it a pleasant jaunt on foot or in a carriage." ("The History of Manchester, Formerly Derryfield, in New Hampshire" by Chandler E. Potter 1856.)

Late in 1911 the Amoskeag Manufacturing Company gifted the land around Rock Rimmon to the City of Manchester as a public park. The Manchester Board of Mayor and Alderman voted, on 6 February 1912, to accept the deed for a parcel of land of 42.88 acres which contained Rock Rimmon, for one dollar. Although not listed as an official park in Manchester's 1914 Annual Report, it was mentioned by 1923 as *Rock Rimmon Park*. The rock itself has been a site for toboggan races, rock climbing enthusiasts and with a short 0.1 mile hike provides a inspiring vista over the City of Manchester and the Merrimack River.

Directions: In Manchester from Interstate I-93, Exit-6, head west 0.3 mile on Wellington Road, cross over Route-28A, you are now on Bridge Street. Continue west for 1.75 miles through Manchester, staying onto West Bridge Street and cross over the Merrimack River on the Notre Dame Bridge, on the other side you will be on Armory Street, turn right onto Coolidge Drive in 0.2 mile. North for 0.2 mile and turn left onto Bremer Street. Follow west for 0.4 mile; turn right on Jolilette, Laval, or Boutwell Street over to Manson Street.

58. Rye Pond Erratic

Rye Pond Erratic – South Stoddard, NH

Location: South Stoddard (Cheshire County)
Delorme Atlas & Gazetteer-New Hampshire: p26, K-3
Parking GPS: N43° 0' 57.93" W72° 3' 26.48" (Rt-123 Kings Highway)
Destination GPS: N43° 1' 9.56" W72° 3' 32.11"
Wow Factor: 5 **Accessibility:** 0.3 walk no path
Contact: Harris Center for Conservation Education; 83 King's Highway, Hancock, NH 03449 | phone (603) 525-3394 | fax (603) 525-3395
Harris Center Super Sanctuary: www.harriscenter.org (603) 525-3394

Information: This large glacial erratic is on the opposite side of Rye's Pond from Route-123; it is located in part of the Harris Center Super Sanctuary and Virginia C. Baker Natural Area. I do not have any historical or folk lore about. It is included for I have noticed it so many times as we visited the Willard Pond boulders or the Harris Center East Side Trails Conservation area. Stopped a few times, but never took that extra effort and time to bushwhack over my estimated 0.3 mile. All I have is a curiosity factor, would it make a good fishing rock or is it just attractive to be on the other side idling the time away.

Direction: In Stoddard, Route-9, travel south on Route-123 towards Hancock for 2.1 miles, at the south end of Rye Pond a small unimproved pull-off for parking, watch for rocks embedded in ground.

59. Simmonds Rock - a.k.a. Pennichuck Rock

Simmond's Rock – Merrimack, NH

Location: Merrimack (Hillsborough County)
Delorme Atlas & Gazetteer-New Hampshire: p22, H-2
Parking GPS: N42°48' 18.33" W71°29' 21.43" (Do not block gate)
Destination GPS: N42° 48' 12.10" W71° 29' 24.94"
Wow Factor: 7 **Accessibility:** Short hike 0.1 mile on dirt access road.

Information: Simmond's Rock a.k.a Pennichuck Rock has been used many times as a boundary maker in establishing early settler's property, when Massachusetts Colony was being sectioned off. Native Americans and early settlers were said to seek shelter here as the front facing has a large over-hang slanted boulder with the rear having a shallow indented shelter cave. This lone jumbled heap of boulders is 25-feet in height, 50 feet in length and 30 feet wide. Unfortunately, the rock has graffiti, broken glass and campfire remnants. Simmonds Rock was placed on the New Hampshire Register of Historic Places by the N. H. Division of Historic Places on June 2007.

Directions: In Nashua, from the Interchange 7 of the Everett Turnpike, Route-101A and Route-3; follow Route-3 (Heni Burque Highway) for 0.8 mile and turn left onto Manchester Street. Heading north for 1.7 miles, turning left onto Al Paul Lane, go 0.5 mile, there is a gated service road with a small brick utility building. Park without blocking the gate. Simmons Rock is 0.1 mile on your left. Note: that the rock is closer behind the western corner parking lot of Heron Cove Office Park, but has parking issues associated with that location.

60. Stoddard Powerline Boulders

SP-1 – Split Rock – Power line – Stoddard, NH

Location: Stoddard (Cheshire County)
Delorme Atlas & Gazetteer-New Hampshire: p26, I-3
Parking GPS: N43° 3' 59.48" W72° 3' 23.90" (Route-9 pull-off)
Parking GPS: N43° 3' 26.55" W72° 4' 45.03" (Route-123 parking)
Destination GPS: Individual GPS locations below.
Wow Factor: 5-7 **Accessibility:** Moderate-plus, no marked trail.

Information: The course of this power line from Route-123 north towards Stoddard and runs parallel to Route-9 for 1.5 miles separated by a 100 yard buffer of woodland until it crosses Route-9 and continues east. Brush and bramble can make the power line trek quite an ordeal, just remember it might be easier to hike in and when you are out of time or your limit is reached, cut down through the woodland buffer and return to your starting point via the highway. The Stoddard area has many glacial boulders, the power line is no exception and we certainly did not see all. We left a few for you to discover. Use Google Earth to reconnoiter.

Speaking of discovery, our original exploration in the Stoddard area, was to seek and locate the *"Lion's Head Rock"* as seen in an old postcard post below. In our quest, we never found its location, but in pursuit located we discovered that Stoddard has many glacial erratics strewn throughout its landscape and woodlands. It may still be sitting out there, especially among this multitude of power line boulders. With just the right light or point of view, you may find it! Of course if someone in the Stoddard area knows its location, please contact me.

Lion Head Rock – Stoddard, NH

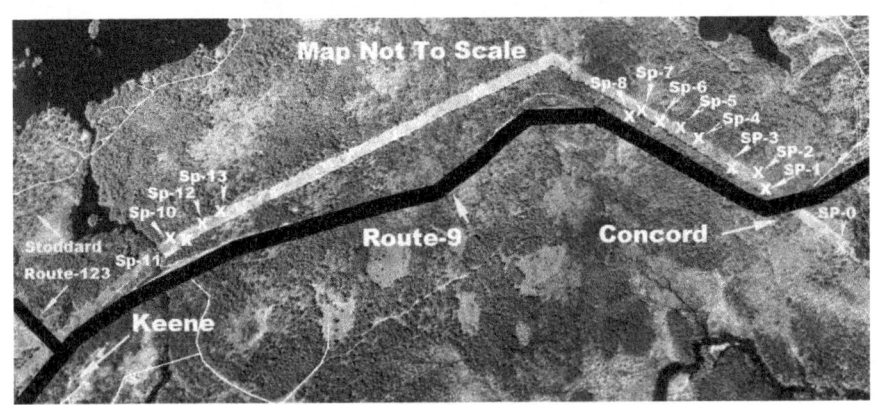

Power line Erratic Map – Stoddard, NH

SP-0: N43° 3' 56.89" W72° 3' 14.92" (Colossal Rock) *WOW 8*
Large 18 foot boulder, located downhill from Route-9 east.

SP-1: N43° 3' 59.90" W72° 3' 26.10" (Split Rock) *WOW 8*
Large 16 foot rock cleaved in half with curved over-hang on one side. On eastern end, above and near Route-9.

SP-2: N43° 4' 1.52" W72° 3' 28.28" (Perched Rock) *WOW 7*
One precariously 12 foot boulder atop another with small 2 foot rock wedged between.

SP-3: N43° 4' 0.30" W72° 3' 28.50" (Cluster A) *WOW 5*
Large 16 foot boulder with several smaller rocks, not very remarkable.

SP-4: N43° 4' 3.09" W72° 3' 35.45" (Erratic) *WOW 5*
Large 16 foot boulder we passed and just documented.

Sp-6 – Balanced Rock – Power line - Stoddard, NH

SP-5: N43° 4' 3.81" W72° 3' 38.10" (Cracked Rock) *WOW 7*
Large 16 foot boulder, large remarkable split-crack on one end.

SP-6: N43° 4' 3.93" W72° 3' 40.29" (Balance Rock) *WOW 7*
Surprised to find this Small 8 foot rock balanced atop a 3 foot base.

SP-7: N43° 4' 4.81" W72° 3' 44.01" (A Rock) *WOW 6*
Small 12 foot erratic with one side intact with the other half reduced to rubble.

SP-8: N43° 4' 3.60" W72° 3' 47.10" (Roadside) *WOW 5*
Woodland boulders, 12 to14 feet in height, next to Route-9, insignificant, but we passed by it.

SP-10: N43° 3' 37.60" W72° 4' 33.35" (ABC Rocks) *WOW 8*
Three, 14 foot to 16 foot boulders which look as to have been sliced into sections from a roast.

SP-10 - ABC Rocks – Power line – Stoddard, NH

SP-11: N43° 3' 37.23" left W72° 4' 32.25" (Sheer Rock) *WOW 8*
Rock with 16 feet to 18 feet sheer frontal face, a pit in middle-front allows addition depth.

SP-5 – Cracked Rock – Power line - Stoddard, NH

SP-12: N43° 3' 38.90" W72° 4' 31.90" (The Wall) *WOW 6*
On top of hill with various sized boulders in an over-sized stone wall alignment.

SP-13: N43° 3' 40.10" W72° 4' 30.20" (Hill Top Rocks) *WOW 6*
Cluster of rocks atop of hill, nothing very significant.

SP-13 - Hill Top Rock – Power line - Stoddard, NH

Directions: From either Keene or Concord, follow Route-9 to the junction of Route-123 north which goes to Stoddard. We parked on the both the eastern end off Route-9 and a small 1 car pull-off a short way up Route-123 on the right. While we saw no posted signs, this area does have safety hazards associated to high voltage transmission lines. As always, in season check for ticks during and after your outdoor sojourns.

61. Stoddard Rocks

SD-4 – Impressive Rock – Stoddard, NH

Location: Stoddard (Cheshire County)
Delorme Atlas & Gazetteer-New Hampshire: p26, H-3
Parking GPS: N43° 6' 22.50" W72° 4' 56.90"
Destination GPS: Individual GPS locations below.
Wow Factor: 8-10 **Accessibility:** Moderately difficult, 5.0 miles hike RT.

Information: The outstanding Stoddard Boulders are located on a remote hilltop on the east side of Highland Lake. While the terrain is not daunting, it will require some energy to the summit and back. Fortunately, a trailhead with legal parking is located over by Pickerel Cove, off Shedd Hill Road. The Trail is well marked with red & white triangular markers and with signs at major junctions. You will reach the Stoddard Rocks via Pioneer Lake and the Old Dodge Farm then by a loop trail up and over to the rocks, back the way you came.

Starting from the parking area, head northeast on a meandering foot path that will be paralleling a *private, keep out road*. After 0.6 mile, you will turn left onto an old forest road for 100 yards, on your right pass through a gate and continue 0.3 mile; you will arrive at Pioneer Lake's southern shore. Turn sharply left, uphill, west and away from the lake following the trail for 0.3 mile; you will arrive at the Old Dodge Farm

Turn right, following the road through fields and back down into the woodlands. Continue northeast on this trail until you reach the intersection for the Stoddard Rocks Loop Trail. Turn left, uphill, 0.3 mile, a small foot path, slightly steeper, will be on you right. The first *Hillside Boulder* will be in 100 yards and the rest in 0.1 miles. After the boulders, the trail will head south downhill and back to the loop trail junction, return the way you came.

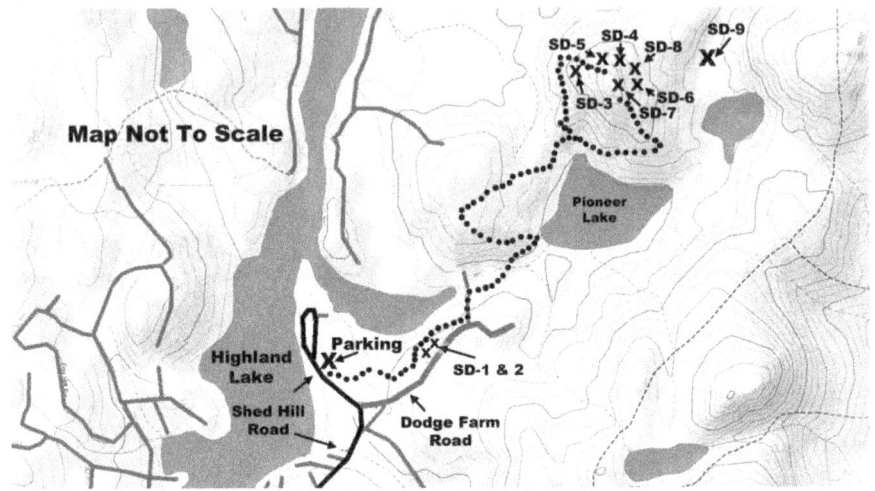

Map to Stoddard Rocks – Stoddard, NH

SD-8 – Humongous Rock – Stoddard, NH

SD-1: N43° 6' 24.50 left W72° 4' 35.36" (Trail Rock) *WOW 4*
Small 10' trail side split rock. Rather insignificant.

SD-2: N43° 6' 26.87" W72° 4' 35.12" (Trail Rock) *WOW 4*
Small trail side split rock.

SD-3: N43° 7' 18.64" W72° 3' 56.79" (Hillside Rock) *WOW 7*
Approaching from the west, first major and impressive boulder encountered Being on the hillside it will have a Hi-Lo approach.

SD-4: N43° 7' 17.17" W72° 3' 50.52" (Impressive Rock) *WOW 10*
This 35 foot boulder is impressive sitting center stage among other large boulders.

SD-5: N43° 7' 17.16" W72° 3' 51.12" (Big Split Rock) *WOW 9*
Two 18 foot boulders cleaved in half with a large passageway between them.

SD-6: N43° 7' 16.43" W72° 3' 50.47" left (Potato Rock) *WOW 6*
Roundish 16 foot boulder and part of the gateway with SD-7.

SD-7: N43° 7' 16.41" W72° 3' 50.62" (Gateway Rock) *WOW 7*
The other half of the gateway between boulders.

SD-8: N43° 7' 16.10" W72° 3' 50.20" (Humongous Rock) *WOW 10q.*
Massive and humongous 30 foot boulder. (See photo above.)

SD-9: N43° 7' 18.65" W72° 3' 45.47" (Guessim Rock) *WOW?*
Seen on Google earth, no trail found, GPS and bushwhacking required, looks downhill and northeast from summit; rather large to be seen on Google Earth, be the first to visit and let me know.

SD-3 – Hillside Rock – Stoddard, NH

Directions: Follow Route-123 north off Route-9 towards Stoddard. In 1.8 miles you will pass Island Pond, off on the right, at the Stoddard Fire Station, Shedd Hill Road will begin. In a short distance, cross a small bridge and bear left following Shedd Hill Road for 2.25 miles, look for a small 3-4 car parking area on your right. If you reach the boat launch go back 0.1 mile.

62. The Rinks Boulder

The Rinks Boulder – Exeter, NH

Location: Exeter (Rockingham County)
Delorme Atlas & Gazetteer-New Hampshire: p23, A-14
Parking GPS: N42° 59' 40.82" W70° 58' 6.34"
Destination GPS: N42° 59' 43.20" W70° 58' 4.44"
Wow Factor: 9 **Accessibility:** 0.1 walk no path
Contact: Town of Exeter- Exeter Conservation Commission. 10 Newfields Road. Exeter, NH 03833 (603) 778-0591
Trail Map: http://exeternh.gov/bcc/trail-maps

Information: This 25-foot boulder is isolated, but readily accessible with a short 100 yard+ walk from behind the Exeter Skating Rink. The short transition from the parking area into the woodlands can be tedious; however once into the woodlands it is open and easily navigable. Certainly the *"Rinks" boulder (a.k.a. Exeter Boulder)* is the most phenomenal erratic in the area, there are others located in the nearby adjacent Henderson-Swasey Town Forest. This area has more erratics listed; but developed more for the mountain bike enthusiasts with an elaborate network of trails. The latest trail map offered by the Town of Exeter, no longer lists these boulders. In addition, there are more trails and boulders just north of Route-101 in Oakland Town Forest in Newfields and can be access by a tunnel under Route-101.

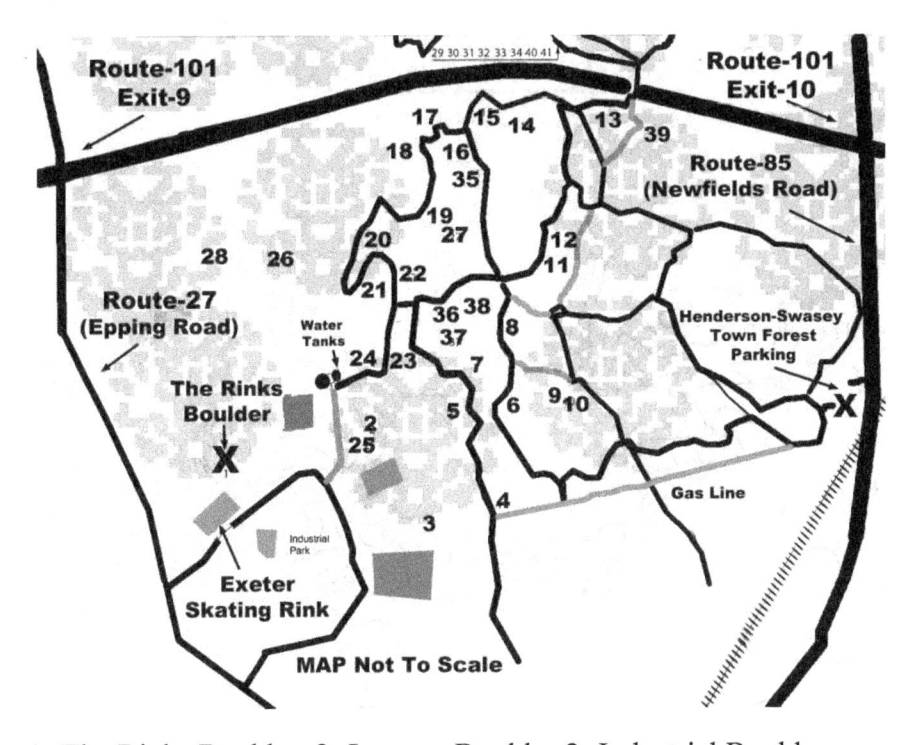

1: The Rinks Boulder **2:** Lantern Boulder **3:** Industrial Boulder
4: Quarryman Boulder **5:** Mid-Point Boulder **6:** Intro Boulder
7: Hallucinogen Boulder **8:** Fort Rock Boulder **9:** Super Slab
10: Kahtulu Boulders **11:** Camel Toe Boulder **12:** Camels Hump
13: Tunnel Boulder **14:** The Fling Boulders **15:** Tall Boy Boulder
16: The Shire **17:** Orange Peel **18:** Far Away Boulders
19: Swamp Side Boulder **20:** Hillside Boulder **21:** Pond Boulder
22: Girl Friend Rock **23:** Black Magic Boulder **24:** Beaver Boulders
25: Gas Rock **26:** Cell Tower Boulder **27:** Hidden Boulder
28: Boulders of Mystery **29:** Highway Boulders **30:** In Between Bldr

Directions: The Ricks Boulder; From Route 101 use Exit-9 and onto Route-27 (Epping Road) south for 0.7 miles. Turn left onto Industrial Drive. The Exeter Skating Rink is 0.1 mile on the left; 40 Industrial Drive Exeter, NH. We parked behind the building, into the woods with the boulder up to your right.

Henderson-Swasey Town Forest Parking; From Route-101, use Exit-10 onto Route-85 (Newfields Road) south for 0.3 miles. Just before the railroad trestle, on your right, a small unimproved dirt road heads west and back to a dirt parking area.

63. Thompson Farm Boulders

Fran (L) and Dan Butler (R) Butler @ Thompson Farm Bldr – Durham, NH

Location: Durham (Strafford County)
Delorme Atlas & Gazetteer-New Hampshire: p29, H-14
Parking GPS: N43° 6' 24.35" W70° 57' 21.26" (Woodland entry point)
Destination GPS: N43° 6' 30.01" W70° 57' 21.18"
Wow Factor: 9 **Accessibility:** 0.1 walk woodland path
Contact: College of Life Sciences and Agriculture Rudman Hall, 46 College Road, Durham, New Hampshire 03824

Information: The Thompson Farm Boulders a.k.a. Wiswall Boulders consists of several small granite boulders with a massive 18-feet center piece. These remarkable boulders are located on 204 acres that is owned and managed by University of New Hampshire.

The closest access is from the intersection of Packer Falls Road and Wiswall Road. Opposite of the intersection, on the east side of Packer Falls Road, a small opening can be found leading into the woodland. No kiosk or signs noted. Parking is a concern for the neighborhood and for traffic safety. It's best to park further down on Wiswall Road and walk to the entry. Once within the woodlands, a clearly worn path is seen, head west to the rocks in 0.1 mile.

Directions: In Newmarket, at the junction if Route-108/ Route-152, head west on Route-152 (South Main Street) for 0.2 mile and turn right onto Packers Falls Road. Head north for 2.4 miles, Wiswall Road will be on the left. It's best to park some distance from the intersection and the immediate houses of that vicinity.

64. Tippin Rock - Shirley Hill

Tippin Rock – Swanzey, NH

Location: Swanzey (Cheshire County)
Delorme Atlas & Gazetteer-New Hampshire: p19, G-12
Parking GPS: N42° 49' 47.71" W72° 16' 54.78"
Destination GPS: N42° 49' 25.93" W72° 17' 14.15"
Wow Factor: 6 Accessibility: easy side of moderate, 0.5 mile trail.
Contact: Monadnock Conservacy 15 Eagle Court 2nd Floor, PO Box 337, Keene, NH 03431-0337 ·603-357-0600 www.monadnockconservancy.org

Tippin Rock – 1900's – Swanzey, NH

Information: A local landmark or hiking destination for over 100 years, *Tippin Rock* also shares a yet another *rocking rock* legend; "with a shove of your shoulder under the right spot" you can make 40 tons of granite rock gently, like a baby's cradle."

A marked hiking trail leads to the Tippin Rock and Hewes Hill cliffs. The trail starts in a hay-field on Warmac Road, rises up to the Tippin Rock, continues on to a stunning lookout, and then makes its way across the top of the cliffs. The trail to Tippin Rock from the field is about 1/2 a mile and an easy walk with an elevation gain of 320 feet. From the field to the ledges outlook and back is 1.8 miles, round trip.

Visitors are reminded to remain on marked trails, no motorized vehicles, fires or camping.

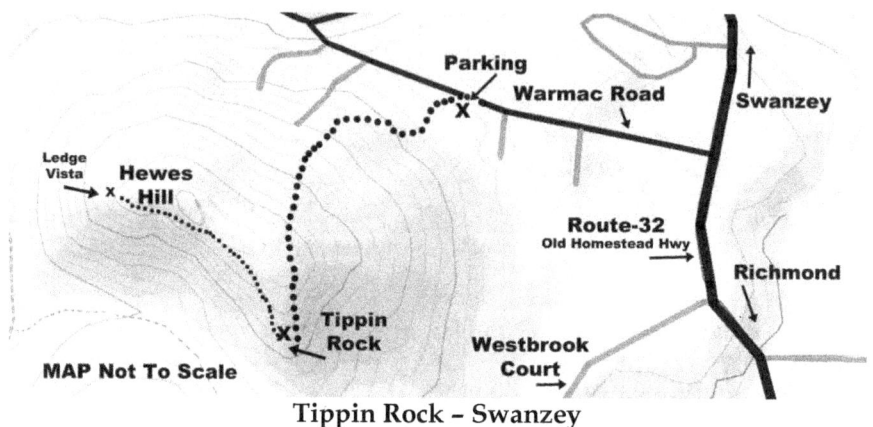

Tippin Rock – Swanzey

Directions: From Swanzey center, follow Route-32 (Old Homestead Hwy) south for 3.3 miles, turn right onto Warmac Road. Head west on Warmac Road for 0.4 mile, on the left look for the opening to a hay field across from the Chebaco Kennel. The blue blazed Tippin Rock trail starts in the back right corner of the field, do not drive across the field, park near the road side.

From the field the trail begins as a narrow path, but will become a larger fire road type trail. The slope is minimal and you'll reach Tippin Rock in 0.5 mile. One can continue westerly from Tippin Rock, along the summit to reach the Hewes Hill Overlook vista.

65. Vincent Rock a.k.a. Big Rock Rock

Vincent Rock a.k.a Big Rock – Epping, NH

Location: Epping (Rockingham County)
Delorme Atlas & Gazetteer-New Hampshire: p29, J-12
Parking GPS: N43° 2' 33.60" W71° 1' 59.15"
Destination GPS: N43° 2' 33.60" W71° 1' 59.15"
Wow Factor: 8 **Accessibility:** Road Side – Private grounds
Contact: http://www.heddingcampground.com

Information: Incorporated in 1863, Hedding Camp Ground is a long term and multi-generational Christian Community maintained for the benefit of Christian people seeking inspiration, quiet, relaxation and pleasure. In a few words: *Hedding is all about Christian fellowship, family, history, nature, laughter, and sharing, both in good times and bad.* Having recently reached their Sesquicentennial Anniversary in 2012, the community has maintained growth from a rustic lifestyle to now with a two-fold purpose: celebrating Hedding's heritage and reaching out to the community. In recent summers they are holding more public concerts, more public suppers, and will work harder to share the Hedding ambience with the greater Epping community.

The camp is open from mi-April through mid-October. During this period cottage owners, their families and invited guests are permitted the use of the grounds and facilities in compliance with the established Rules and Regulations of the Association. During the off season (mid-October through mid-April), only approved winter residents and their guests may be on grounds, unless prior approval has been granted by the Board of Trustees. All non-winter residents entering the grounds must check in with the Director of Winter Security.

Located at the end of Hedding Avenue which passes through the camp ground, *Vincent Rock* a.k.a *Big Rock* apparently was a popular summer ritual for many childhood memories, it was a challenge and conquering the top was a rite of passage shared by older campers to the younger. Our visit found Vincent Rock easily identified by the 6" engraved lettering upon its front facing.

Directions: In Newfields at the junction of Route-85 and Route-87 head north on Route-87 for 4.5 miles. On you left, Hedding Avenue, a dirt road enters into the community area.

Access to the rock's location is a concern for anyone venturing into the camp ground which is heavily occupied by children and is a private community with safety, privacy or security concerns. Vehicle usage and a 15 mph speed limit along with other rules and regulations are provided on their web site. You must check to see if your presence will be inappropriate for any activities being held at that time for residents.

66. Willards Pond Balance Rock

WP-1 Balance Rock – Willard Pond – Antrim, NH

Location: Antrim (Cheshire County)
Delorme Atlas & Gazetteer-New Hampshire: p26, K-4
Parking GPS: N43° 0'59.30" W72° 1'15.29"
Destination GPS: Individual GPS locations below.
Wow Factor: 9 **Accessibility:** Moderate 1.0 marked trail.
Contact: N.H. Audubon 84 Silk Farm Road - Concord, NH 03301
(603) 224-9909 www.nhaudubon.org
Membership or donation fee is accepted.

Information: The De Pierrefeu-Willard Pond Wildlife Sanctuary at nearly 1700 acres is New Hampshire Audubon's largest property. Much of the land owned by NHA has come about through the foresight and generosity of Elsa De Pierrefeu Leland and her family. Surrounding the 100 acre Willard Pond, a diverse mixture of woodlands encompasses Bald Mountain and Goodhue Hill. A scattering of glacial erratic boulders deposited by receding glaciers, along with an abundance of wildlife, creates a unique and attractive area to hike and explore. Willard Pond itself is a remarkable flat water canoe or kayak destination.

WP-3 - Entry Boulder – Willard Pond, NH

From the parking area, walking back down Willard Pond Road, on your left, within 100 feet is Wp-2 a roadside 14 foot tall erratic, just pass here within 50 feet is *Memorial Boulder* with its dedication inscription (see below). Your next boulder on your left is *Turning Rock,* WP-3: N43°0'57.90" W72°1'13.00" here starts the yellow blazed *Mill Pond* loop trail which heads east and will connect with the *Goodhue Trail* and returns back by Willard Pond. However, it's the woodlands across the road where no marked path was noted. One needs to funnel into the woodlands bushwhacking approximately 100 feet to find the Wp-1 *Balance-Cave Rock*. The juxtaposition of three large boulders is clustered to provide the explorer an impressive Indian Cave and Balanced Rock to ponder.

<u>From Memorial Rock on Willard Pond Road</u>
**In Loving Memory of
Elsa Tudor De Pierrefeu
1878 – 1967
Who Preserved This Land
For Peace Among All Beings.**
*They shall not hurt nor destroy
In all my holy mountain
For the earth shall be full
Of the knowledge of the Lord
As the waters cover the sea.*
Isaiah 11:9

<u>Tamposi Trail:</u> Is readily found in the lower left southern corner of the parking area. It is well marked with yellow blazes and has a moderate climb that passes by some impressive glacial erratic within the first 0.5 mile. One can continue to the top of Bald Mountain The Tamposi Trail will split, stay right for quicker but steeper to the Bald Mountain ledges and for exceptional views of Willard pond. Staying left is slightly longer with a steady ascent.

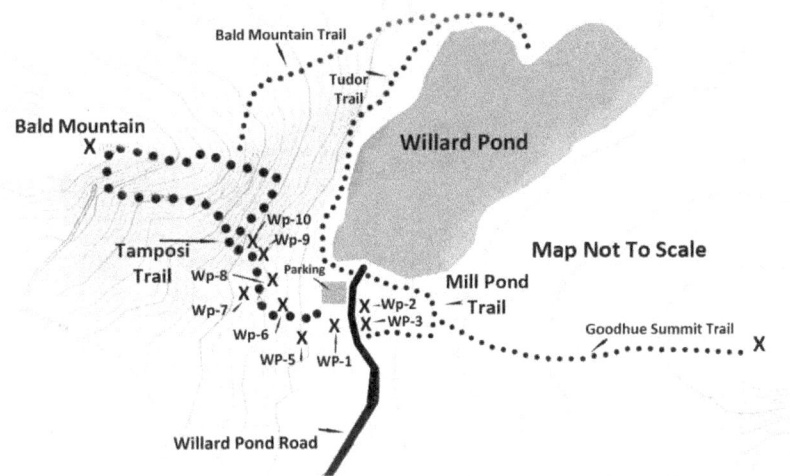

Tamposi Trail Erratic's - Willard Pond - Antrim, NH

Wp-1: N43° 0' 57.40" W72° 1' 14.00" (Balance Rock) *WOW 10*
An impressive trio of large boulders creates a balanced rock and shelter cave. Located just south of the parking area and requires minimal effort to access.

Wp-2: N43° 0' 58.26" W72° 1' 13.67" (Roadside Boulder) *WOW 6*
Large 14 foot boulder is roadside, just down from parking lot.
The memorial boulder to Elsa Tudor De Pierrefeu. is 50-feet pass this erratic.

Wp-3: N43° 0' 57.90" W72° 1' 13.00" (Turning Rock) *WOW 5*
Small erratic boulder on roadside also is entry point for the Mill trail east. FYI: On the opposite side of the road and a short 50 yard easy bushwhack brings you to Wp-1-Balance-Cave Rock.

Wp-5: N43° 0' 55.50" W72° 1' 16.80" (House Rock) *WOW 7*
Very large 20' boulder, 75 yards downhill off Tamposi trail at very beginning.

Wp-6: N43° 0' 59.10" W72° 1' 22.50" (Perched Rock) *WOW 5*
Situated on trail, nothing overly dynamic, good for quick and short break.

Wp-7: N43° 1' 0.79" W72° 1' 27.48" (Rockin Rock) *WOW 9*
Awesome leaning rocks with very large "Bear Cave" between them.

Wp-8: N43° 1' 1.90" W72° 1' 27.50" (Flat Top Rock) *WOW 8*
Large boulder with slight lemon squeeze, located on trail with easy access to top.

Wp-7 – Rockin Rock – Willard Pond, NH

Wp-9: N43° 1' 6.30"N W72° 1' 27.60" (Big Rock 1) *WOW 8*
Large 16 to 18 foot boulder, off trail, but passes relatively close.

Wp-10: N43° 1' 7.00" W72° 1' 27.50" (Big Rock 2) *WOW 8*
Large 16 foot boulder, the trail passes by relatively close.

Wp-8 - Flat Top Rock – Willard Pond, NH

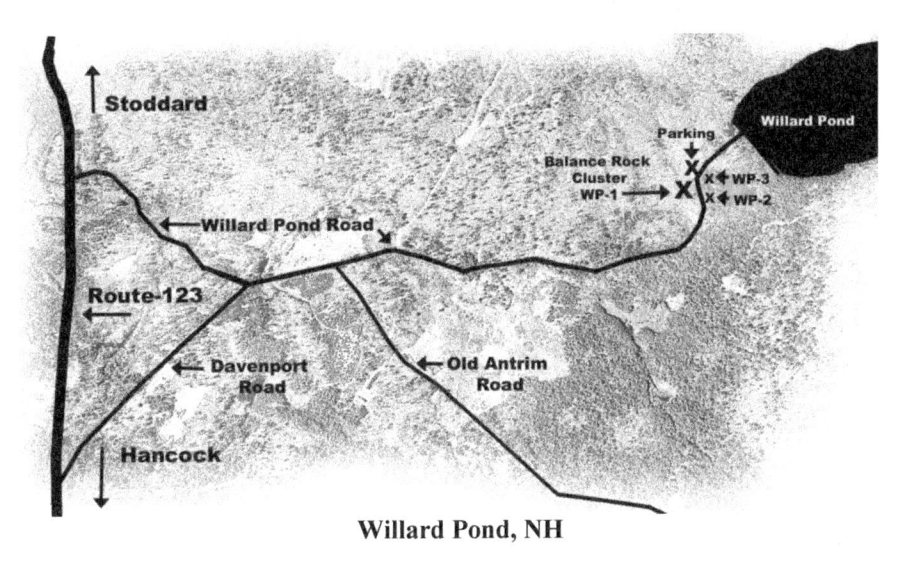

Willard Pond, NH

Directions: From Keene, follow Route-9 East, 15.0 miles into South Stoddard, at junction Route-123 towards Hancock. Follow Route-123 south for 3.4 miles, turning left onto Willard Pond Road. Continue 0.5 mile onto Davenport Road, continue left and shortly bearing left again, continue to follow Willard Pond Road, within 1.5 mile, a large improved dirt parking area for many vehicles appears on your left.

Wp-5 – House Rock – Willard Pond, NH

67. Wolf Rock

Wolf Rock – Mason, NH

Location: Mason (Hillsborough County)
Delorme Atlas & Gazetteer-New Hampshire: p21, J-10
Parking GPS: N42° 44' 48.30" W71° 45' 52.60"
Destination GPS: N42° 44' 56.87" W71° 45' 34.29"
Wow Factor: 6 **Accessibility:** 0.5 mile on unmaintained Scripts Road
Contact: Mason Historical Society-Public Library Director
(603) 878-3867 Email: library@masonnh.us

Information: Legend in the early days of Mason, Reverend Francis Worcester one night found himself surrounded by wolves as he traveled in the gloom of late evening. To elude the marauding wolfs he jumped upon the top of *Wolf Rock*, the rock is high and steep allowing a man to scale it, but preventing the wolfs from jumping up. The reverend spent the chilly night cold, but safe from wolfs.

The legend really isn't that far-fetched with the understanding if wolves were a concern for one's safety back then. The rock would be a convenient and suitable location for the reverend to quickly scale and maintain a defensive position on its top. However, noting the dog on top of the rock in the postcard (next page), if the Reverend Francis Worcester had been besieged by a pack of Collies we would have a different legend. lol ☺ In addition, I see that the rock facing at the time of the postcard does not appear to have the engraving now seen.

Wolf Rock, Mason, N. H. On this rock, in the early days, a Minister was besieged by wolves.
Wolf Rock – circa 1920's – Mason, NH

Directions: Off Route-123, Mason town center, follow Meeting House Road northeast for 0.3 mile. On your right, just prior to the Meeting House Memorial site and with the old 1771 Town Pound foundation across the street, is an unimproved parking area among some tall pine trees, this would be Scripts Lane. Park and hike down this old road behind the old Meeting House and Cemetery site for 0.4 miles. On your left, the first prominent path goes back some distance, but this is not for Wolf Rock, just past this path lies the correct path. Wolf Rock is only 50 feet from the old road and is hidden amongst the Mountain Laurel. The words *Wolf Rock* are engraved into the front surface which is facing the road.

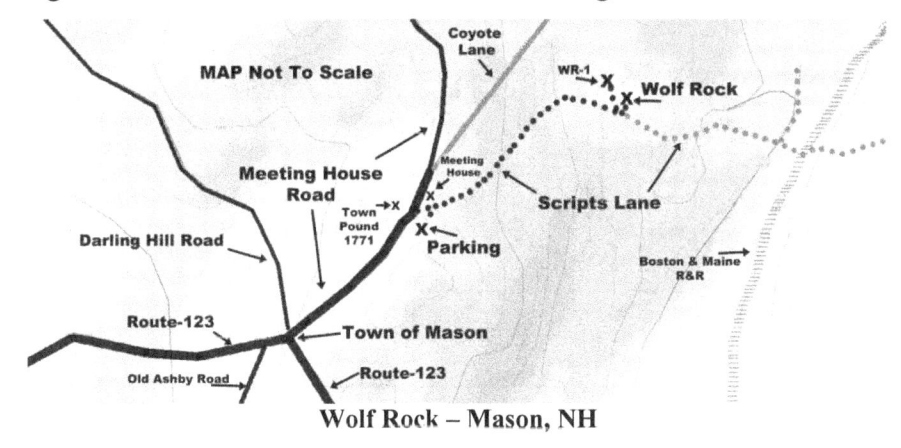

Wolf Rock – Mason, NH

Vermont

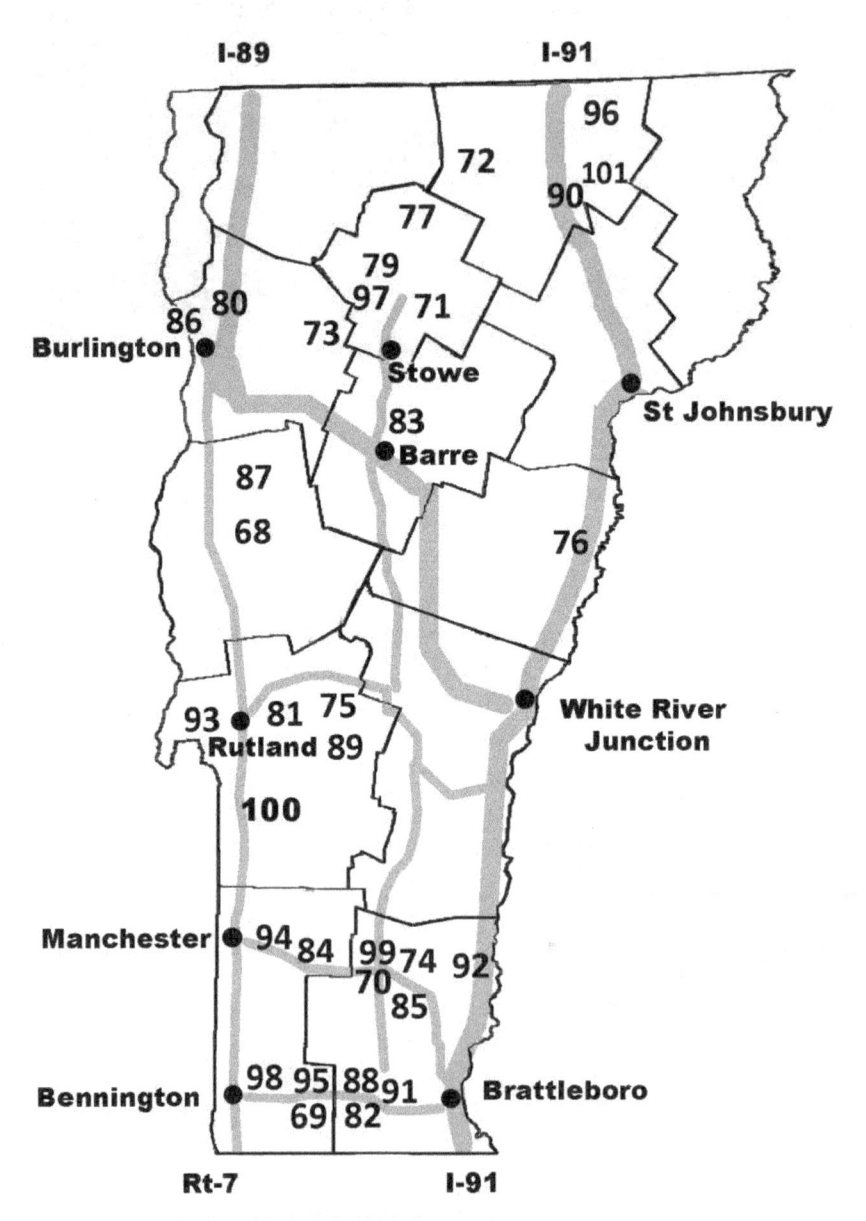

I-89   I-91

96
72
101
77 90
79
80 97 71
86   73
Burlington   Stowe
83
Barre   St Johnsbury
87
68   76

93 81 75
Rutland 89   White River Junction
100

Manchester 94 84 99 74 92
70
85

98 95 88 91
Bennington   69 82   Brattleboro

Rt-7   I-91

MAP No To Scale – For Reference Only

Vermont

68. Abbey Pond Boulders (Middlebury)
69. American Legion Balance Rock: (Readsboro)
70. Balance Rock: (Jamaica)
71. Balance Rock: Mt Elmore (Lake Elmore)
72. Balance Rock: (Westfield)
73. Cantilever Rock: Mt. Mansfield (Underhill)
74. Creature Boulders: (Grafton)
75. DEKD Boulders: Appalachian Trail (Killington)
76. Devils Den - Wright's Mountain: (Bradford)
77. Devils Gulch: Long Trail (Eden)
78. Devil's Rock: Lake Willoughby (Westmore)
79. Dog Head Rock: (Johnson)
80. Ethan Allan Park Boulders (Burlington)
81. Green Mountain Lodge Ruins: (Killington)
82. Green Mountain Giant: (Whitingham)
83. Hope Cemetery: (Barre)
84. Indian Head: (Windham)
85. Jamaica Ball Field: (Jamaica)
86. Lone Rock Point: (Burlington)
87. Lord's Prayer Rock a.k.a Bristol Rock: (Bristol)
88. Medburyville Bouldrs: (West Wilmington)
89. Mouse Rock: (Killington)
90. Mt Hor Boulders-Willoughby State Forest: (Sutton)
91. Perched Rock Brickhouse Road: (Whitingham)
92. Petroglyphs: Bellows Falls-Town of Rockingham
93. Pine Hill Park Glacial Erratic: (Rutland)
94. Power Line Boulders: (Windham)
95. Searsburg Boulders: (Searsburg
96. Sentinel Rock: (Westmore)
97. Smuggler's Notch: Vermont
98. Split Rock: Appalachian Trail (Woodford)
99. Target Rock: (Grafton)
100. White Cliffs Ice Beds - Cairns: (Wallingford)
101. Willoughby Lake: *The Boulders* (Westmore)

68. Abbey's Pond Boulders

Abbey's Pond Boulder – Middlebury, VT

Location: Middlebury (Addison County)
Delorme Atlas & Gazetteer-Vermont: p33, A-9
Parking GPS: N44° 1' 50.98" W73° 5' 17.49"
Destination GPS: N44° 1' 55.06" W73° 5' 8.95"
Wow Factor: 6 **Accessibility:** Easy 0.1 mile on trailside.
Contact: Middlebury Ranger Station. 1007 Route 7 South Middelbury, VT 05753 (802) 388-4362
Information: The land adjacent to the road and parking lot is private property. Please be respectful of the ownership; No fires or camping, No horses, mountain bikes, or motorized vehicles. Easy hike to the rock and just another 0.1 mile to Abby's Pond Cascades: N44°1'59.00" W73°5' 5.10"
Directions: From Middlebury travel south 4.0 miles on Route-7 to where it intersects with Route-125. Travel east on Route-125 for 0.6 mile to the intersection with Route-116. Travel north on Route-116 for 4.4 miles and look for a sign for the Abbey Pond Trail on the right. Turn right onto a gravel road and follow the right spur to the trailhead parking at 0.3 miles. From the parking lot, the trail leads into the woods and climbs moderately to a bridge at 0.2 miles. The trail continues beside a stream to a second stream crossing that has no bridge, but can be crossed on rocks. Ascending steadily after the second stream crossing, the trail climbs to yet a third stream crossing after which the terrain is gentler. The trail arrives at the outlet of Abbey Pond at 2.1 miles.

69. American Legion Balance Rock

American Legion Balance Rock – Readsboro, VT

Location: Readsboro (Bennington County)
Delorme Atlas & Gazetteer-Vermont: p21, K-13
Parking GPS: N42° 46' 13.20" W72° 56' 55.80"
Destination GPS: N42° 46' 13.20" W72° 56' 55.80"
Wow Factor: 8 Accessibility: Roadside.
Contact: American Legion Post 29, 66 Tunnel St Readsboro, VT 05350 (802) 423-7562

Information: A notable elongated and large balance rock sits next to the American Legion Post 29 Readsboro. Its additional height serves as a beacon for the American flag situated atop of this boulder. Glacial erratics were placed in their delicately balanced positions as the last of the ice flows receded relatively just a short several thousand years ago. In general, New England is no stranger to the many huge or uniquely placed erratics with the Readsboro and Whitingham area having many significant glacial boulders that are presently left and hidden with the regrowth of the surrounding woodlands. Uniquely, this balance rock is literally in the backyard and almost if not part of the patio.

Directions: From Wilmington at the junction of Route-9 and Route-100, follow Route-100 south for 13.5 miles continuing through Jacksonville, Whitingham and into the center of Readsboro. Turn south onto Tunnel Street, just after you cross the bridge, the immediate right is the location of the American Legion at the end a short side street. The balance rock is behind the post. Note: the post, patio and pavilion are private property and may have a proprietary interest or post activities on their property.

70. Balance Rock. Jamaica

Balance Rock – Jamaica, VT

Location: Jamaica (Windham County)
Delorme Atlas & Gazetteer-Vermont: p26, K-4
Parking GPS: N43° 5' 1.52" W72° 45' 7.84"
Destination GPS: N43° 5' 3.00" W72° 45' 7.90"
Wow Factor: 7 **Accessibility:** Easy 75 yards off Route-30.

Information: Jamaica Balance Rock is a hidden gem of a roadside attraction just south of Jamaica on Route-30. There are no signs or overt indication other than a small roadside pull-off, barely used, with a faint foot path up a small crag; a stony rise and the 8-feet by 12-feet boulder perched on an evidently small even apex.

From the University of Vermont Libraries, through an excerpt we are provided a glimpse on the lifestyle of Porter Thayer who in 1916 was a contemporary photographer and entrepreneur: *Porter Thayer was born Porter Charlie Thayer on January 6, 1882 on Main Street in Williamsville, Vermont. He grew up in the red house called the Tillotson Place in the Parish section of Newfane, Vermont. He photographed Windham County, Vermont, beginning in 1906 through around 1920. The postcard craze that most likely reached Vermont by about 1905, was perhaps the impetus for Porter Thayer starting up a photographic business. His diaries tell that he sold 1,197 postal cards during a six-month period at the height of his career. The cards were for sale as souvenirs to*

Balance Rock –1916 – Thayer, Porter C. (Porter Charlie), 1882-1972

summer tourists at small general stores, local inns, boarding houses and hotels. Local folks purchased his photographs as well, especially around the Christmas season, to send to distant relatives. Around 1911 he recorded that he had 720 customers. Eventually he photographed in all the towns within a 25 mile radius of his home in Newfane……. A Brattleboro, Vermont directory of 1909 lists Porter as advertising that he would come to anyone's home and make images for a reasonable fee……..Porter Thayer perfectly fits the archetype of the town photographer. He traveled the narrow dirt roads in his buggy, behind his faithful mare Lady, who accompanied him daily. ….. He used two cameras: a 5 x 7 and a 6.5 x 8.5 view camera and made glass dry-plate negatives. He traveled with stacks of postcards to be delivered at stores along the way to his days work.
Written by Jessica Weitz and Forrest Holzapfel, 2010

Balance Rock, Jamaica, Vt., Box 3, Porter Thayer Collection, Local History/Genealogy, Brooks Memorial Library, http://cdi.uvm.edu/collections/item/bmlthayerT247 (accessed December 06, 2017)

Directions: From East Jamaica at the intersection of Route-30 and Route-100, travel north 1.1 miles towards Jamaica. Shortly after Chaplin Lane, on your right, but before the rocky roadside crag is the Balance Rock. If you start to pass over the West River you have gone by, return 0.1 mile.

71. Balance Rock - Mt Elmore

Balance Rock – Mt Elmore - VT

Location: Elmore (Lamoille County)
Delorme Atlas & Gazetteer-Vermont: p47, E-8
Parking GPS: N44° 32' 23.42" W72° 32' 9.25"
Destination GPS: N44° 31' 56.40" W72° 32' 51.40"
Wow Factor: 9 **Accessibility:** Moderate to difficult 3.5 mile round trip
Contact: Elmore State Park 856 VT Route 12 Lake Elmore, Vermont 05657 802-888-2982 e-mail;parks@vermont.gov https://vtstateparks.com

Information: Many people use the Elmore State Park for its wonderful 219 acre Lake Elmore with beach, camping, picnic and rental pavilions. Others enjoy the hiking trails that loop up and over Mt. Elmore 2,608-feet summit, vistas, fire tower and its awesome balance rock. There is a per-person fee unless you meet the various criteria for youth or senior citizen, Veteran waiver or reduced charges through seasonal passes.

There are two trails to the summit; Fire Tower Trail, the shortest and steepest approach to the fire tower and southern end of Mt

Elmore (1.9 miles) versus the Ridge Trail that ascends at a longer gradual grade (2.2 miles), but only 1.5 miles to the Balanced Rock.

First, you park up at the end of the entry road off Route-12, 0.75 mile. From the parking area, hike north 0.3 mile, follow the dirt road until you reach the Ridge Trail turn-off on you right. This path will also bring you up and down the ridge south, to the fire tower. Along the way you will eventually encounter the Balance Rock another fine example of these natural wonders within the New England Region.

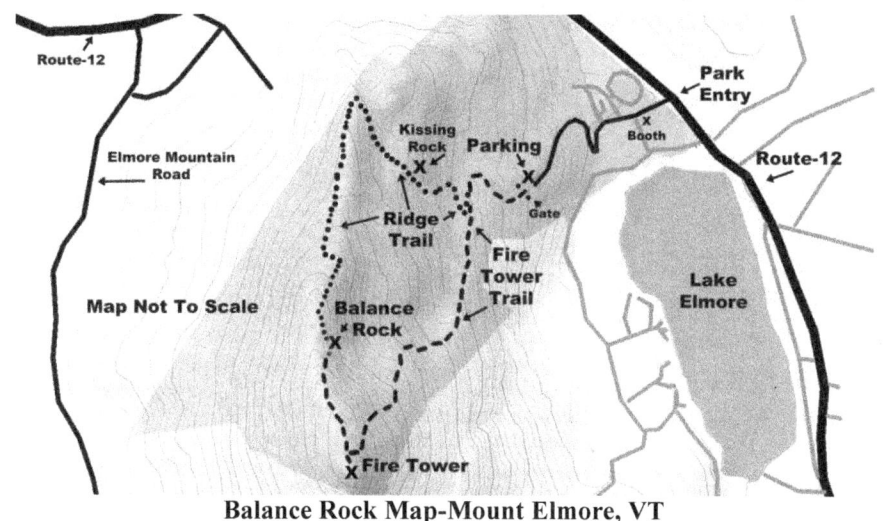

Balance Rock Map-Mount Elmore, VT

Directions: Off Interstate I-89, use Exit-8 into Montpelier, from its center, head north on Route-12 for 22.0 miles use the 2nd entry on your left after Lake Elmore. Park has entry/parking fee.

Balance Rock – Mt. Elmore, VT

72. Balance Rock - Westfield

Balance Rock – Lowell, VT

Location: Lowell (Orleans County)
Delorme Atlas & Gazetteer-Vermont: p53, F-9
Parking GPS: N44° 50' 38.00" W72° 28' 50.35"
Destination GPS: N44° 50' 39.70" W72° 29' 6.80"
Wow Factor: 9 **Accessibility:** Easy side of Moderate, 0.5 mile round trip.

Information: Just 11 miles south of the Canadian border, Westfield's Balance Rock is not frequently visited, the trail head itself is difficult to locate and was only by chance that I located the old, small wooden, decaying sign, plopped and over grown on the ground. However, our reward for the hassle and frustration is one of the best top ten balance rocks I've been awed by in the New England region. The trail was not well marked, you can sense the old overgrown road as you follow back as it heads westerly for 0.2 mile, you should sense the ridge in front of you, bear left, sweeping clock-wise up-hill; (in Spring or Fall as you look ahead the rock should be seen from a distance)

Directions: Our approach starts from the interchange of Route-100 and Route-58 in Lowell heading west on Route-58; in 1.9 miles pass the Buck Hill Road and continue west for additional 0.9 mile. Here you turn onto Green Hill Road heading north which will become Balance Rock Road as you enter Westfield. From this intersection the where Monteith Road enters on your left, continue on Balance Rock Road north for 0.3 mile, the trail head will be on your left. The only landmark I can note is a house with a small duckfire pond on the left, set back away from the road about 100 yards and before the small un-kept pull-off, watch the drainage ditch as you pull in or out.

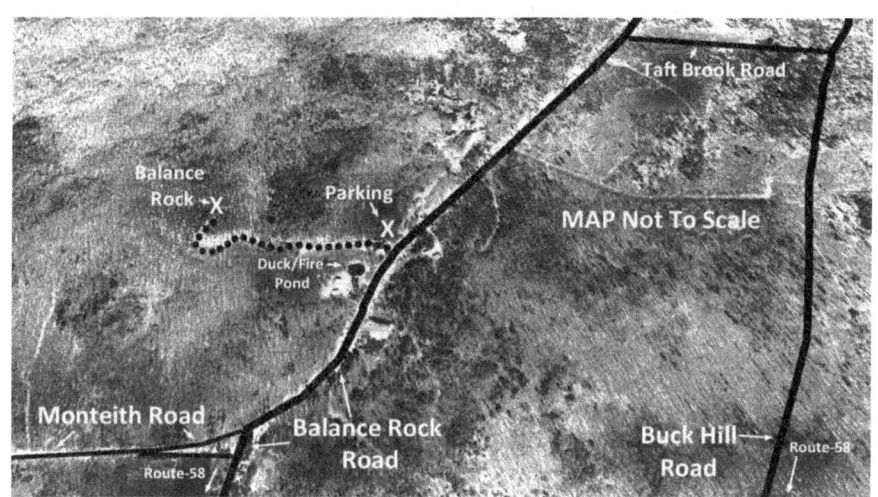

Map for Balance Rock – Westfield, VT

Lateral view of the Balance Rock. - -Westfield, MA

73. Cantilever Rock. Mt Mansfield

Cantilever Rock – Mt Mansfield – Underhill, VT

Location: Underhill (Chittenden County)
Delorme Atlas & Gazetteer-Vermont: p46, E-1
Parking GPS: N44° 31' 45.20" W72° 50' 34.50"
Destination GPS: N44° 32' 29.50" W72° 49' 51.81"
Wow Factor: 9 **Accessibility:** Moderate to difficult 1.5 mile up to rock.
Contact: Underhill State Park 352 Mountain Road Mailing PO Box 249 Underhill Center, VT 05490 (802)899-3022 www.vtstateparks.com

Information: From Underhill and the western side of Mount Mansfield, this moderate to strenuous hike up the Sunset Ridge Trail is the easiest route to *Cantilever Rock*. The Sunset Trail is the also recommended route down or up the mountain for completing a loop with Laura Cowles, Halfway House, or Maple Ridge trails. Seasonal staff can be found May through October. There may be a parking fee. Trailers, buses and RV's are not recommended due to tight road conditions and the lack of turn around ability.

Start from the Underhill State Park parking area located at the end of Mountain Road. From here the to the Sunset Ridge trail head, follow the old dirt CCC Road for 1.0 mile; or follow the Eagle Cut hiking trail to the trail head for 0.7 miles. Follow the Sunset Ridge Trail north, the trail for Cantilever Rock is 0.5 mile up and at this spur trail; (GPS N44°32'26.50" W72°49'49.10") turn left and follow 0.1 mile to the rock. Did not feel like a WOW-10, for the rock itself is rather inaccessible being 40-feet over head, still very remarkable.

Clyde Smith walks the "Walks the Plank"- Cantilever Rock, VT

Some describe the rock as: *This is a giant overhead rock that protrudes from the cliff like a knife blade."* others have said, *it's a Viagra billboard.* Technical Rock climbers do have history here; "Walking the Plank" is shown in these images by John Couture photographed in 1960's. I do see rope in the set-up; it must have been a rite of passage or challenge to get up to its base and then out to the tip.

Directions: From Interstate I-89, take exit-11, heading north on Route-2 briefly, immediately near the interchange, turn onto Route-117 (River Street) heading north for 3.3 miles. Turn right onto Skunk Hollow Road towards Jericho. Follow for 2.5 miles, bear left merging with Plains Road into Jericho 0.5 mile away. In Jericho, turn right onto Route-15 heading east towards Underhill for 2.7 miles. Turn right onto River Road, go 2.8 miles into Underhill Center, from there, continue for 1.0 mile on what is now Pleasant Valley Road, turn onto Mountain Road, follow 2.6 miles until you reach the Underhill State Park-Ranger Station and some facilities.

Cantilever Rock – Mt Mansfield _ Underhill, VT

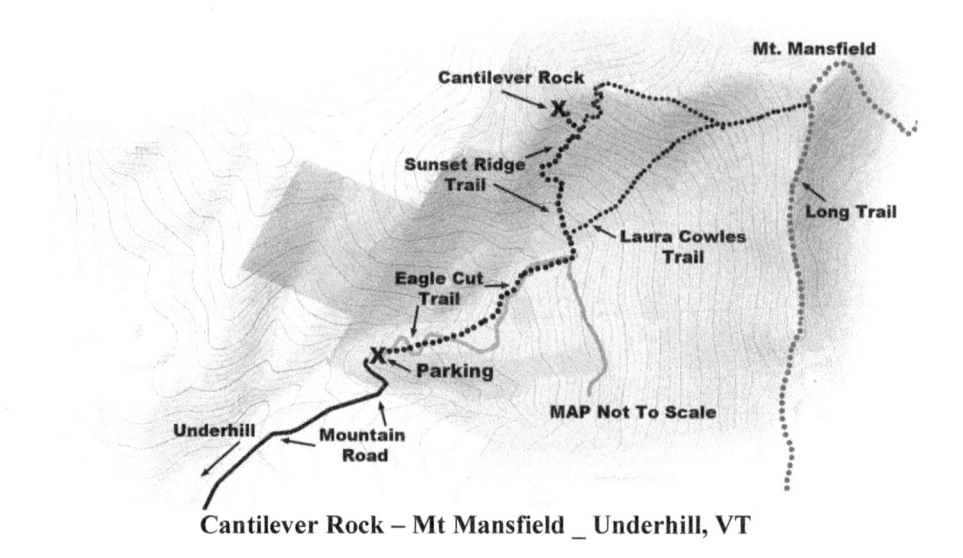

74. Creature Boulders

Creature Boulders – Grafton, VT

Location: Grafton (Windham County)
Delorme Atlas & Gazetteer-Vermont: p26, I-7
Parking GPS: N43° 8' 49.02" W72° 34' 38.22"
Destination GPS: N43° 8' 53.80" W72° 34' 42.52"
Wow Factor: 8 **Accessibility:** Moderate 0.2 mile, easy uphill path to site.
Contact: Windmill Hill Pinnacle Association. 35 Sleepy Valley Road. Athens, VT 05143 www.windmillhillpinnacle.org (802) 869-1388

Information: This 207-acre property was recently acquired and conserved in 2010 with a mission to conserve land in the Athens Dome area of Grafton and Athens Vermont. The Creature Rock area is physically in the town of Grafton VT. It is currently developed and managed by the Windmill Hill Pinnacle Association and a committee called the Athens Dome at Grafton Conservation Committee. This immense cluster of glacial erratic boulders were named "Creature Rock" from children who actively or imagined animal sounds coming from within crevices that look appealing as a shelter caves. An excellent PDF map is obtainable from the above contact web site.

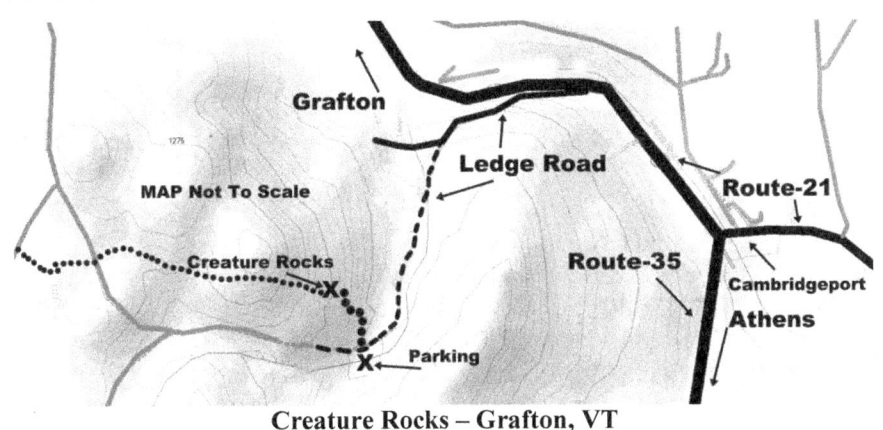

Creature Rocks – Grafton, VT

Directions: From the center of Grafton, follow Route-35 south for 3.5 miles. Ledge Road, a dirt road, will enter on your right at an angle, follow Ledge Road 1.0 mile to a large dirt parking area where the Creature Rock Trail crosses, park at this trailhead. From behind the Kiosk, take the Creature Rock Trail (white blazes) westerly about 0.2 miles. You will see creature rock on your left which consists of a prominent cluster of very large boulders with shelter cave-like openings. Ledge Road does continue from the Ledge Road trail head parking area, but is not passable safely by most vehicles, nor permissible for any motorized vehicle.

75. DEKD Boulders

DEKD-3 – Sliding Rock – Killington, VT

Location: Killington (Rutland County)
Delorme Atlas & Gazetteer-Vermont: p30, B-2
Parking GPS: N43° 40' 23.11" W72° 47' 57.11"
Destination GPS: Individual GPS locations below.
Wow Factor: 7 **Accessibility:** Easy side of Moderate 0.5 mile to boulders.
Contact: Green Mountain Visitor Center. 4711 Waterbury-Stowe Road. Waterbury Center, VT 05677-7035 gmc@greenmountainclub.org (802).244.7037 https://www.greenmountainclub.org/

Information: Readily accessible, this large boulder field is located heading east on the Appalachian Trail. Your first boulder, DEKD-1 will be found on your right in 0.1 mile, continue another 0.1 mile to DEKD-2 again trail side, DEKD-3 will be found 100 feet south from DEKD-2. Continuing east on the AT where DEKD-4 will be found on the trail side within 200 feet up on your right. Boulders; DEKD 5, 6 &7 will be found on the opposite side of the AT as you continue east on the AT all located within the next 0.1 mile from DEKD-4. While boulders here are not gigantic, I definitely sense that more boulders are waiting for off-trail explorers to discover. I do see many of these boulders having an interest for bouldering. Those telltale chalky hand-prints along with cleared or tamped woodland floor near their base say so. The rocks just make the woodlands fun to roam some off trail. I try to imagine the generations of cultural landscapes over the years. The rocks stay stoic with secret whispers.

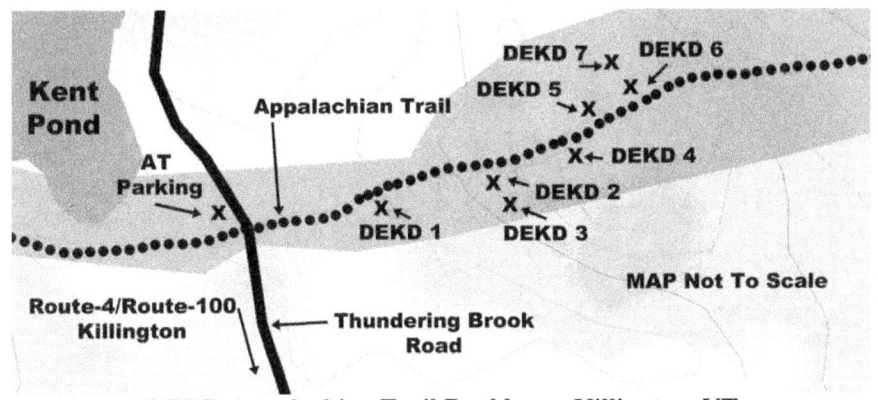

DEKD Appalachian Trail Boulders – Killington, VT

DEKD-1: N43° 40' 23.30" W72° 47' 48.82" (Rocking Horse)*WOW-6*
Not a Hugh rock 12-feet high, have no idea how the name was derived at.

DEKD-2: N43° 40' 23.34" W72° 47' 41.11" (Red Elf) *WOW-7*
Another not overly Hugh rock, 14 feet high. At least "Red Elf's' live in the woods?

DEKD-3: N43° 40' 22.64" W72° 47' 39.39" (Sliding Rock) *WOW-8*
Impressive height of 18 feet, a pinnacle with sloping sides. Slightly off trail, down behind DEKD-2

DEKD-4: N43° 40' 24.71" W72° 47' 38.74" (Dirty Crack) *WOW-7*
Appears to be another popular climbing boulder with trample ground near its trail-side facing. A good 14 feet of boulder with a spruce tree growing on its top.

DEKD-5: N43° 40' 24.70" W72° 47' 35.07" (Bug Rock) *WOW-6*
Long boulder, 12 feet in height, with a small chunk stone split off its rear. If I remember here the black flies were fierce.

DEKD-6: N43° 40' 24.52" W72° 47' 33.12" (Fat Bastard) *WOW-7*
A good size 16 feet tall by 30 feet in length boulder. Located on trail side. Name does work.

DEKD-7: N43° 40' 24.93" W72° 47' 33.50" (Pig Rock) *WOW-6*
Not very tall, only 12 feet in height by 30 feet long, laying on its side slanted down into a gully. Located within a cluster of similar sized rocks, just off-trail, not very far behind DEKD-6.

DEKD-4 – Dirty Crack – Killington, VT

Directions: From the center of Rutland, follow Route-4 east for 11 miles, uphill and until you reach the junction Route-100 north (on your left) and the Killington Road to Killington Ski Resort off on your right. Continue pass this junction on Route-4 for another 0.5 mile turning onto Thundering Brook Road on your left. Travel 0.4 miles till you see the Appalachian Trail crossing and parking. If you reach the shoreline of Kent Pond you have traveled pass the AT parking area.

DEKD-6 –Fat Bastard – Killington, VT

So what does the DEKD acronym stand for? I truly did not find anyone or anything about the origins of the DEKD Boulders label. However, if you do Google the question, the search brings one to Astronumerological Analysis and meaning of DEKD a somewhat wordy analysis of numbers and meanings. Below are some excerpts, visit: http://acronymsmeanings.com/full-meaning-of/dekd/dekd-stands-for-dekd-means/ for more information.

D: is intense vitality and is the letter connected with business; When it is the main consonant in a name the individual is inclined to over-work themselves, yet frequently discover accomplishment in their lives; this letter demonstrating independence and broadmindedness ; increase common information, its relentless and moderate, careful and confidence takes it back to itself.

E: is by and large a pleasant, cherishing and merciful soul; can be inconsistent and somewhat flaky on occasion; The equivalent lengths demonstrate a level of reasonableness to the outside world; They stretch out outwards showing an ability to learn, think extensively and be more fiery in comprehension.

K: speaks to a man that goes to extremes; Individuals with K as their first introductory are solid willed and persuasive. Adversely, K's can be disappointed with life and regularly take their discontent out on others. It demonstrates an appealing identity, its openness shows resistance and is prepared to help. K is likewise enthusiastic and culture arranged.

 In Vermont, the Appalachian Trail coincides with the Long Trail from the Massachusetts border to Maine Junction at Willard Gap just north of U.S. 4, and then swings east to cross the Connecticut River near Hanover, New Hampshire, a distance of 149.8 miles. The GMC maintains the AT from the Massachusetts border to Vt. 12. to Norwich. For more information about the Appalachian Trail, contact the Appalachian Trail Conservancy.

 Vermont and the Long Trail hold a prominent place in the history of the Appalachian Trail. It may have been on or near the summit of Stratton Mountain, after construction of the Long Trail was begun, that the idea of an extended footpath linking the scenic ridges of the East crystallized in the mind of Appalachian Trail visionary Benton MacKaye.

76. Devil's Den - Wright's Mountain

DD-2 - Entry Boulder – Bradford, VT

Location: Bradford (Orange County)
Delorme Atlas & Gazetteer-Vermont: p36, A-2
Parking GPS: N44° 1' 55.40" W72° 9' 38.26" (Chase Hollow Road)
Destination GPS: N44° 2' 11.20" W72° 10' 8.40" (Creature Rock)
Wow Factor: 8 Accessibility: Moderate-well marked trail, 1.7 round trip.
Contact: The Bradford Conservation Commission. (802) 439-3562
http://www.bradfordconservation.org

Information: The Bradford Conservation Commission (BCC) was officially established in 1990 and the 218-acre Wright's Mountain parcel was purchased from Sylvia Appleton in 1993. In April 2004, the town of Bradford acquired the 60-acre Devil's Den tract and through a conservation restrictions agreement with Upper Valley Land Trust, the Wright's Mountain/Devil's Den area will always be conserved as wildlife habitat and forest land, and open to the public for recreation, education, and enjoyment.

Devil's Den is a readily accessible ravine and has many small and large shelter caves created by many fragmented talus boulders. The yellow blazed Chase Hollow Trail enters and hugs the eastern side of the ravine wall along the base of its cliffs. Not until you reach the back wall is any rock hopping required. However, access to many of the shelter caves will require maneuvering or climbing around to reach their entrances off trail. Devils Den is a remote wilderness and could have wildlife (e.g. porcupine, fox, bats, and other vermin) which may not like your visitation into their home if occupied, just a thought to be aware of.

Creature Rock: By following the yellow blazes of the Chase Hollow Trail all the way into Devil's Den, you may discover Creature Rock. Apparently the Creature has resided here along with the Ravens for several years. Originally, I had assumed the creature would be larger-than-life, but its size was a little more life-like once I spotted it within its well hidden lair. If not for the lack of water, I would have easily and mistakenly thought the creature a carnivorous look alike of the alligator or crocodile. Hence, it surely must be from the dragon family if not that of a very large lizard! **DD-3 - Creature Rock >**

DD-2: N44° 2' 8.40" W72° 10' 6.80" (Entry Boulder)

DD-3: N44° 2' 11.20" W72° 10' 8.40" (Creature Rock)

Directions: To Devils Den via Chase Hollow Road Trailhead; From Interstate 91, take exit-16 for Bradford. Go west on route-25 for 3.3 miles. Turn right onto Chase Hollow Road and go 1.2 miles. Trailhead parking is on the left, and the yellow-blazed trail starts at the north upper corner of the parking lot. Watch for rocks within the parking area.

From the Chase Hollow Trail parking lot, you will junction early on with Joel's Trail, then uphill where it splits with Best Way In/ Best Way Out, (either way is relative easy), enter onto and share Woods Road for a short distance, then at Ernie's Trail junction, exit downhill to Devils Den.

It is to be noted that during the winter months Chase Hollow Road may not be plowed to the parking area. Parking becomes restricted with no parking tolerated within the snowplow turn-around on Chase Hollow Road.

77. Devil's Gulch – Long Trail

Devil's Gulch – Eden, VT

Location: Eden (Orange County)
Delorme Atlas & Gazetteer-Vermont: p52, I-6
Parking GPS: N44° 45' 50.02" W72° 35' 16.28" (Route-118 Eden)
Destination GPS: N44° 44' 44.80" W72° 36' 27.30" (Devil's Gulch)
Wow Factor: 8 Accessibility: Moderate-well marked trail, 4.0 miles RT.
Contact: Green Mountain Visitor Center. 4711 Waterbury-Stowe Road. Waterbury Center, VT 05677-7035 gmc@greenmountainclub.org (802).244.7037 https://www.greenmountainclub.org/

Information: This can be an excellent loop trail hike. From Devil's Gulch everything is higher ground, walking down to it, is the option. You will go south on the *Long Trail* 2.0 miles, this starts relatively as a stroll down the ridge, along the way a vista of Mud Pond and Ritterbush Vista, the trail will descend steeply, the Long Trail maintenance crew provides well placed stone stairways which help greatly. At the intersection of the *Babcock Trail* and the AT/LT trails, to your left, descends down to Ritterbush Pond. To your right, going north is the 2.0 mile ***return trail.*** With a lesser incline, this is a favorable or optional return route rather than the one you just descended. You'll skirt along the western length of Mud Pond and turning out onto Route-118, 0.4 mile below the parking area. The *Babcock Extension* crosses Route-118, it returns to the parking area via woodlands or you can hoof it out on the pavement back to the parking area.

From the *Babcock Trail* junction, The *Devil's Gulch* is close; continue south and you will see the entry ladder going up and passing through some boulders into the Gulch. The prominent boulder *Devils Gate* is readily seen for it is massive and tall, a fern and moss covered behemoth, up-ended, leaning on top of another fern covered behemoth, creating a large and long shelter cave. All the rocks and ground cover have a great display with little islands of lush greenery of fern and moss. As you return; you can either return by staying on the steeper *Long Trail* north all the way back to the parking area or at the *Babcock Trail* junction turn left returning by Mud Pond back to Route-118.

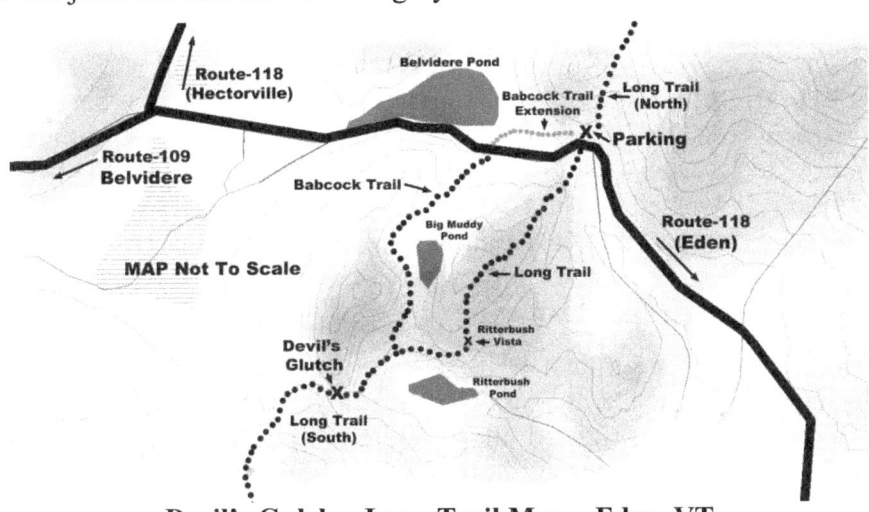

Devil's Gulch – Long Trail Map – Eden. VT

Directions: From the Junction of Routes-100 and Route-118 in Eden, turn north on Route-118 (Belvidere Road) and go 5.0 miles. At the top, on a long sweeping curve, turn right into the entry for the *Long Trail Trail* head parking.

78. Devil's Rock

Devil's Rock – Lake Willoughby – Westmore, VT

Location: Westmore (Orleans County)
Delorme Atlas & Gazetteer-Vermont: p54, J-5
Parking GPS: N44° 43' 32.25" W72° 2' 7.19"
Destination GPS: N44° 43' 32.25" W72° 2' 7.19"
Wow Factor: 7 **Accessibility:** Roadside

Information: It may not be sanctioned and there is no lifeguard, but the rock is a well-known landmark for the swimming, jumping and/or diving opportunities it presents. A painted larger-than-life, red devil is located on the front (not seen in photo) and can be only viewed from the lake. In addition, it is suggested that its moniker *Devil's Rock* is because of an image of a skull lying on its side can be seen reflected in still water.

Directions: From Interstate I-91, Exit-23, follow Route-5 north through Lyndon for 9.5 miles until in West Burke Route-5A branches off on the right. Follow Route-5A north for 6 miles where you will come to Lake Willoughby, continue north on Route-5A along the lake's eastern shore for 0.7 mile where on your left a small and limited pull-off for 2-3 cars is noticeable on the lake side of the road. A gap in the guardrail allows entry to the top of Devil's Rock.

79. Dog Head Rock

Dog Head Rock – Johnson, VT

Location: Johnson (Lamoille County)
Delorme Atlas & Gazetteer-Vermont: p46, B-5
Parking GPS: N44° 37' 18.10" W72° 40' 41.80"
Destination GPS: N44° 37' 21.60" W72° 40' 38.40"
Wow Factor: 9 **Accessibility:** Public access, easy 0.1 mile path.

Information: For me the profile of Dog Head Rock resembles a short snouted Black Lab swimming in water. While the profile can be viewed down-stream, the up-stream view is more appealing for your closer to the profile and the waterfall. That said in the spring time or when high water flows, this location of a narrowed body of ripping water becomes a class 4-5 rapids. If you did not come with the intention of swimming, then mind your step and watch out for wet or smooth slick rock surfaces.

Directions: From Waterbury, Interstate I-89, Exit-10 take Route-100 north into Stowe, continue through Stowe on Route-100 north for 9.5 miles where it will junction with Route-15 in Morristown. Turn left and head west on Route-15 for 6.75 miles into Johnson, in the center of Johnson, turn left onto Railroad Street, in 0.3 mile and just after you cross the Lamoille River Bridge, turn left onto River East Road. Travel along the river southerly for 1.0 mile. The road will widen and a narrow parking pull-off area is located on your left where the bike path and Lamoille River seem to come together, from here it's no more than quick 100 yard walk to the Dog Head Rock and Falls.

80. Ethan Allen Park Boulders

EA-3 Boulder – Ethan Allen Park, VT

Location: Burlington (Chittenden County)
Delorme Atlas & Gazetteer-Vermont: p44, F-6
Parking GPS: N44° 30' 16.10" W73° 14' 23.03"
Destination GPS: As listed below.
Wow Factor: 7 **Accessibility:** Easy. Path or paved gated access road
Contact: Burlington Vermont Department of Parks and Recreation 1006 North Ave, Burlington, VT 05408 (802) 864-0123

Information: Prior to the park, this elevated ridge was referred to as *"Indian Rock."* This land was used as an Abenaki camp site with fishing on the shores of Lake Champlain and as a strategic lookout. Ethan Allen Park was named after the revolutionary war hero, who did indeed own this land himself for a period of time in the 1780's. Later through a series of land ownership transfers of title, the park grew to 67 acres and was set aside for public usage. The park is presently maintained by volunteers and the Burlington Department of Parks and Recreation. On the lower southwestern side, just above the playground and below the tower at street level, you will find a group of small boulders 14-feet to 16-feet in height. Lurking under the summer tree canopy, the diffused and shaded light seems to camouflage their hideout. The rocks in many ways are just average, especially in contrast to the dense residential neighborhood just across the street, still for young or old it does provide escapism or a location to get away from it all just across the street.

These stand-alone boulders certainly do seem to have their share of attention, from young boulderer's strengthening or honing their climbing skills or with younger youngsters scampering among these stone fortifications as action figures, freeing the world from evil, Ogre's, Witches and Zombie's that live here!

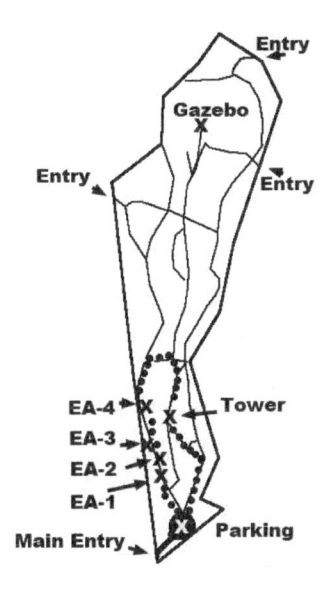

EA-1: N44° 30' 21.90" W73° 14' 25.40" *(WOW 6)* A bigger rock than I expected, large 16' in height, squarest on one side, roundish on the other. First boulder on the left, trail side.

EA-2: N44° 30' 23.10" W73° 14' 25.90" *(WOW 6)* 14' feet in height, square shaped in the rear with its top cresting like a wave. Second boulder on left, trail side.

EA-3: N44° 30' 22.70" W73° 14' 27.00" *(WOW 7)* One side is a 16' tall slab, next to a 14 foot boulder separated by a large crack. Located downhill closer to roadside from trail.

EA-4: N44° 30' 25.30" W73° 14' 27.60" *(WOW 5)* Two large prominent boulders that narrows the trail creating a constricted upper entry point or gateway.

EA-Tower: N44° 30' 23.4" W73° 14' 25.67" *(WOW 10)*

EA-2 Boulder – Ethan Allen Park, VT

The Tower built in 1905 was renovated and stabilized in 1942, closed for safety in1974, later after being rejuvenated, the tower re-opened in 1983. The recent renovations include, all the interior stairways being replaced, the native Redstone and Marble cut stone received masonry repairs or replacement. The tower is the best attraction we encountered during this short loop hike. It looks like a castle fortress and from its top vantage point the 360° panoramic view is awesome. The tower gates are unlocked each morning from Memorial Day to Columbus Day by passionate neighborhood volunteers.

There is a gazebo in the northern section of Ethan Allen Park, situated on top of Pinnacle Hill and was re-built in 1937 replacing the original wooden gazeboes with one made of stone. Being on the tallest of hilltops within the park boundaries, it has always been remembered for once having a remarkable scenic vista of the North Burlington area. Presently, brush growth obscures these panorama views.

Directions: In North Burlington, traveling north on Route-127, use the North Avenue and Beaches exit. Follow the interchange out, stay in the right lane, turn right onto *North Avenue* heading north. Travel 0.3 mile and turn right onto the *Ethan Allen Parkway*, take the immediate first right into the entry of Ethan Allen Park and parking area.

81. Green Mountain Club Lodge

GMC Cabin Boulder – Killington, VT

Location: Killington (Windham County)
Delorme Atlas & Gazetteer-Vermont: p30, B-1
Parking GPS: N43° 39' 47.60" W72° 49' 57.30"
Destination GPS: N43° 39' 46.60" W72° 50' 0.30"
Wow Factor: 6 Accessibility: Unmark path to dilapidated rubble site .
Contact: Green Mountain Club 4711 Waterbury Stowe Rd, Waterbury Center, VT 05677 (802) 244-7073 https://www.greenmountainclub.org/

Information: James Taylor conceived the Long Trail in 1910, in 1911, a group of 23 people, including Mr. Taylor, got together in Burlington, VT and formed the Green Mountain Club. The GMC is the founder and maintainer of the *Long Trail*, the oldest established long distance hiking trail in America. It was their job to begin cutting the Long Trail, and to provide trail maintenance and protection. Since its inception the GMC has served the Long Trail System through trail building and maintenance, maps, sanitation, protecting natural resources from overuse or development, educating and safeguarding special natural areas.

In 1923, the *Long Trail Lodge* was constructed to be the base of the GMC and the heart of the Long Trail. The lodge was constructed of logs and lumber found in the woods in close proximity of the construction site. The lodge encompassed other elements of the mountains as well, including a natural rock wall that was built into the lodge. The most fascinating thing about the lodge was that the

An excerpt found the above post card: *The lodge is built into a wooded hillside surrounded by deciduous trees with no leaves at this time. There is snow on the ground as well. A very large, lichen covered, glacial erratic sits in the middle of the image, partially blocking view of the lodge.* If you look to the other end of the porch on the right end, you'll note another large glacial erratic.

It was inconclusive that both of the above boulders could be one in the same.

The Long Trail actually ran right through the lodge, and meals were given to any who desired them. The former Long Trail Lodge was sold by GMC in 1954 and destroyed by fire in 1968. There are ruins just west of the Sherburne Pass trail head parking lot, but the land is owned by Killington Resort. It's not managed and conditions are not very safe. If you visit, please take care. I was seeking the large erratic seen in front or part of the GMC Lodge, there are a couple of remarkable boulders among the ruins. A novel area and is difficult trying to imagine where the original GMC Lodge's components were located. Then there are some "structures" which appear to be contemporary after-thoughts. Examination of these ruins did not appear to support the descriptions of natural material for posts and rafters used in the original construction, nor did the layout seem to concur or agree with photographs of the complex.

Either way, everything is a relic or everything seen was totally being reclaimed by the forest. Older topographic maps do show the Long Trail converging at this the old lodge's location.

Green Mountain Club Structure - 2017 – Killington, VT

Directions: In Rutland, at the junction of Route-7 and Route-4, follow Route-4 east, uphill towards Killington for 9.0 miles. Just 0.5 mile pass the entry to Pico Mountain Ski Resort is the Shelburne Pass parking area where the Long Trail crosses. Across the street is Deer Leap Rocks. You will pass on your right the parking area for the Appalachian Trail just prior to this large LT parking area. There is a path leading west from the southern end of the LT parking near the kiosk. Apparently we are not the first visitors to visit the ruins with a well-worn path in place.

82. Green Mountain Giant

Green Mountain Giant – Front – Whitingham, VT

Location: Whitingham (Windham County)
Delorme Atlas & Gazetteer-Vermont: p21, J-13
Parking GPS: N42° 45' 54.95" W72° 54' 27.09"
Destination GPS: N42° 46' 29.30" W72° 54' 7.32"
Wow Factor: 9 **Accessibility:** Moderate 1.0 mile to rock on dirt road/trail.

Information: Known as the "Green Mountain Giant" since at least the 1861, when Edward Hitchcock, state of Massachusetts geologist and president of Amherst College, gave it that name. The boulder measures 40' across, has an average width of 32 feet and 125feet in circumference. It is estimated to weigh 3,400 tons. Although located within a tract of the Green Mountain National Forest, the glacial erratic sits on private land. The approach on the dirt road which turns into a snowmobile trail from Atherton Meadows Wildlife Management access off Route-100 seems to be permissible.

Described in Hitchcock's 1861, "Report on the Geology of Vermont"; *But the most gigantic specimen with which we have met, lies on the naked ledges on a high hill on the farm of Jonathan Dix, in the west part of Whitingham.* I enjoy the thought that all around the area was deforested and how easy it must have been compared to today's forest regrowth which now obscures the scenic panoramic vistas and hides massive objects such as the many glacial erratics, unseen until one literally bumps into it.

Green Mountain Giant – Whitingham, VT

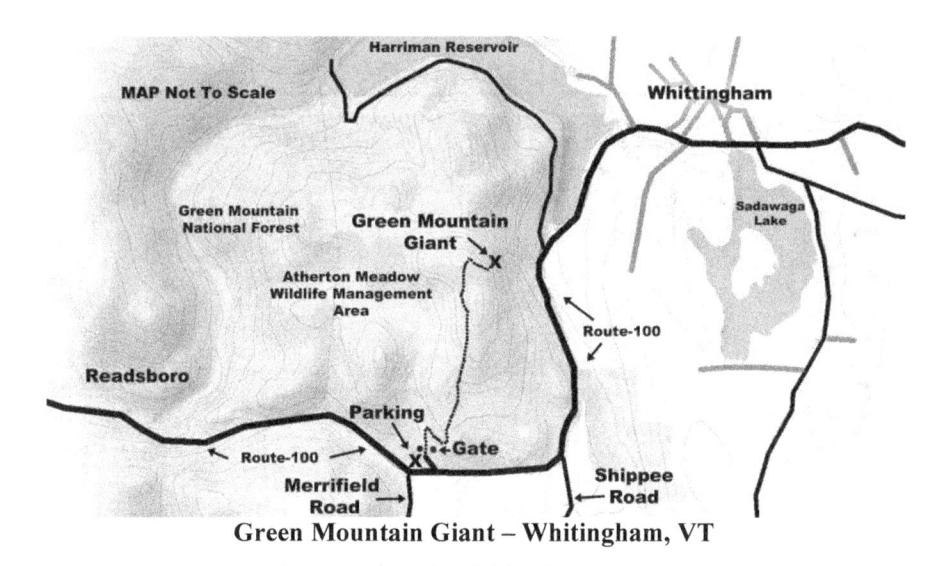

Directions: From the center of Whitingham, follow Route-100 west for 2.7 miles, a small dirt road which has parking for 2 to 3 vehicles will be on your right. A heavy timbered sign is posted at this road entry "Atherton Meadows Wildlife Management Area." Should you pass this turn off, Merrifield Road very shortly will be on the left. Pull into and off Route-100, park here without blocking the gate. Walk pass the gate heading north and follow the logging road. The road and trail is presently unmarked about the Green Mountain Giant. The road will shortly have a switchback heading east and then will switch back continuing north. After 0.9 mile the road will narrow and become more trail oriented; soon at a junction of posted snowmobile trails, turn sharply right, head east for 0.1 mile, the Green Mountain Giant will be easily seen on your left, set back off the trail slightly.

Green Mountain Giant – Rear- Whitingham, VT

83. Hope Cemetery

C - Hope Cemetery – Barre, VT

Location: Barre (Washington County)
Delorme Atlas & Gazetteer-Vermont: p41, E-9
Parking GPS: N44° 12' 37.71" W72° 30' 0.15"
Destination GPS: N44° 12' 37.71" W72° 30' 0.15"
Wow Factor: 7 **Accessibility:** Public access, easy walking.
Contact: *Hope Cemetery*-201 Maple Ave, Barre, VT 05641
(802) 476-6245 cemeteries@barrecity.org Hours 7 a.m. to 5 p.m.
Rock of Ages-560 Graniteville Road, Graniteville, Vt.; (802) 476-3119

Information: Hope Cemetery was established in 1895 and originally consisted of 53 acres which has grown to 65 acres. It was designed and planned by the renowned landscape architect Edward P. Adams. Skilled artisans from around the world settled in Barre for the quality of the grey granite from its quarry that is used in tombstones and memorials sold throughout the United States. As I am told, every memorial in Hope Cemetery is Barre Granite. While the majority of the headstones are more traditional, many have been commissioned as custom figures, bas-reliefs and ornate engravings.

Consider that cemeteries are usually attractively landscaped, meticulously mowed and often adorned with flowers or ornamental shrubs. Hope Cemetery goes one step further and provides the visitor some stunning examples of stone sculptures and insight into the cultural influence of how people deal and view the inevitable onset of death. A visit here is not about the macabre, but the joy and celebration of life in death. Shown here are only a few of the prominent headstones. Nearby, the Barre *Rock of Ages* quarry that produces the stone is also open for tours and visits.

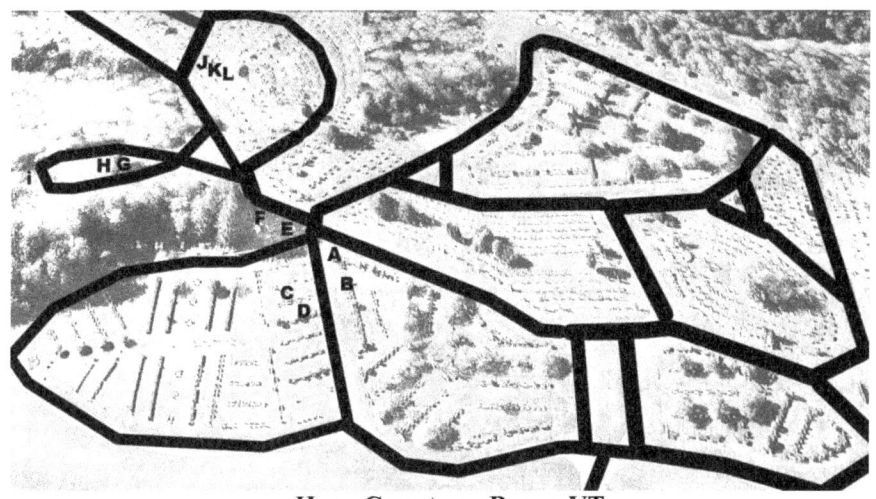

Hope Cemetery- Barre, VT

Prominent Tombstone Sculptures - Hope Cemetery – Barre, VT

A: N44° 12' 37.70" W72° 29' 59.60" (Soccer Ball)
B: N44° 12' 37.90" W72° 29' 59.00" (Cube)
C: N44° 12' 37.10" W72° 29' 59.10" (Car)
D: N44° 12' 37.20" W72° 29' 58.20" (Plane)
E: N44° 12' 37.20" W72° 30' 0.40" (Pyramids)
F: N44° 12' 36.60" W72° 30' 1.40" (Sailboat)

G: N44° 12' 35.40" W72° 30' 3.20" (Beds)
H: N44° 12' 35.30" W72° 30' 3.20" (Louis Brusa)
I: N44° 12' 33.60" W72° 30' 3.40" (Angelo)
J: N44° 12' 36.50" W72° 30' 5.10" (Elia Corti's)
K: N44° 12' 36.70" W72° 30' 5.20" (Urn)
L: N44° 12' 36.75" W72° 30' 4.84" (Cole)

Directions: Interstate I-89 Exit 7, go east on Route-62 for 4.0 miles. In Barre, cross Main Street (Route-302), continue north 0.7 mile on Route-14. The main gate of Hope Cemetery will be on your left.

84. Indian Head

Indian Head – Windham, VT

Location: Windham (Windham County)
Delorme Atlas & Gazetteer-Vermont: p25, G-12
Destination GPS: N43° 11' 31.77" W72° 56' 46.60"
Wow Factor: 8 Accessibility: Roadside on Route-30

Information: This painted rock is done extremely well and sits on the southern side on Route-30 between Manchester and Windham. Since I've first seen it, has been repainted once including its creative and bold tribal paint genre.

Directions: From Exit-4 off Route-7 in Manchester, go east on Route-11 and Route-30 for 5.0 mile, turn right staying on Route-30 east for 1.4 miles. The painted Indian will be on the right.

85. Jamacia Ballfield

Jamacia Ballfield Outcrop – Jamacia, VT

Location: Jamacia (Windham County)
Delorme Atlas & Gazetteer-Vermont: p26, K-3
Parking GPS: N43° 4' 32.55" W72° 44' 5.57"
Destination GPS: N43° 4' 32.90" W72° 43' 54.50"
Wow Factor: 6 **Accessibility:** Easy 0.1mile to rocks, woodland, no path.

Information: One of the first locations in Vermont which really didn't pan out for finding boulders. However, in lieu of erratics or boulders, at the time, the rocky and tall out-crop here was being climbed by a young boulderer, her enthusiasm was charismatic, so I have kept it listed. Easy access and easy to locate.

Directions: At the ball field located directly at the junction of Route-100 north from Wilmington and with Route 30 (West River Road) in Jamaica. At the ball field entry; park and walk down Route-30 east for 0.1 mile to find this ledge slightly away from the roadway. Its base will be lower than the roadway.

86. Lone Rock - Lone Rock Point

Lone Rock a.k.a. "Bishop's Rock" – Burlington, VT

Location: Burlington (Windham County)
Delorme Atlas & Gazetteer-Vermont: p44, F-5
Parking GPS: N44° 29' 47.96" W73° 14' 24.59"
Destination GPS: N44° 29' 16.94" W73° 14' 56.68"
Wow Factor: 7 **Accessibility:** Easy to moderate-limited public access-fee.
Contact: The Episcopal Church in Vermont | 20 Rock Point Road, Burlington, VT 05408 | 802.658.6233 bishopbooth@dioceseofvermont.org

Information: Lone Rock Point in Burlington is part of what is known as the Champlain thrust fault and is located on the eastern shore of Lake Champlain at the north end of Burlington Harbor. For geologists, this locality is one of the finest exposures of a thrust fault in the Appalachians because it shows many of the fault zone features characteristic of thrust faults throughout the world. This upward thrust of rock layers is well exposed with impressive 80-feet cliffs along with a rocky shoreline. At the tip of Rock Point is the stand-alone, off shore *"Lone Rock"* and has been a popular hiking destination and a well photographed landmark. For more academic geological information contact the University of Vermont in Burlington or Google it.

The 130 acres of Lone Rock Point trails and rocky shoreline is private property. You may request permission to access the land at the main office as you enter or their web site which lists passes, fees and regulations: (**www.rockpointvt.org/rock-point-passes**)

Since 1855, Rock Point Episcopal Diocesan Center has welcomed friends or neighbors attracted to its natural beauty and its peaceful environment. Serving as an administration center to the Episcopal Church in Vermont, thousands of people come to Rock Point to find a place to walk, seek solitude, learn, play, sing, pray, think, share, and just too be. You need to park on the church grounds to enter the trails. Note: There are some restricted areas for Summer Camps and other activities which usually will be posted.

The cliffs and shoreline during the summer months have liability concerns to the Diocese and a stricter approach has been implemented for certain activities. There is absolutely no water access for swimming, cliff jumping or diving.

Stereographic Photo of Lone Rock Point – Burlington, VT

Rock climbing has been another topic of concern and primarily banned for some time. However, the 2017-2018 seasons under a special use agreement signed between CRAG-VT and the Episcopal Diocese of Vermont, climbing permission has tentatively been restored. All climbers <u>must</u> get a Rock Point Property Pass via the process described here; **www.rockpointvt.org/rock-point-passes** Guidelines can be found here; **www.cragvt.org/rockpoint**

The Lone Point Rock itself is located off the mainland and considered accessible by watercraft or if frozen via the ice, but you cannot walk the shoreline to reach it or beach onto the shoreline.

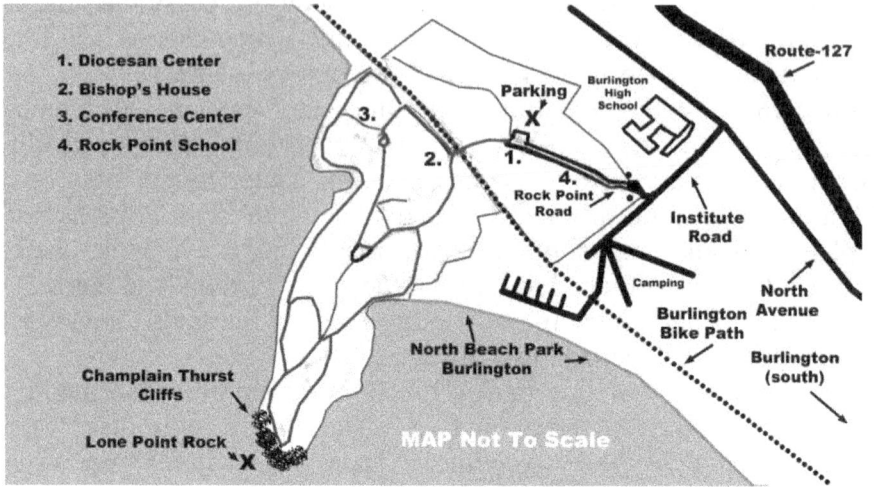

Map labels:
1. Diocesan Center
2. Bishop's House
3. Conference Center
4. Rock Point School

Other map features: Parking, Burlington High School, Rock Point Road, Institute Road, Camping, Burlington Bike Path, North Avenue, Burlington (south), Route-127, North Beach Park Burlington, Champlain Thurst Cliffs, Lone Point Rock, MAP Not To Scale.

Lone Rock Point – Burlington, VT

Directions: In North Burlington traveling north on Route-127 use the North Avenue and Beaches exit. Follow the interchange out, stay in the left lane and turn onto North Avenue heading south. Travel 0.4 mile and turn right onto Institute Road at the Burlington High School and athletic field. Travel 0.2 mile, just after the High School, on your right is the entry into the Rock Point Episcopal Center with two brick pillars. The required parking area is 0.2 mile in, on your right with a gravel area for approximately 30 cars.

Vertical Photo above: **Mrs. Irving Kennedy and friends at Lone Rock Point in Burlington, circa 1890.**

87. Lord's Prayer Rock

"Lord's Prayer Rock" – Bristol Rock – Bristol, VT

Location: Bristol (Addison County)
Delorme Atlas & Gazetteer-Vermont: p39, H-10
Parking GPS: N44° 7' 45.50" W73° 4' 5.80"
Destination GPS: N44° 7' 46.55" W73° 4' 7.72"
Wow Factor: 7 **Accessibility:** Roadside

Information: A 19th century physician, Joseph C. Greene, of Buffalo, NY, had the idea to have the Lord's Prayer engraved on a slanted rock just east of Bristol. Supposedly the inspiration to do so stemmed from his youth growing up in South Stacksboro where one of his jobs was delivering logs to the Bristol sawmill. The difficult decent down the mountain consisted of switchbacks and river crossings, until reaching this particular slanted rock, he would say a silent prayer thanking the Lord that the worst of the journey was behind him. What is known that in 1891, Dr. Greene did pay to have the Lord's Prayer engraved onto the slab, including his full name as seen in the lower left corner. Another version of the rock's engraved origin is that Greene, evidently a religious soul, was upset by the cursing and swearing of passing logging wagon drivers. So he had the prayer carved to make them think twice before taking the Lord's name in vain.

The best angle on photographing the Lord's Prayer Rock is achieved by standing in the middle of the road which on this very busy road is risky and reciting the Lord's Prayer just might be a good policy before doing so. It is also known as Bristol Rock and as a landmark there are many renditions of photographs and postcards showing the slanted rock with many calling it a "Ramp to Heaven." Community discussion concerning the rock in 1957, 1974, and 1985, was heighten each time the roadway was talked about its improvement. Discussion on removing a portion of the rock, moving the rock away from the roadway or widening the road, were either too costly and that no assurances could be made that no damage to the landmark would result.

Directions: From Middlebury, travel north on Route-7 for 8.0 miles to the junction of Route-7 and Route-17 in New Haven Junction. Turn right onto Route-17 and continue east, through New Haven and into Bristol in 5.5 miles. From the center of Bristol, continue east on Route-17 for 0.6 mile, on your right is the Lord's Pray Rock and a small improved parking/picnic area for several cars.

"Lord's Prayer Rock" – Circa 1915 – Bristol, VT

88. Medburyville Boulders

The General – Medburyville, VT

Location: West Wilmington (Windham County)
Delorme Atlas & Gazetteer-Vermont: p21, G-13
Parking GPS: N42° 52' 13.99" W72° 55' 29.57"
Destination GPS: As listed below.
Wow Factor: 6-10 **Accessibility:** GPS guided bushwhack only.

Information: At all locations I venture onto for discovery, I deal with the four "P's", Parking, Paths and Private Property: Parking is instantly important; leaving your car with hopes of returning to it is paramount. Finding *No Parking Signs* or *Vehicles will be Towed* catches my attention instantly. Paths are very important. A kiosk with Maps, Rules and Regulations along with blazed trail and signs indicating to you that; *This is the Way,* are your friends. Property with public access is usually not an issue for most places have amazing amounts of acres has been set aside as public parks. However, whenever posted *No Trespassing Violators-will be shot*! I usually tend to think this means me.

So, this location on this hillside in Medburyville has a field of glacial erratics and does not have a bona-fide parking area, any paths or signs, nor is it overtly posted against trespassing. Another twist is that boundary markers show the boulders are posted as being within the Green Mountains National Forest. Obviously private ownership along the entry roadway is problematic for access, lack of paths, parking and private property concerns.

Our strategy then requires a bushwhacking and flanking maneuver from the west. Still no paths or blazed trails are found, prior usage of the GPS coordinates placed in Google Earth will create the map for destinations. This approach will not be for everyone, but is valid for exploration on this hillside with some very large or unusual erratics found and probably more to be discovered.

The General: N42° 52' 3.40" W72° 55' 12.10" *WOW-10*
A big surprise, a very tall 30-35-feet and surrounded by a few other interesting erratic's. One of the largest boulders we saw this day.

Major: N42° 52' 3.20" W72° 55' 12.20" *WOW-8*
Located a short distance east of the General. A 18-feet, roundish boulder perched upon a rocky ledge, the front has a slanted over-hang.

Colonel: N42° 52' 2.80" W72° 55' 13.90" *WOW-7*
Triangular facing, 16-feet tall, uphill from the General.

Captain: N42° 52' 2.40" W72° 55' 13.60" *WOW-7*
Large evenly split rock just above the Colonel. 12-feet in Height.

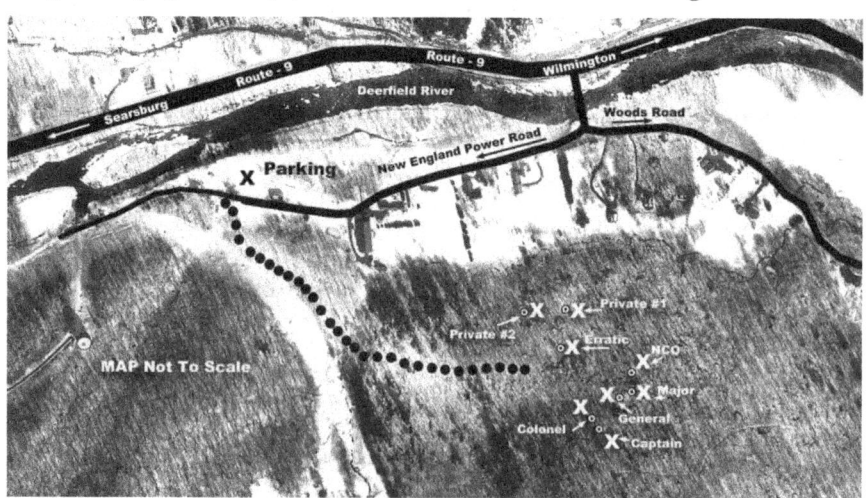

Map for Medburyville Boulders, VT

NCO: N42° 52' 4.00" W72° 55' 11.30" *WOW-7*
Downhill from the General & Major, a massive 14-feet high, 30-feet long.

Erratic: N42° 52' 5.90" W72° 55' 14.50" *WOW-6*
Not remarkable very remarkable and was downhill to the Private #1

Private #1: N42° 52' 7.10" W72° 55' 13.80" *WOW-8*
A large Hi-Lo boulder nestled into the hillside. Uphill end is 16-feet tall, with the downhill side reaches up 30-feet.

Private #2: N42° 52' 7.20" W72° 55' 16.10" *WOW-7*
A small roundish boulder 16-feet from the downhill facing, small over-hang shelter suitable for getting out of the rain.

Major – Medburyville, VT

Private #1 – Medburyville, VT

Directions: From Wilmington, at the junction of Route-100 and Route-9, head west on Route-9 for 2.7 miles. Turn left onto Woods Road which starts as a small bridge and crosses the Deerfield River into Medburyville. On the other side, turn right onto New England Power Road; follow for 0.3 mile past the last house on the left, but before the electric sub-station. A small dirt service road which comes down from the power lines is where we parked, do not park on or block this road. From here we walked up this service road and skirted into the forest just left of the power line avoiding its bramble and walked 0.2 mile southeasterly. Then head east and traversed the hillside in search of the boulders. (See Map Above.)

89. Mouse Rock

Mouse Rock – Bear Mountain Road – Killington, VT

Location: Killington (Rutland County)
Delorme Atlas & Gazetteer-Vermont: p30, D-3
Destination GPS: N43°36'20.53" W72°46'27.06"
Wow Factor: 6 **Accessibility:** Roadside

Information: I have always enjoyed the creative aspect of an individual's imagination in transforming an "insignificant" roadside stone with a touch of paint and having it become a cartoonish creature. Coincidentally, many New England roadways have these "Folksy Art" creation sites that have existed for years if not for several decades or generations. Cultural acceptance of their efforts are rejected by some and embraced by others. More often than not, someone within a community will step-up and pick-up the touch-up repainting, trimming of brush along with litter patrol for these landmark locations. I guess they become the ultimate "Pet Rock."

Directions: From the northern junction of Route-4 and Route-100 in Killington, drive south for 5.0 miles. Off Route-4 and Route-100 turn up East Mountain Road which is just 0.1 mile south of the Killington Resort SKYESHIP Gondola terminal. Continue 1.3 miles up to where *Bear Mountain Road* will enter on your left. Turn onto Bear Mountain Road and drive up 0.62 mile where the *Mouse* will be on your right roadside.

90. Mt. Hor - Willoughby State Forest

MH-1 – Roadside Boulder - Sutton, VT

Location: Sutton (Caledonia County)
Delorme Atlas & Gazetteer-Vermont: p54, J-5
Parking GPS: N44° 42' 35.90" W72° 2' 41.10"
Destination GPS: Assorted GPS list below.
Wow Factor: 4-5 **Accessibility:** Roadside to 0.1 mile no trails
Contact: Willoughby State Forest www.vtstateparks.com (802) 535-8410 ANR.Parks@vermont.gov
Vermont State Parks 1 National Life Drive, Davis 2 Montpelier, VT 05620 parks@vermont.gov (888) 409-7579

Information: To be honest, I wouldn't go too far out of the way for this boulder field. Firstly, not an impressive set, although *"one man's trash is another's treasure."* My original informational search for images did provide a couple of good size boulders. During our visit, we did not locate any overly impressive boulders at this time. However, we were under a viscous assault from a marauding swarm of black flies and under pressure with time constraints. Yet, since we were there, we persevered and chose to present them here anyway. While my knee-jerk reaction and brief visit may not be totally valid, some boulderer's just might find or see potential for these erratics differently, so check it out anyways. Good luck.

MH-1: N44° 42' 35.60" W72° 2' 42.20" (Roadside Boulder) *WOW-5*
One of the larger boulders located roadside.

MH-2: N44° 42' 35.20" W72° 2' 42.40" (Axe Head Rock) *WOW-5*
Narrow 12-feet tall boulder with a shape that looks like one could affix a handle to create an axe.

MH-3: N44° 42' 33.70" W72° 2' 41.40" (Puny) *WOW-4*
Small not remarkable rock 10-feet in height.

MH-4: N44° 42' 33.30" W72° 2' 41.20" (Split Rock) *WOW-5*
Roundish 12-feet boulder split in equal half, one side more erect than the other

MH-5: N44° 42' 35.70" W72° 2' 40.00" (Erratic) *WOW-4*
A wedge shaped rock, 12-feet at its highest and sloped downwards to 4-feet.

MH-4 – Split Rock - Sutton, VT

Directions: From the beach at the south end of Lake Willoughby follow Route-5A south for 0.6 mile and turn right into the parking lot which has the gated "CCC" road. If the gate is open proceed up and in 0.5 mile bear right towards the Hebert Hawkes Trailhead. The boulders will be on your left in another 1.0 mile just before heading uphill to the Hebert Hawkes Trailhead. The CCC Road is well built and maintained; you'll also pass by a terrific vista of the southern end of Lake Willoughby and Mt Pisgah.

91. Perched Rock

Perched Rock – Brickhouse Road – Whitingham, VT

Location: Whitingham (Windham County)
Delorme Atlas & Gazetteer-Vermont: p21, J-14
Parking GPS: N42° 48' 10.86" W72° 53' 37.97"
Destination GPS: N43° 8' 6.96" W72° 26' 26.24"
Wow Factor: 5 **Accessibility:** No path-GPS bushwhack to Rock location.

Information: While this erratic is not overly significant, the area surrounding of Harriman Reservoir (also known as Lake Whitingham) was created by the Harriman Dam at the south end of the lake, the dam is named for Henry I. Harriman, engineer for the New England Power Company. As part of a hydro-electric system, the dam was constructed within 1 year with over 1,500 men and has a unique feature called the "Glory Hole" to assist the spillway to maintain water level during high water levels or flood stage. When in 1923, the waters of the Deerfield River began to fill the 2,200 acre lake; some residents of Mountain Mills had to hastily gather their belongings as the waters rose to their doorways to engulf their former homes and village. The submerged foundations of a mill and other buildings can occasionally be seen when seasonal drawdown lowers the waterline revealing much of the coastline. The maximum depth of the reservoir is normally 185 feet.

Directions: From the junction of Route-9/Route-100 in Wilmington, follow Route-100 south for 9 miles, through Jacksonville and into

Whitingham center. From the center of Whitingham continue on Route-100 approximately 0.2 mile, Brickhouse Road will be on your right. Follow Brickhouse Road 1.0 mile to its end.

After parking at the end of Brickhouse Road continue northwest on the dirt access road which continues from the parking area. This road if followed will bring one to the Harriman Reservoir shoreline in 0.5 miles. However, the rock is very close to the parking area, but one needs to walk 0.1 mile down the dirt road and bear left, off the dirt road, through a section of hemlock, across an old stone wall uphill in a southwesterly direction for 0.1 mile to locate this distinctive rock, on the southeastern hillside at the 1840-foot elevation. A map is not provided here, so a GPS check on Google Earth or other map application will significantly assist in its location. The driveway at the end of Brickhouse Road is private property, so please return back the way you approached.

92. Petroglyphs

Petroglyphs – Bellows Falls, VT

Location: Bellow Falls; Town of Rockingham (Windham County)
Delorme Atlas & Gazetteer-Vermont: p27, I-10
Parking GPS: N43° 8' 5.50" W72° 26' 26.90"
Destination GPS: N43° 8' 6.96" W72° 26' 26.24"
Wow Factor: 8 **Accessibility:** Difficult location, not well marked.

Information: Reverend David McClure from Dartmouth College wrote about the petroglyphs in his notes in 1789 and their origins are still a lingering mystery. Reverend David McClure suggests that Abenaki native populace had significant and cultural burial sites along this section of the Connecticut River.

That are several rudimentary images each simplistic in design, hauntingly captivating and some ambiguously seeking for one interpretation. The surviving two stone blocks have carvings of several circles and with three dots inside have a graphic representation of faces with some containing pairs of lines that radiate out from the top. The engravings age are not known, are they only 300 years ago or is it 3,000 years? There are other arguments for the images to represent extraterrestrial, alien or religious symbolism. The fact they have survived the natural erosive forces of water and ice or generations of municipal growth and decline throughout New England States. Unfortunately, not all petroglyphs have survived; journals list or present drawings that indicate many were destroyed by bridge or hydro-canal construction.

Directions: From the Interstate I-91, use Exit-5 to Bellows Falls.
Head east on Westminster Street for 0.6 mile turning left onto Route-5 north. Travel on Route-5 north, for 2.5 miles, in Bellows Falls at the junction of Route-5 and Route-121, bear right onto another Westminster Street. Continue for 0.3 mile and turn right onto Bridge Street, travel 0.2 mile, across the Hydro-Canal until you reach the detour and barrier for the old Vilas Bridge. The last of the known Bellows Falls petroglyphs are located on a couple of large boulders found slightly south and below the defunct Vilas Bridge that crosses the Connecticut River. Just prior to the bridge, on your right is a small unnamed access road, approximately 75-feet south from the corner will put you above the location of one of the easier seen petroglyphs. The only markings are two yellow painted rectangles upon the top of the boulder. You can locate and view them from above or to access them at rivers edge, you will need to follow a small bushy trail down, to a steep, long and smooth stone ledge, this can be hazardous if it's wet, wintery; you are improperly geared or have been drinking: (I wouldn't recommend sandals.) A small parking area and the access path to the river's edge is another 150-feet along the access road on the left, the unmarked path will descend steeply and what goes down, must come back up!

93. Pine Hill Park

PH-1 Elephant Rock - Rutland

Location: Rutland (Chittenden County)
Delorme Atlas & Gazetteer-Vermont: p29, D-11
Parking GPS: N43° 36' 58.38" W72° 59' 28.74"
Destination GPS: Individual GPS locations below.
Wow Factor: 7 Accessibility: Easy to Moderate trail system.
Contact: Pine Hill Park. 2 Oak St Ext, Rutland, VT 05701 (802)775-7976
pinehillpark@gmail.com   www.pinehillpark.org

Information: Found in the northwest corner of Rutland, Pine Hill Park has 300 acres with 16 miles of snowshoeing, running, hiking and mountain biking trails. Geocaching is another past time found here, with a few glacial erratic's frequently targeted. The park is stewarded by the Pine Hill Partnership, a non-profit organization run by volunteers. The park has a very enthusiastic crew of young and older volunteers keeping the trails in good repair and upgrading the present system. The only issue I found is the trails are plentiful, maybe just too plentiful. A maze of trails which can be a little daunting for first time visits, I do suggest to visit the Pine Hill Park web site to obtain a PDF map of the trail map to assist.

PH-1: N43° 37' 0.20" W72° 59' 33.00" (Elephant Rock) *WOW-7*
Largest Glacial Erratic we found 12-feet tall by 40-feet long, easy to climb and find 150-feet from parking area, located at main entry. (Trail marker #1)

PH-2: N43° 36' 52.40" W72° 59' 39.00" (Hippo Rock) *WOW-6*
Roundish 12-feet high. Located on Furlough Trail above trail marker #40.

PH-3: N43° 37' 11.80" W72° 59' 26.70" (Box Rock) *WOW-5*
Small 10-foot flat top rock, on the lower Giorgetti Trail, near trail marker #3.

PH-2 Hippo Rock - - Rutland, VT

Users of Pine Hill Park do so at their own risk.
The park is open for day use only.
No camping. No fires.
Keep the park clean and beautiful. Pack out what you pack in.
Some trails are pedestrian use only, or closed due to wet conditions.
Please obey posted restrictions on trail use.
Please park in the designated area at Giorgetti Park.
Dogs must be on leash at all times.
Please stay on blazed trails.
Respect private landowner's property.
Disruptive behavior is prohibited.
Disturbing, removing, defacing, cutting or damaging plants, animals or man-made features in the park is prohibited.
No hunting in the park.
Discharge of firearms, bow and arrows, paintball guns or fireworks is prohibited in the park.
.Pine Hill is a city park and there is no smoking allowed in any city park including Pine Hill and the Giorgetti Athletic Complex.

Directions: In Rutland, from the junction of Route-7 and Route-4, follow Route-4 downtown and west for 0.4 mile turning onto Grove Street. Head north for 0.5 mile on Grove Street, turning left onto Crescent Street and head west for 0.4 mile, turn right onto Preville Avenue to its end, and enter into the Giorgetti Athletic Complex at 2 Oak Street Extension. The trail Head is on the western side of the parking area, where the little tin-man statue will welcome you.

Serpentine Rock – Photograph Pre 1917 - Grafton VT

Serpentine Rock – 2017 - GPS: N43° 11' 28.30" W72° 37' 20.00"

Serpentine is a group of semi-precious minerals, often green in colour, cuts easily, polishes well, and has an attractive appearance as an architectural decorative stone for their pseudo marble-like qualities. Its name originates from the similarity of the rock's textured appearance, to that of the skin of a snake. When polished it produces a patterned appearance and has a slippery waxy feel. The ability to insulate and resist the transfer of heat also makes it a valuable insulator. This particular boulder is still in position after 100 years; however a large boulder in the background in the *top photograph* has disappeared perhaps to "Boulder Quarrying."

Located on private property–no directions provided.

94. Power Line Boulders

PW-2 – Whale Rock - Windham

Location: Windham (Windham County)
Delorme Atlas & Gazetteer-Vermont: p25, G-12
Parking GPS: N43° 12' 25.56" W72° 58' 13.35"
Destination GPS: Individual GPS locations below.
Wow Factor: 8 Accessibility: Moderate Bushwhack no marked trail.

Information: Of interest here is a comparison between the natural growth of forest versus the terrain of the power line with maintenance or continuous growth reduction methods. The boulders on the power line are readily approached (as your wade through the briars) and are easily seen or photographed. Versus, the woodland over-growth, the decaying logs and surrounded by large trees that camouflage its location or obscures it size. I'm sure for the people who are drawn into this area, get their enjoyment from being off-the-beaten path, on game trails or otherwise has seen little development other than the surrounding natural forest growth.

WP-2 N43° 12' 27.40" W72° 58' 21.20" (Whale Rock) *WOW-8*
A profile of a whale breeching the surface by a good 20 feet in height.

WP-3 N43° 12' 27.02" W72° 58' 22.77" (Trio Rocks) *WOW-7*
A trio of 10 foot to 12-feet boulders lying in the open above Whale Rock.

WP-4 N43° 12' 28.24" W72° 58' 24.15" (Bear's Den) *WOW-8*
A large elongated, 14 foot high boulder 40 feet long, rear split open. Location is north of WP-3 into the woodlands 100 feet.

PW-5 – Mammoth Rock - Windham

WP-5 N43° 12' 24.40" W72° 58' 34.30" (Mammoth Rock) *WOW-9*
Tall 20 feet by 25 feet high meatball. On the northern tree line west of WP-4.

WP-6 N43° 12' 23.37" W72° 58' 34.81" (Leaning Rock) *WOW-8*
Open small cluster of rocks with largest 14 foot boulder tilted at 45 ° with a small end overhang. Just a short distance south of WP-5.

WP-7 N43° 12' 23.12" W72° 58' 34.52" (Two Face Rock) *WOW-7*
Large wedge shape, 14 feet in height, with two faces, both sides each apparently utilized by boulderers. Located in the open terrain next to WP-6.

WP-8 N43° 12' 22.00" W72° 58' 33.30" (Big Rock) *WOW-9*
Tall 25 foot boulder in height, a detached front chunk with a walk-through fissure between them.

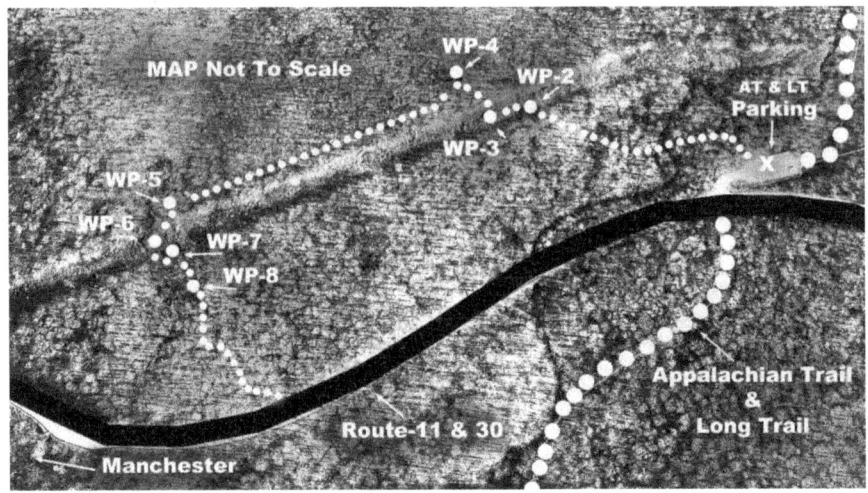

Power Line Boulder – Windham, VT

PW-8 - Big Rock – Windham

Directions: From Manchester, off Route-7 at Exit-4. Follow uphill Route-11 and Route-30 east for 4.3 miles. On your left, a paved parking area for 25 cars is for the Appalachian Trail and Long Trail crosses the highway. From the left rear of the parking area, a snowmobile trail heads back and downhill, over a small wooden bridge for crossing a brook, shortly after crossing get off trail and bushwhack north until you reach the power line and you will see WP-2 *Whale Rock*. Just a short 150-feet west on the power line will be WP-3 *Trio-Rocks*. North into the woodland is WP-*4 Bear's Den* boulder. Further west 0.2 mile is the WP-5 *Mammoth Rock*. Note walking parallel to the power line in the woods can be easier than bramble and Briar found sprawling across the power lines. South and in the open WP-6 *Leaning Rock* and WP-7 *Two Face Rock* will be found side by side. Below these two locations, south of the power lines is WP-8 *Big Rock*. From here we continued south through the lower woodlands and quickly returned to the highway below to hike back up Route-11 and Route-30 for 0.2 mile back to the AT/LT parking area.

95. Searsburg Boulders

SB-1 - Hi-Lo Boulder - Searsburg, VT

Location: Searsburg (WindhamCounty)
Delorme Atlas & Gazetteer-Vermont: p21, G-13
Parking GPS: N42° 52' 31.00" W72° 56' 3.00" (Heather Road-Dirt)
Destination GPS: See list below.
Wow Factor: 8 Accessibility: No blazed trail-GPS bushwhack only.

Information: This boulder field is located in Searsburg, on top a small hill above Route-9 (Molly Stark Highway) and probably is visited mostly by hunters or mushroomers. No trails, signs, postings for or against parking. The acreage is located within the Green Mountain National Forest; Regulations would still apply out-lined by the U.S. Forestry Department. I reconnoitered the area through Google Earth and other Topographic Maps such as the National Geographic series.

Fortunately, a small road is located off of Route-9, the road was in good repair and the CR-V (*Chris's Recreation Vehicle*) had no problems. The parking GPS will get you to vicinity, but you'll have to evaluation, *where* to park, by what you drive, do not to block the road. We parked at where a snowmobile trail crosses Heather Road. By starting here you will have a moderate walk, if parking down on Lind Lane or Route-9 you will require a more strenuous climb up. You'll want to locate the snowmobile trail to where it heads westerly uphill. If not, some trail sense might enable you to follow suitable terrain until it opens into a previously logged open woodland, most patches of evergreen were small and predominately on lower slopes.

SB-1: N42° 52' 32.50" W72° 56' 20.30" (Hi-Lo Boulder) *WOW-8*
First significant boulder we came upon, uphill side has 16 foot facing, with the down-slope end extending up to 26 feet. This stand-alone boulder is located in dip between a small southern hill and the higher northern hill.

SB-2: N42° 52' 30.40" W72° 56' 19.30" (Erratic) *WOW-7*
Slightly down the southern slope towards the west. Not as significant. Was the lowest location of the findings below the Hi-LO boulder.

SB-3: N42° 52' 34.20" W72° 56' 25.40" (Birch Boulder) *WOW-6*
A 12-feet gum drop shape boulder, presently a good size Silver Birch tree has taken root for some time; I think the rock will win! Half-way up hillside above the SB-1 Hi-LO boulder

SB-4: N42° 52' 35.90" W72° 56' 22.70" (Perched Rock) *WOW-6*
A small 5 foot rock, attractively balanced or perched on a 6 foot trailing boulder adjacent boulder Cluster. Just below the crest of hill near the SB-5.

SB-5: N42° 52' 36.90" W72° 56' 22.30" (Hilltop Boulder) *WOW-9*
Either side is an exception 40 feet in length, 18 feet tall which tapers down closer to 12-feet on one end..

SB-5 – Hilltop Boulder – Searsburg, VT

Directions: In Wilmington, at the junction of Route-100 and Route-9, head west on Route-9 for 3.5 miles. Heather Road will be on your right; it has an appearance to be a driveway and runs up between residential properties. However, follow the dirt road, north for 0.27 mile to the Parking GPS vicinity. In respect to your elevation, this location is about even to the destinations by heading west from the road. Pay attention to where you traverse, for you'll probably return the same way out as in.

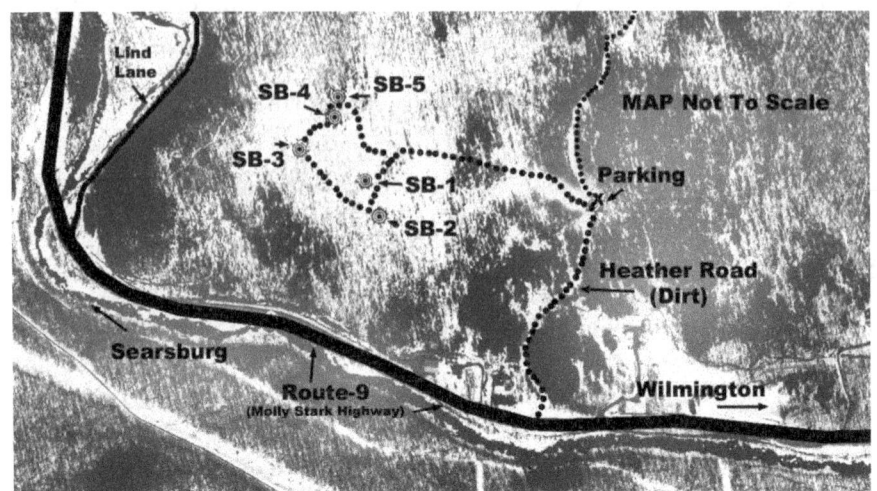

Searsburg Boulder Map – Searsburg, VT

SB-2 Erratic – Searsburg, VT

96. Sentinel Rock

Sentinel Rock – Westmore, VT

Location: Westmore (Orleans County)
Delorme Atlas & Gazetteer-Vermont: p54, G-6
Parking GPS: N44° 47' 26.78" W72° 1' 40.37"
Destination GPS: N44° 47' 27.40" W72° 1' 42.80"
Wow Factor: 8 **Accessibility:** 100 yard walk to rock from parking area.
Contact: Department of Forests, Parks and Recreation; St. Johnsbury Office 374 Emerson Falls Road. St. Johnsbury, VT 05819 (802) 751-0110
E-mail: ANR.Parks@vermont.gov Web-https://www.vtstateparks.com/ Northeast Parks Regional Manager; Vermont Dept. of Forests, Parks & Recreation 5 Perry Street, Suite 20 Barre, VT 05641 (802) 476-0181

Information: In 1997, Windsor Wright donated a 356-acre portion of his family-owned Sentinel Rock Farm to the State of Vermont. The Wrights donated the property to the Department of Forests, Parks and Recreation (DFPR) with the intent that the state conserve the natural and scenic resources of the property and manage it for public use and enjoyment. The term "Sentinel Rock Farm" refers to a large glacially deposited boulder in a meadow of the property, from which, there is a spectacular 270 degree view to the west and southwest. Relatively a new Vermont Parks & Forests property, the long term management proposals of the 356 acres include development of educational and recreational experiences with minimal impact upon the historical resources of the property. In short, the fields and pasture surrounding the farmhouse and Sentinel Rock shall be kept open to preserve the view. Unfortunately, the farm structures were not feasible for restoration and were removed. However, in itself the remarkable panoramic view of the northern

Lake Willoughby remains. The iconic Sentinel Rock also remains with the telltale evidence of boulder quarrying. A portion of the boulder that remains near the Sentinel Rock was removed and used for the rock foundation of the McLaughlin farm around 1890. Drill marks can be seen on the edges of the boulder and its remnants.

Directions: From Interstate I-91 at Exit-23, follow Route-5 north through Lyndon for 9.5 miles until in West Burke, Route-5A branches off on the right. Follow Route-5A north for 6 miles where you will come to Lake Willoughby, continue north on Route-5A along the lake's eastern shore for an additional 4 miles until you reach the center of Westmore. On your right, turn onto Hinton Hill Road heading east, in 0.5 mile, bear right at the fork and continue on Hinton Hill Road for 1.3 miles and bear left to the parking area.

97. Smuggler's Notch

SN-k – Roots Boulder – Smuggler's Notch

Location: Stowe (Lamoille County)
Delorme Atlas & Gazetteer-Vermont: p46, E-2
Parking GPS: N44° 33' 19.61" W72° 47' 44.39"
Destination GPS: Individual GPS locations below.
Wow Factor: 8-10 **Accessibility:** Easy to moderate, roadside to 0.1 mile
Contact: Smugglers' Notch State Park 6443 Mountain Rd, Stowe, VT 05672 (802) 253-4014
Vermont State Parks Reservation Center (888) 409-7579 M-F, 9 AM-4 PM
www.vtstateparks.com

Information: Traffic through the notch can be slow and tedious, a narrow roadway, cars backing out and pedestrians on roadways with bicyclists, requires patience and tolerance. At the top of the notch, Route-108 snakes through a series of colossal roadside boulders. Some activities in the notch include: hiking, bouldering, cave exploring, ice climbing, sight-seeing and biking. Parking is first come and loosely defined as finding a space amongst the numerous pull-off between bolder sites. During the Fall Foliage season, a massive increase of tourists can add to the chaos when traveling through the notch.

This is a premier location for boulderer's in Vermont with plenty of boulders to go around. It appears that most of the boulders are from the surround cliffs and are not glacial erratics. The names I have used for labels comes from some of the climbers or Google information. The boulders are part of Vermont's Smugglers' Notch State Park and there are currently no access issues. Conditions are best in the spring and fall, but because of its high elevation, Smugglers' Notch stays relatively cool in the summer. In addition, Route-108 is also seasonal with the Smugglers Notch being gated during winter months. Access is allowed, but you will need to hike 1 mile up.

SN-a – Big Freaking Boulders – Smuggler's Notch, VT

SN-a: N44° 33' 19.20" W72° 47' 45.71" (Big Freaking Boulders) *WOW-9*
Twin boulders, cubed in shape, impressive for the area they occupy, located next to road.

SN-b: N44° 33' 19.90" W72° 47' 45.60" (Backyard Boulder) *WOW-8*
A cluster of boulders with

SN-c: N44° 33' 20.98" W72° 47' 45.48" (Asteroid) *WOW-8*
Squat 16 foot high boulder, set back above the road and getting slightly overgrown with saplings

SN-d – Highlander Boulder – Smuggler's Notch, VT

SN-d: N44° 33' 19.19" W72° 47' 44.17" (Highlander) *WOW-8*
A tall 24 foot boulder. Popular for its southern climbing wall and 2-tiered ascent.

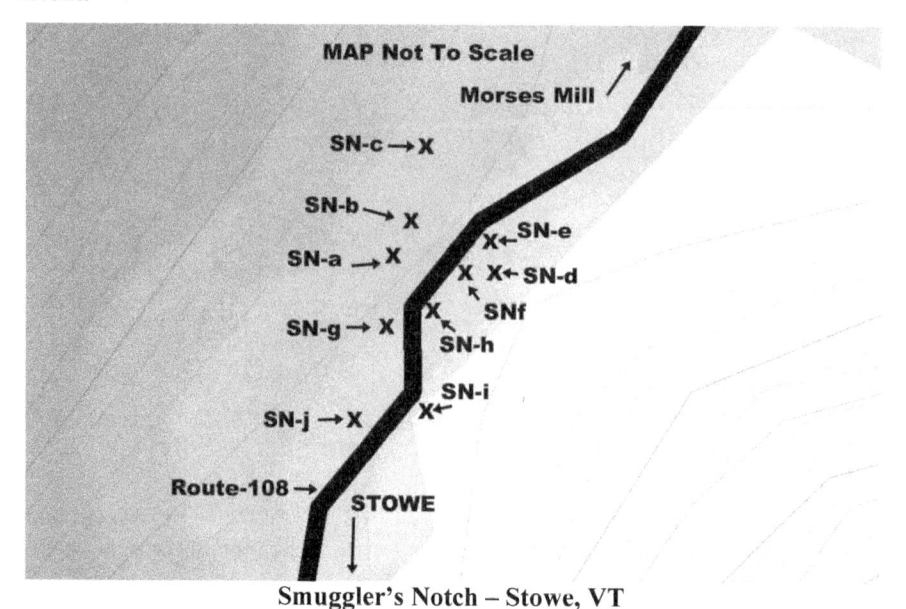

Smuggler's Notch – Stowe, VT

SN-e – Leaning Rock – Smuggler's Notch, VT

SN-e: N44° 33' 19.68" W72° 47' 43.99" (Leaning Rock) *WOW-8*
Just behind the SN-d T*he highlander*, leaning rock lays atop of another creating a tunnel to the delight of many children who can walk through without bumping their head.

SN-f – The Mantel – Smuggler's Notch, VT

SN-f: N44° 33' 19.41" W72° 47' 44.64" (Mantel Rock) *WOW-7*
Large ramped 12-feet high boulder, easy walk up with crest directly over roadway. In front of SN-d and north of SN-h.

SN-g: N44° 33' 18.50" W72° 47' 45.50" (Chuff Boulder) *WOW-7*
Roadside boulder 14-feet in height.

SN-h: N44° 33' 18.61" W72° 47' 44.98" (Shark Finn Rock) *WOW-8*
Tall 12 foot, triangular upright rock a.k.a. Shark's Tooth. Sits right upon roadway and actually constricts the road-curve at the highest place in the notch.

SN-i: N44° 33' 17.70" W72° 47' 45.00" (Wheaties's Rock) *WOW-7*

SN-j: N44° 33' 17.50" W72° 47' 46.00" (Roadside) *WOW-7*

SN-k: N44° 32' 53.68" W72° 47' 37.44" (Roots Boulder) *WOW-9*
Large 25 foot boulder with large tree still growing atop with it roots sprawling across the surface. Locate 0.6 mile below the main Smuggler's Notch on Route-108 driving up from Stowe.

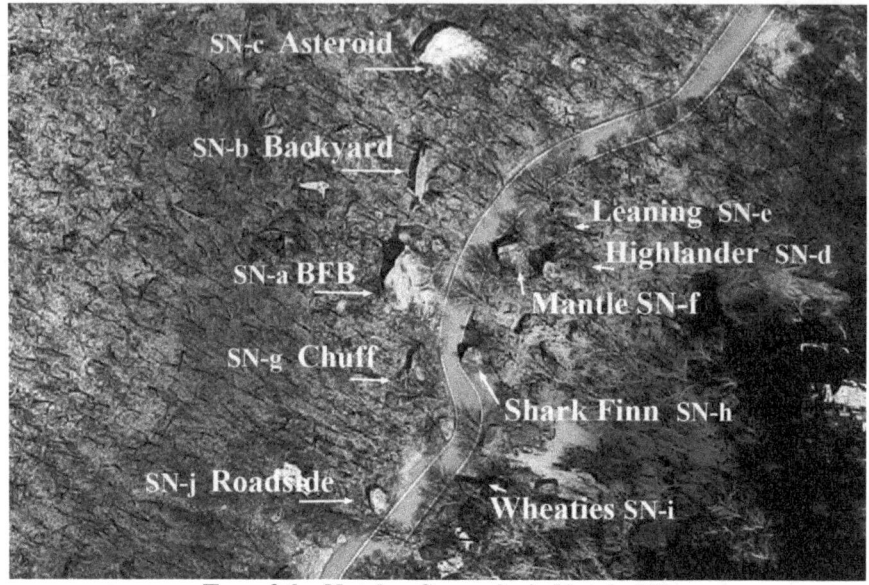

Top of the Notch – Smuggler's Notch, VT

Directions: From the center of Stowe, follow Route-108 north for 9.5 miles until you reach Smuggler's Notch

98. Split Rock - Appalachian Trail

Split Rock - Appalachian Trail – Woodford, VT

Location: Woodford (Bennington County)
Delorme Atlas & Gazetteer-Vermont: p21, G-9
Parking GPS: N42° 53' 6.60" W73° 6' 55.74"
Destination GPS: N42° 53' 7.60" W73° 6' 35.10"
Wow Factor: 8 **Accessibility:** Long & Appalachian Trail moderately steep.
Contact: Green Mountain Club 4711 Waterbury-Stowe Rd, Waterbury Center, VT 05677 (802) 244-7073 E-mail: gmc@greenmountainclub.org www.greenmountainclub.org/

Information: The Long Trail along with the Appalachian Trail will cross Route-9 in Woodford. From the trail head parking lot you head north and up for 0.6 mile to reach this landmark on the trail. The trail starts behind the kiosk, quickly runs along a stream and shortly will cross the stream with a large footbridge. Continue the hike up until the split rock is encountered. The trail passes through its Hugh crack. This hike provides a quick destination and with a 1.5 mile round trip good bit of exercise.

Directions: From the junction of Route-7 and Route-9 Bennington, follow Route-9 (Molly Stark Highway) east, through downtown and up into the mountains. After 5.0 miles, the trail crossing is evident and labeled, with a large paved parking area there is room for over a dozen vehicles.

99. Target Rock

Target Rock - Grafton

Location: Grafton (Windham County)
Delorme Atlas & Gazetteer-Vermont: p26, H-6
Parking GPS: N43° 9' 45.23" W72° 36' 51.35"
Destination GPS: N43° 9' 51.12" W72° 37' 11.22"
Wow Factor: 6 Accessibility: Viewed from Grafton Ponds Outdoor Center parking area.
Contact: Grafton Ponds Outdoor Center 783 Townshend Road Grafton, Vermont 05146 (802) 843-2400

Information: For us the viewing of *Target Rock* was from the Grafton Pond Outdoor Center on Route-35 in Grafton. From the parking area look to the west and among the bushes on the hillside *Target Rock* will be seen readily The origin of *Target Rock* is said to have been a painted marker for a local man who in the 1940's and 1950's flew his airplane and from the air would use the target to indicate he was near a runway to land. This does have credence for back when rural airports had only grassy runways, control towers often did not exist. In addition, many town halls or barns would paint their roofs with the associated town's name and provide directional arrows or other symbols to aid pilots in determining where they were.

Directions: From the center of Grafton at the junction of Route-121 & Route-35, follow Route-35 south for 0.75 mile, on your left is the entry to Grafton Pond Outdoor Center.

100. White Cliffs Ice Beds & Cairns

Ice Bed Rocks Base – White Cliffs, VT

Location: Wallingford (Rutland County)
Delorme Atlas & Gazetteer-Vermont: p-29, I-12
Parking GPS: N43° 27' 3.00" W72° 56' 36.60"
Destination GPS: N43° 26' 59.80" W72° 56' 45.70" (Ice Bed Vista 1)
Destination GPS: N43° 26' 58.20" W72° 56' 53.30" (Ice Bed Vista 2)
Destination GPS: N43° 26' 45.60" W72° 56' 59.80" (Ice Bed Rocks)
Wow Factor: 8 **Accessibility:** Easy side of Moderate, 2.0 miles round trip.
Contact: **Green** Mountain & Finger Lakes National Forests Office 231 North Main Street. Rutland, VT 05701 (802) 747-6700
https://www.fs.usda.gov/greenmountain

Ice Bed Rocks

Information: From the southwest corner of the parking lot follow Ice Beds Trail. Follow the blue blazes, the trail quickly begins to ascend steeply and after a series of switchbacks you'll be on top. The spur trail to the left leads to a view of the northern side of the White Rocks Cliffs. Continuing on the Ice Bed Rock trail south leads you to the second vista in less than 0.2 mile. Off on the left, access requires some rock hopping; this vista provides a grander view of the cliffs, its talus boulder fields and the valley south. Continue following the blue blazes as the trail begins to descend, and within 0.5 mile cross a small stream and bridge. The trail flanks to the left and shortly arrives to the base of the Ice Bed Rocks. As you near, you can feel the cool and refreshing thermal breeze emitted from the rock field. We visited in early August and experienced a radical drop in temperature around the base of this massive entanglement of large and small boulders. During winter, ice forms deep within the nooks and crannies of this extensive rock pile. Protected, the ice can last late into the summer as the ice slowly melts. The Ice Bed Rock field is extensive in size, ascending 1500 feet and a sloped width 500-800 feet across. With an astonishing number of medium and very large jumbled boulders, hundreds of shelter caves can be discovered amongst them. Exploring this rock field alone should be on the side of caution for its isolation and any assistance if needed will be scarce.

White Cliffs from Vista #2 – Wallingford, VT

White Cliffs Cairns – Keewaydin Trail

Destination GPS: N43° 26' 34.70" W72° 56' 33.10" (Cairns #1)
Destination GPS: N43° 26' 40" W72° 56' 40" (White Rocks Cliff Vista)
Destination GPS: N43° 26' 32.40" W72° 56' 35.90" (AT Boulder)
Destination GPS: N43° 25' 54.70" W72° 56' 32.20" (Cairns #2)
Wow Factor: 6 **Accessibility:** Moderately difficult trail 5 miles round trip.

Information: The Keewaydin trail head is found at the eastern end of the parking lot. The trail quickly begins to ascend along the Bully Brook on your left and will join the Appalachian and Long Trails in 0.4 mile. Continue following the AT/LT trails south which will wind around and ascend from the northeastern rear of White Cliffs. You will reach the White Rocks Cliff Vista Spur trail in 1.5 miles. The spur trail leads to the vista in 0.2 of a mile to the western side of the cliff. At this junction we found a scattering of cairns presumably created by many of the hikers making the trek north or south on the AT/LT trail. Photographs found on-line indicate a large multitude of these cairns were constructed perhaps in some sort of hiker's tradition or by other conceptual rituals such as "Peace Piles." This man-made sculptured environment expectantly creates a surreal experience amongst the isolation and solitude found along these ridgeline woodlands. In addition, following the AT/LT trail further south for 1.0 mile brings you to an additional cairn rock garden integrated into or onto several large erratic boulders. In both locations, the cairns ranged in construction from being somewhat intricate, balanced precariously, placed in trees or just a run-of-the-mill rock pile. For this particular experience, the number of cairns which had eroded into rubble either through time or weather was disappointing. For some, constructions of cairns are intrusive, others find them artistic and others worry about mistaken trail markers.

Cairn Rock Garden #2 – Appalachian Trail – Wallingford, VT

Appalachian Trail/ Long Trail Boulder – White Cliffs, VT

Directions: From Route 7 in Wallingford, follow Route-140 east 2.1 miles to the junction of Sugar Hill Road on the right. Turn onto Sugar Hill Road and follow for 0.2 miles to picnic area and trail head parking. This gated access road is dirt and can be slightly washed out.

101. Willoughby Lake - "The Boulder's"

"The Boulder's" – Lake Willoughby – Westmore, VT

Location: Westmore (Orleans County)
Delorme Atlas & Gazetteer-Vermont: p54, J-5
Parking GPS: N44° 43' 11.10" W72° 1' 49.00"
Destination GPS: N44° 43' 11.10" W72° 1' 49.00"
Wow Factor: 4 **Accessibility:** Street viewed.

Information: In 1921, Mr. Elmer Darling built *The Boulders Dance Casino* and *The Boulders Tea Room*, the tea room was connected to the casino by a covered boardwalk. Reported in earlier years, the Casino earned a profit of $1,223.28; the Tea Room earned $132.72. In 1935, David I. Grapes bought *The Boulders Tea Room and Casino* and started developing and expanding the property. Across the road he acquired a total of 14 cottages for rent. Incidentally, along with the 1935 purchase of the Darling property included a 35-foot oak & mahogany passenger boat he renamed the *Mountain Maid*. It was refitted with a fine Chrysler marine engine and was operated as a passenger boat for the enjoyment of the public. With David Grapes death in 1943, ownership to all the properties passed to his son Clarence Grapes. Offerings to guests renting out the cottages now included a dining room, souvenir shop, tennis court, a dairy bar, croquet, shuffleboard, table pool, Ping-Pong, and other games. They could fish, hike, take a boat ride, attend The Boulders Theater, or just relax. Clarence Grapes died in 1969 and the property management quickly withered and was eventually purchased by Ernest Robie of Bristol, New Hampshire. In 1979, Bruce and Mary-Jo Scott of East Ryegate leased *The Boulders* with the dream of revitalizing and bringing *The Boulders* back to life. They hoped to show movies, open a coffee shop, a gift shop, a game room and to re-open the restaurant. The Scotts, along with their family moved into the old Tea Room. However, *The Boulders*, in their deteriorated state required greater expensive repairs than expected, coupled with the burden of governmental regulations and within a short time they realized their quest was futile. Presently, all the cottages have been sold off and the remaining two building of *The Boulders Tea Room and Casino* are the only remembrances of their good ole days.

What ever happen to the *Mountain Maid*? In a somewhat dilapidated condition in 1975, two college students purchased the Mountain Maid with hopes to restore it for use on Lake Champlain. It was moved to the Shelburne Shipyard and was placed in dry dock to be refurbished. A photograph was found that was taken in the 1980's of it being restored, but no further information has been readily found.

Directions: From Interstate I-91, Exit-23, follow Route-5 north through Lyndon for 9.5 miles until in West Burke Route-5A branches off on the right. Follow Route-5A north for 6 miles where you will come to Lake Willoughby, continue north on Route-5A along the lake's eastern shore for less than 0.2 mile where the large roadside erratic is located on your right.

Maine

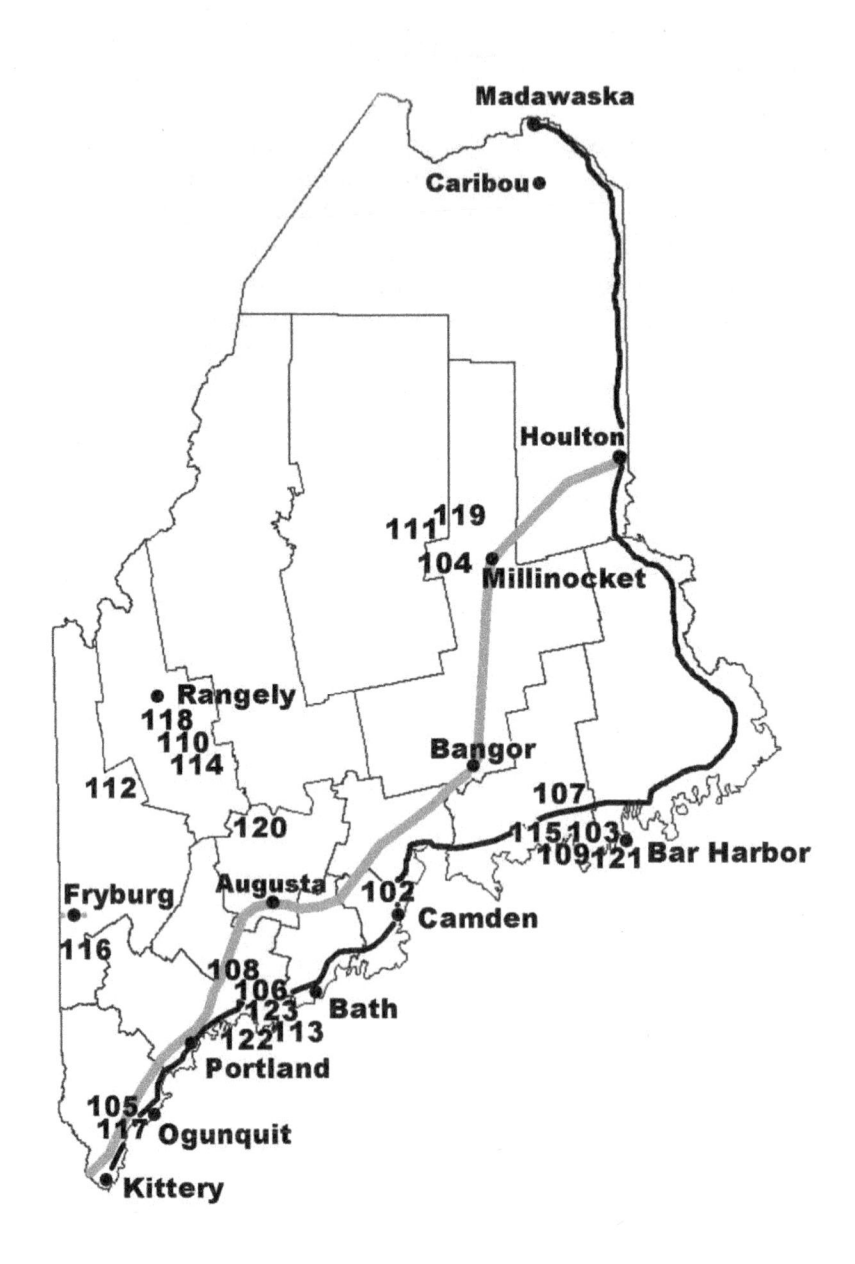

MAP Not To Scale – For Reference Only.

Maine

102. Balance Rock: Fernald's Neck Preserve (Lincolnville-Camden)
103. Balance Rock: Shore Walk (Bar Harbor)
104. Balance Rock Upper Jo-Mary Lake: (Millinocket)
105. Balance Rock: Orris Falls Conservation (South Berwick)
106. Big Green Thing-Painted Rock (Brunswick)
107. Big Rock: Little Webb Pond: (Waltham)
108. Bradbury Mountain Boulders: (Pownal)
109. Bubble Rock: Acadia National Park (Mt Desert Island)
110. Daggett Rock: (Phillips)
111. Debsconeag Wilderness- Ice Cave
112. Devil's Den: (Andover)
113. Flag Rock-Painted: (Phippsburg)
114. Gnome Rock House-Painted Rock (Avon)
115. Jack-O-Lantern Rock-Painted Rock (North Ellsworth)
116. Jockey's Cap (Fryeburg)
117. Kenyon Hill Preserve: (South Berwick)
118. Piazza Rock Appalachian Trail: (Sandy River Plantation)
119. Pockwockamus Rock-Painted: (Baxter State Park South Entry)
120. Snapper Rock: (Rome)
121. The Beehive; Acadia National Park: (Bar Harbor)
122. The Pebble: Curtis Farm (Brunswick)
123. Wally Rock-Painted Rock (Phippsburg)

102. Balance Rock - Fernald's Neck Preserve

Balance Rock – Lincolnville, ME

Location: Lincolnville (Waldo County), Camden (Knox County)
Delorme Atlas & Gazetteer-Maine: map 14, C-3
Parking GPS: N44°15'38.0" W69° 06'34.7"
Destination GPS: N44°15' 24.4" W69° 06'39.5"
Wow Factor: 8 Accessibility: Marked trails-Easy hiking 0.4 of mile
Contact Info: Coastal Mountains Land Trust. 101 Mount Battie Street, Camden, ME 04843 (207)236-7091 www.coastalmountains.org

Information: Established in 1969, the 328-acre Fernald's Neck Preserve occupies much of a peninsula that juts out into Megunticook Lake, a large body of water within Lincolnville and Camden. With nearly 4.0 miles of shoreline, the preserve has about 3.5 miles of interior walking trails. A color coded trail map is posted at the parking area and is available through the organizations web site.

Dogs are not permitted. Hunting is prohibited within the preserve. All fires and camping are prohibited. All motorized vehicles, bicycles or horses are not allowed on the preserve. Groups larger than 12 require permission before using the preserve. (e.g. schools)

A highlighted feature within the preserve is the balanced rock referred to as "The Big Boy" and being a 12 feet by 20 feet, the glacial erratic lives up to its moniker. In 1991, the preserve acquired the 3-acre property which included Balance Rock. A plaque mounted high on the rock reads "Balance Rock Dedicated to the memory of Vinton O Harkness and Elizabeth Harkness. August 1990."

Directions: From Camden (junction of US-1 & Route-52), drive north 4.75 miles on Rt-52 (Mountain Street), turn left onto Fernard's Neck Road, continue 0.5 mile bearing left at the fork in road. The road will become dirt; the gated parking area for Fernald's Neck is another 0.5 mile. The preserve is closed at 7:30 p.m.; the gate closes and is locked sharply at 7:30 p.m.

From the parking area, follow the blue trail south for 0.2 mile through the field and into the woods, bear left, then shortly taking your left again onto the orange trail which within 0.1 mile will bring you to the balanced rock and it location on the water's edge.

103. Balance Rock: Shore Walk

Balance Rock – Bar Harbor, ME

Location: Bar Harbor (Hancock County)
Delorme Atlas & Gazetteer-Maine: map 16, B-4
Parking GPS: N44° 23' 19.85" W68° 12' 5.20" (Grant Park)
N44° 23' 29.08" W68° 12' 15.24" (Agamont Park-Town Pier)
Destination GPS: N44° 23' 19.9" W68° 12' 00.1"
Wow Factor: 7 **Accessibility:** Public access via historic ocean shore-path.
Contact: Town Hall 93 Cottage Street Bar Harbor ME 04609
(207) 288-4098 www.barharbormaine.gov

Information: The famous Shore Path dates to 1880 and for more than a century grants access to Balance Rock and other spectacular ocean front scenic views. The Balance Rock is closest and readily accessible from Grant Park parking area located at the end of Albert Meadow Lane. The Shore Path also begins and is accessible from Agamont Park with parking at the town pier. Agamont Park has picnic tables, restrooms, Wi-Fi and overlooks Frenchman Bay. From here, Shore Path begins and follows the shoreline south, past many historic Inns and Cottages providing a level and easy 0.75 mile walk down to Wayman Lane along Bar Harbor's eastern shore. While Wayman Lane is an access point, little to no parking is provided here. Parking is always an issue, a reminder that Bar

Harbor strictly enforces traffic regulations. In addition, please note that much of the *Shore Path* crosses private property, stay on the path. The Bar Harbor Village Improvement Association maintains the path on behalf of the granting landowners.

Directions: Cross over Thompson Island on Route-3 from the "Mainland" onto Mount Desert Island, Route-3 will bear left into Bar Harbor. Follow Route-3 for 10 miles, at the junction of Route-3 and Route-233, turn left staying on Route-3 for 0.5 mile into the downtown area of Bar Harbor. In the center of the town, with the Village Green on your left, Route-3 will sharply turn right onto Main Street. YOU will turn left, travel 50 feet and take the first right onto Albert Meadow Lane, follow to the end staying left for the parking area of Grant Park. The Balance Rock is 100 yards from the parking area on the shoreline, easily seen and approachable at low tide. For Agamont Park; you turn left onto Main Street, travel straight through this touristy and very busy area for 0.2 mile until it intersects with West Street, turn right to Town Pier parking and Agamont Park. From this entry for the Shore Path, walk south 0.3 mile, at Grant Park the Balance Rock is seen on your left.

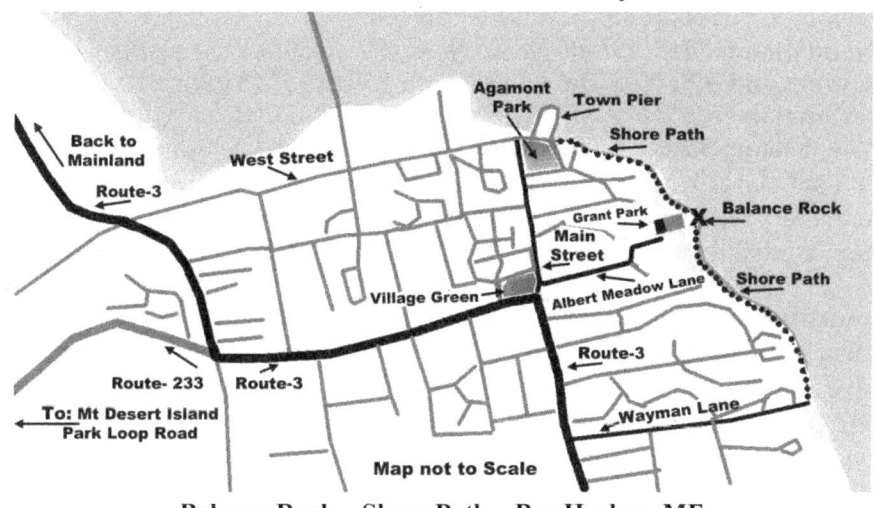

Balance Rock – Shore Path – Bar Harbor, ME

104. Balance Rock - Upper Jo-Mary Lake

Balance Rock – Jo Mary Lake (upper) – Millinocket, ME

Location: Millinocket (Penobscot County)
Delorme Atlas & Gazetteer-Maine: map 42, B-5
Parking GPS: N45° 36' 1.27" W68° 56' 3.82"
Destination GPS: N45° 36' 18.30" W68° 56' 36.50" (Viewing Point Z)
Destination GPS: N45° 36' 11.47" W68° 56' 35.31" (Viewing Point Y)
Destination GPS: N45° 36' 11.19" W68° 56' 38.87" (Balance Rock)
Wow Factor: 8 **Accessibility:** Difficult-No path-All bushwhacking
Contact: North Maine Woods, Inc. P.O. Box 425, 92 Main Street Ashland ME 04732 (207)435-6213 info@northmainewoods.org http://northmainewoods.org/

Information: Access to the Balance Rock of Upper Jo-Mary Lake is not a user friendly jaunt. First the access roads are not paved and have seasonal mud or snow considerations. This back road network of roads are created, owned and regulated by North Maine Woods, Inc. In addition, there is no actual trail to follow, strictly a bushwhack adventure through recently harvested woodland. While the forest has already started to reclaim the open land with briar and brush, the closer to the lake and shoreline, the more of a older growth barrier of evergreen trees and brush is encountered.

The easiest approach would be by boat or canoe for the balanced rock sits off shore 100-feet. In the summer time it would a fun swim out to it; cross-country skiing or snowshoeing in winter over the ice would be other options. The reward of viewing a most unusual balanced rock, the chance of watching a Moose browsing at water's edge or a glimpse of the elusive Loons makes the effort worth it. For sure this location has not become over run by tourists.

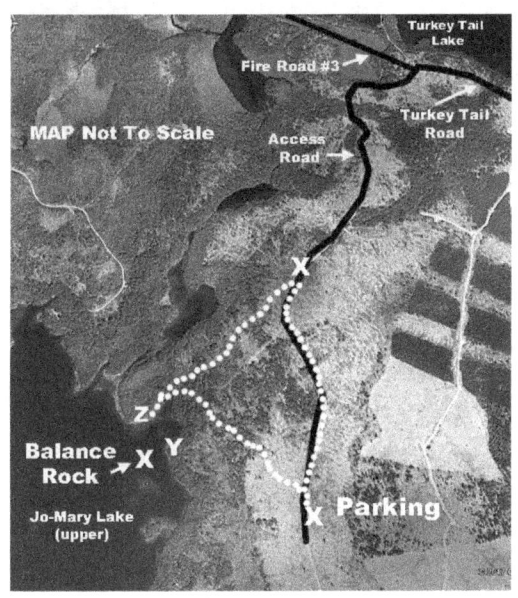

The trek down to the shoreline from the parking area will not be as difficult if; GPS is used along with prior examination through a map application for the area. (e.g. Google Earth.) For viewing the rock, all you need is to reach a stretch of the shoreline near it. While on the other hand, you do not want to be languishing, or wandering through thickets and wasting time or energy. The initial descent went quickly and then started encountering thickets of evergreen and our destination coordinates shifted from point Y, to a more northerly lakeside location point Z.

Returning to the road where you parked, you will need to bushwhack east until you find the dirt access road. Our flanking maneuver swept us northerly and stumbling upon an old logging road, taking its path did head back towards the access road. Although, the last few hundred feet of the old road faded back into briar and bramble, it turned out better than doing a total bushwhack and all we needed to do was walk back up the access road to our parked car.

Visiting this area after the fall foliage season has the advantage of leaves off the trees, the elimination of pesky mosquitoes and cooler weather for bushwhacking which often can be a bit more strenuous, challenging and wearisome.

Balance Rock Map – Jo-Mary Lake, ME

Directions: From Millinocket, head south on Route-11 for 9.5 miles, turn right onto *Lincoln Ridge Road* (Point-A), travel northeast for 3.75 miles, you will merge onto *Turkey Tail Road* (Point-B), stay heading west, travel for 1.0 mile, on your right *Buckham Camp Road*, bear left at that fork (Point-C) *Turkey Tail Road* continues west for 1.0 mile where *Fire Road* #3 (Point-D) will enter on the right, you continue left, onto a smaller dirt logging road which shortly should start to head south. Continue on this road 1.75 miles to the parking vicinity. Your approach should be looking west, towards Jo-Mary Lake; approximately 0.4 mile west and slightly downward towards the shoreline.

A: Lincoln Ridge Road: N45° 34' 8.74" W68° 50' 35.21"
B: Turkey Tail Road: N45°36'42.39" W68°53'20.95"
C: Buckham Camp Road: N45° 36' 53.70" W68° 54' 33.60"
D: Fire Road #3: N45° 37' 11.68" W68° 55' 29.81"

In this upstate Maine region, there is a vast network of roadways owned and regulated by North Maine Woods Inc. along with per person usage fees and other rules, contact or check on their web site for locations, current conditions, check points and other information: info@northmainewoods.org or www.northmainewoods.org

105. Balance Rock: Orris Falls Conservation Area

Balance Rock – South Berwick, ME

Location: South Berwick (York County)
Delorme Atlas & Gazetteer-Maine: map 2, E-4
Parking GPS: N43° 16' 7.90" W70° 41' 41.40" (Emery Road)
Parking GPS: N43° 16' 47.80" W70° 43' 12.70" (Thurrell Road)
Destination GPS: N43° 16' 15.6" W70° 42' 06.3" (Balance Rock)
Wow Factor: 9 **Accessibility:** Marked trails-Easy hiking 0.4 of mile
Contact:, PO Box 151, South Berwick, ME 03908 Office Location: Beach Plum Farm 610 Main St, Ogunquit ME 207-646-3604 email : info@gwrlt.org

Information: Located just a short drive from Ogunquit Beach, the quick ride over twisting and turning back roads will surprise you on just how unique this conservation land is; a waterfall, look-out ledges, glacial erratic field and one impressive *Balancing Rock*. The 171 acre Orris Falls Conservation Area has access from either Thurrell or Emery's Bridge Roads by rights-of-way through private land, so please respect property boundaries. From either entry point a small parking area can be found for 2 or 3 cars. Most hiking can be assumed as getting there and hiking back the way you came. From Emery Bridge Road, a quick and easy 0.5 mile access to glacial erratic's and *Balance Rock* can be found. The short hike has you pass by a large erratic with a couple of headstone memorials, a large split rock, then a short spur trail down to the large balance rock.

Orris B- Split Rock – South Berwick, ME

Orris A: N43° 16' 16.70" W70° 41' 56.90" (Grave Rock) (*WOW-6*)
Not an overly remarkable boulder other than a couple of granite head stone settings around the base of erratic. . This rock is on private property and not part of the Great Works Regional Land Trust, Orris Conservation Land property.

Orris B: N43° 16' 15.40" W 70° 42' 1.30" (Split Rock) (*WOW-7*)
Marvelous 14 foot Split Rock, across from small over-grown boulder cluster.

Orris C: N43° 16' 15.82" W70° 42' 1.78" (Rock Group) (*WOW-6*)
Located near turn-off spur down to Balance Rock.

Directions: Heading north on Route-1and just past the center in Ogunquit, take a left onto Berwick Road. Head west on Berwick Road for 1.3 miles, you will cross over Interstate I-95, Ogunquit Road will start on the other side. Continue west 0.5 miles and at the next intersection continue right staying on Ogunquit Road. Continue west for 3.5 miles, the *Emery Bridge Road* is on your left. Travel south for 0.4 miles, on the right a sign and small parking area for 2-3 cars.

Thurrell Road access; west on *Boyd's Corner Road* 1.0 mile after Emery Bridge Road, turn left onto Thurrell Road. Drive south 0.75 miles to a small parking area on your left.

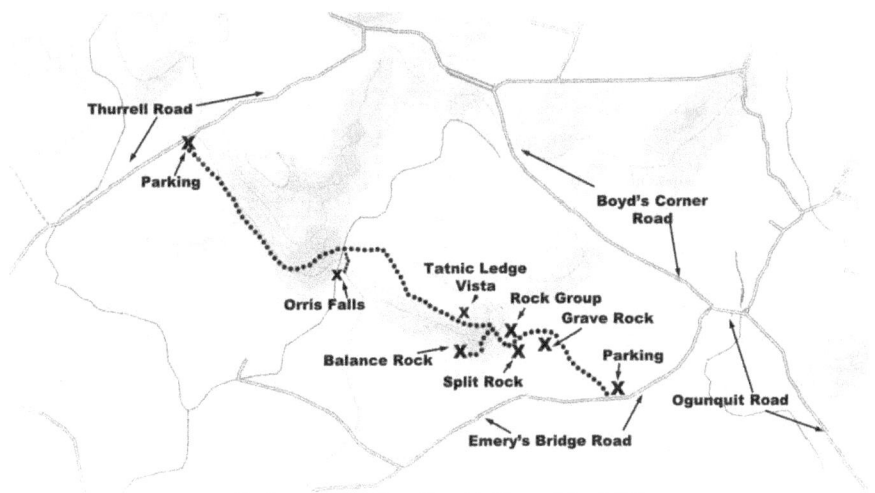

Balance Rock – South Berwick, ME

106. Big Green Thing

Big Green Thing – Brunswick, ME

Location: Bunswick (Cumberland County)
Delorme Atlas & Gazetteer-Maine: map 6, C-2

Parking GPS: N43° 54' 36.5" W70° 00' 50.3"
Destination GPS: N43° 54' 36.5" W70° 00' 50.3"
Wow Factor: 4 **Accessibility**: Road side, Easy 30 yards.

Information: The *Big Green Thing* is a small painted rock located roadside and just above the active Boston & Maine railroad. If you're lucky you might get Amtrak roaring by at 60 mph! In short, be careful, the edge of the gorge is close!! This rock seems to be a toad, frog or lizard with many Geo-cache participants visiting here and from the history of their photos, the *Big Green Thing* has been frequently repainted, each time a different shade of green with some adaptation of detail, placement and color.

Directions: In Brunswick, use Exit-22 off Interstate-295 heading southeast on the interchange exit ramp 0.75 mile towards Route-1. Turn onto Route-1 south (Old Portland Road) and travel 0.6 mile turning left onto Hillside Road, crossing over the railroad tracks below, immediately turn left onto Greenwood Road.
The location of the *Big Green Thing* Rock is immediately on your left within 50 yards. Turn around and park on the correct side of the road. The rock is set back within a small clump of evergreens.

107. Big Rock: Little Webb Pond

Big Rock – Waltham, ME

Location: Waltham (Hancock County)

Delorme Atlas & Gazetteer-Maine: map 24, C-3
Parking GPS: N44° 41' 20.2" W68° 18' 42.8"
Destination GPS: N44° 41' 22.2" W68°18' 44.4"
Wow Factor: 10 Accessibility: Easy hike, small foot path, 100 yards

Information: As a free standing glacial erratic, *Big Rock* is massive in size, its estimated dimension of 30x30x60 feet makes it a very impressive hunk of granite sitting within the woodlands in solitary grandeur. While not as large as *Daggett Rock* which is the largest glacial erratic in Maine, it certainly is a contender for second place. Some have suggested that it resembles the head of a dinosaur with the large crack being the jaw and appears to be munching on some bushes. In addition, this is private land, camping is not permitted and if you pack it in, take back it out.

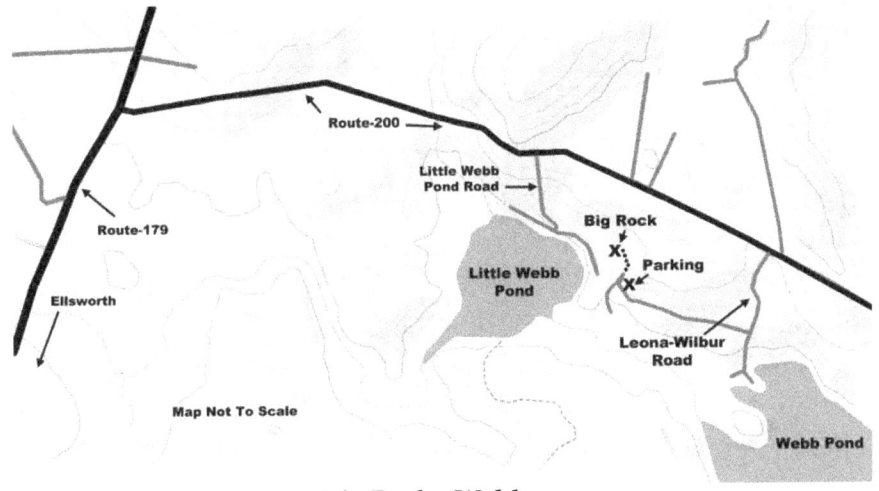

Big Rock - Waltham

Directions: From Ellsworth, travel northwest on Route-1A (State Street) for 1.6 miles, turn on Route-179 traveling north for 10.8 miles, turn onto Route-200 heading east for 2.2 miles, turn right onto Leona-Wilbur Road (a gravel road) heading south for 0.4 mile, turn right for 0.4 mile to large dirt parking area. From the northern area of parking area, follow small path northerly for 100 yards. See the rock.

108. Bradbury Mountain Boulders

BB-5 – Gem Boulder – Pownal, ME

Location: Pownal (Cumberland County)
Delorme Atlas & Gazetteer-Maine: map 5, C-5
Parking GPS: N43° 53' 57.30" W70° 10' 53.40"
Destination GPS: As listed below
Wow Factor: 9 **Accessibility:** Moderate -Short Uphill Bushwhack

Information: Clearly visible in Google Earth, these rocks remain just outside the Bradbury Mountain State Park boundary. While certainly located outside the park's boundary, no postings were noticed in accessing these boulders. However, recent reading has rock climbing being presently suspended. Evidently it is a sensitive area; continue to respect this property with no fires, no camping, carry-in and carry-out philosophy, and keeping you presence low-key will help prevent postings.

BB-1: N43° 53' 57.50" W70° 11' 10.80" (Tree Rock) *(WOW-7)*
Having a flourishing micro-cosmism of ferns and small bushes on top. This 14-feet boulder is the lowest boulder location we visited.

BB-2: N43° 53' 57.80" W70° 11' 12.40" (Pinnacle Rock) *(WOW-5)*
A lone 12-feet semi-gum drop shape boulder, encountered up-hill towards the larger erratic's from Tree Rock

BB-4 – The Hotel – Pownal, ME

BB-3: N43° 53' 58.20" W70° 11' 14.70" (Blob Boulder) *(WOW-7)*
Sprawling 16-foot boulder with a sloped front and long block of stone in the rear

BB-4: N43° 53' 59.20" W70° 11' 14.70" (The Hotel) *(WOW-10)*
A large striking block of stone, colossal 25 to 30 foot boulder. Seems like its volume could contain a Subway, Dunkin Donut and Cumby's stores.

BB-5: N43° 53' 59.60" W70° 11' 16.30" (The Gem) *(WOW-10)*
The front of this mega-rock rise up and juts out like a cruise ship that has run aground. Enormous height and a corresponding length make this rock the largest in this boulder field.

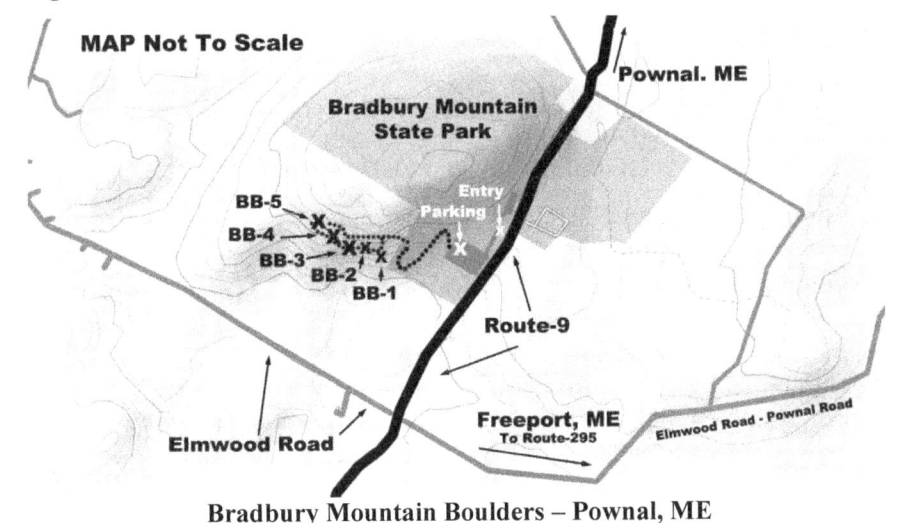

Bradbury Mountain Boulders – Pownal, ME

Directions: From Interstate I-295 at Exit-22 at the interchange of Route-125 and Route -136, head west on Rt-136 for 0.2 mile. Turn left onto Durham Rd, travel south for 0.2 mile turn right, continue west on Pownal Road (turns into Elmwood Road.) After 4.2 miles you will junction of Route-9, turn right heading north for 0.5 mile, turn left for entrance to Bradbury Park. You can enter the park; pay the fee and park at the south parking area. From the parking area, follow the South Ridge Trail for 0.2 mile, bear left and leave the trail just above the hairpin turn, hiking lateral around the mountain's southern slope to the boulder field within 0.1 mile.

109. Bubble Rock: Acadia National Park

Bubble Rock – Bar Harbor, ME

Location: Mount Desert Island (Hancock County)
Delorme Atlas & Gazetteer-Maine: map 16, B-3
Parking GPS: N44° 20' 27.7" W68° 15' 1.7" (Bubble Gap Trail)
Parking GPS: N44° 20' 17.70" W68° 15' 1.81" (Southern Ascent Trail)
Destination GPS: N44° 20' 22.4" W68° 15' 11.5"
Wow Factor: 9 **Accessibility:** Bubble Gap Trail is a Moderate hike. Well marked trail, 0.6 mile. Southern Ascent Trail is steep and more difficult.

Information: Fees, maps, passes and other pertinent information, visit the National Park Service web site: or Acadia National Park, 25

Visitor Center Rd, P.O. Box 177, Bar Harbor, ME 04609 Phone: (207) 288-3338   www.nps.gov/acad/index.htm

The Hulls Cove Visitor Center in Bar Harbor, Maine is open seasonally at different hours. It is closed November 1 through April 14. For information during the winter months, visit the Park Headquarters on Highway 233 near Eagle Lake, just 3 miles (4.8 km) west of Bar Harbor. Portions of the Park Loop Road close for the winter to vehicle traffic.

Directions On Route-3 from the "Mainland" cross over Thompson Island onto Mount Desert Island, Route-3 will bear left into Bar Harbor, you will continue south following Route-102 and Route-198 towards Southwest Harbor. In 4.3 miles, turn left onto Route-198. Continue 1.4 miles, turning left onto Route-233 (Eagle Lake Road) heading east, towards Bar Harbor. Within 4.7 miles just after and passing under a magnificent stone bridge the Acadian Park Loop Road access will be on your left. Travel up the ramp and turn left onto the Park Loop Road access. From Bar Harbor to this same access point, turn onto Route-233 heading west (Eagle Lake Road) off of Route-3, for 1.1 miles turning right onto ramp, left turn traveling south onto the Park Loop Road access.

The Park Loop Road is approximately 20 miles of super scenic roadway, with its eastern side traveling along the coast of Acadia's magnificent seashore and the western side traveling through glacial ponds and mountains with historical landscape along the way.

Heading south, within 0.5 miles you have the option to travel the Park Loop Road clockwise, (which becomes 1-way traffic) or continue south (counter-clockwise) towards the entry to Cadillac Mountain summit road and the Jordon Pond Tea House. Within another 0.5 mile you will pass the Cadillac Summit Road on your left, from here travel south (becomes Jordon Pond Road) for 2.4 miles where the parking area for the Bubble Rock will be apparent on your right. Note: Even these large parking areas will fill up rapidly during summer vacation months and weekends.

Many of the hikers prefer the Bubble Rock Gap Trail up to the 100 ton, Bubble Rock. This trail is well maintained and heavily traveled. The rock is physically located on the South Bubble summit. Just about halfway up the trail will fork, bear left, then within 100 yards, you will turn another sharp left onto to South Bubble summit trail. Within 0.3 mile, on the eastern face of the summit, Bubble Rock can be found in what appears to be a precarious position on the edge of a cliff. Do not miss the terrific view of Jordon Pond from the western edge of South Bubble summit.

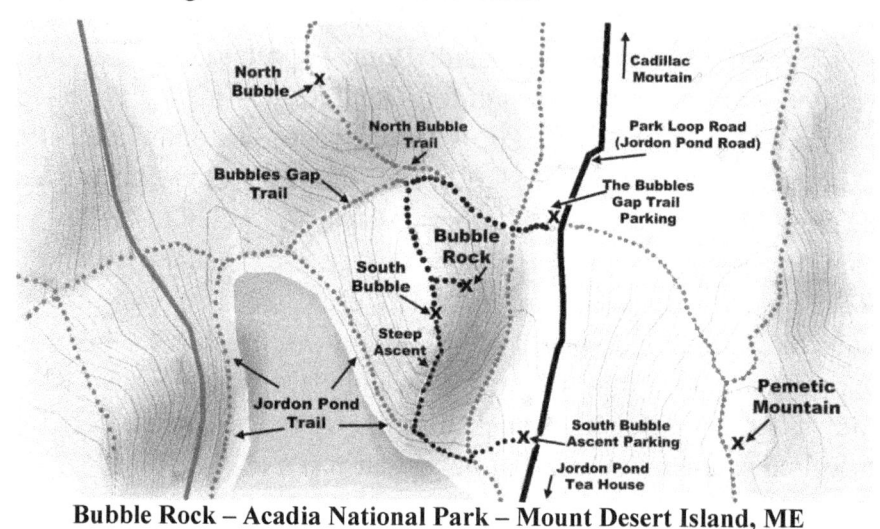

Bubble Rock – Acadia National Park – Mount Desert Island, ME

In addition, just 0.2 mile south of the Bubble Gap Trail parking is a smaller parking area for the South Bubble Ascent Trail, for those who desire a steeper and rockier experience. In 100 yards from the parking area, turn left onto the Jordon Pond Carry Trail; head south for 300 yards, the trail junctions with the Jordon Pond Path and the trailhead for the South Bubble ascent trail will be on the right. From here it's about 0.3 mile to the summit. This approach is steep, yet provides tremendous views all the way up to Bubble Rock.

Take a boat tour of Mount Desert Island or out to Cranberry Island from Northeast Harbor. Visit the beautiful "Asticou Azalea Gardens" at the junction of Route-3 and Route-198 or have a popover with jam at the Jordon Pond Tea house just 1.5 south of the Bubble Rock parking area.

The park offers over 125 miles of hiking trails, many of which reach the granite peaks along with many miles of historical gravel carriage roads suitable for bicycling. Special attractions include miles of marvelous rocky coastline and Thunder Hole. Drive the scenic road to the summit of Cadillac Mountain (1,530 feet), which is the highest point on eastern coastline of the United States.

110. Daggett Rock

Daggett Rock – Phillips, ME

Location: Phillips (Franklin County)
Delorme Atlas & Gazetteer-Maine: map 19, A-4
Parking GPS: N44° 50' 50.3" W70° 17' 54.9"
Destination GPS: N44° 50' 54.6" W70° 18' 17.9"
Wow Factor: 10 **Accessibility:** Public access, easy on 0.4 mile path.

Information: Considered to be the largest glacial erratic in the State of Maine, Daggett Rock is approximately 80 feet long, 30 feet wide, and 30 feet high and is estimated to 8000 tons. Folklore regarding why the boulder is split into (3) large pieces is centered upon a woodsman named Daggett who came upon the rock during a wild thunderstorm. Daggett, inebriated and upset at the storm, climbed onto the rock. In an uncontrollable rage of anger, he took the Lord's name in vain, cursing that he could not be struck down.

A gigantic lightning bolt flashed from the sky followed by a boom of thunder. Daggett was instantly killed and the rock was cracked into the three fragments found today. Popular as a tourist attraction since the 1880's, renewed interest in this location has occurred as a popular location for Bouldering, a freestyle form of rock climbing where large boulders are climbed using only hand/toe holds and without the aid of ropes.

CLEFT ROCK, Phillips, Me   Published by E. S. Bubier

Daggett Rock a.k.a. Cleft Rock - Phillips, ME

Directions: From Phillips at the Route-4 and Route-142, head north towards Kingfield on Route-142 for 1.4 miles. Turn right onto Wheeler Hill Road travel east for 2.4 miles, on your right a small dirt parking area with a makeshift sign is the designated parking are for Draggett Rock. Across the street is a small dirt road which in 0.4 mile will bring you to your final destination.

111. Debsconeag Wilderness: Ice Caves

Ice Cave Entry – Debsconeag Wilderness, ME

Location: Sector T2 R10 WELS (Piscataquis County)
Delorme Atlas & Gazetteer-Maine: map 50, E-5
Parking GPS: N45° 47' 29.60" W68° 58' 41.50"
Destination GPS: As listed below.
Wow Factor: 8 Accessibility: Moderate blue blazed trail 2.1 miles RT.
Contact: The Nature Conservancy 14 Maine Street, Suite 401 Brunswick, ME 04011 (207)729-5181 naturemaine@tnc.org   www.nature.org

Information: Prior to the addition of iron rod steps and hand rails in 2006, I have to wonder how many "explorer's" floundered trying to get out of this icy cave. No matter if ice is present; the dampness within the cave remains slippery year around and caution needs to prevail. The Ice Cave Trail is a well-marked trail with blue blazes and is easy to follow. Additional signs at intersections also provide direction and mileage. To my surprise was the amount of small and large boulders the trail will wind through or pass near. There is a spur trail to a scenic vista before reaching the Ice Cave and continuing downward to the 1st Debsconeag Lake is shortly after the Ice Cave turn-off.

Once at the Ice Cave site, there are many signs asking you to *Stay on the Trail*, environment impact of the ferns, mosses and lichen have become a major concern. Finding the actual *Ice Cave* opening will become obvious, once you find the weather worn iron rod railing with steps that lead down onto another lower series of iron rod steps which you descend down into the cave with. The Railing and steps are very secure, gloves, flashlight and at times ice stabilizers or crampons will insure a safe and interesting exploration. The cave is not overly deep with its main chamber at the bottom 25-feet and you will *squiggle* to reach the inner most chambers.

Debsconeag Lake Wilderness Preserve has 46,271-acres which contains the highest concentration of pristine, ponds and forests in New England. Debsconeag means "carrying place," named by native people for the portage sites where they carried their birch-bark canoes around rapids and waterfalls. *The Nature Conservancy* is a private, nonprofit conservation organization dedicated to the preservation of the plants, animals, and natural communities that represent the diversity of life on Earth by protecting the lands and waters they need to survive. Given their focused biodiversity conservation mission, the Conservancy takes a precautionary approach to human uses on the lands they manage. Please respect these policies when visiting their preserves so that future generations can continue to enjoy the great places of Maine. Visit www.nature.org

The Debsconeag Lakes Wilderness Area preserves Guidelines.

Hunting and fishing are allowed according to state laws and regulations.

Vehicles are restricted to designated roads.

Mountain biking is prohibited.

ATVs are not permitted anywhere in the reserve.

Snowmobiling on pre-existing or established trails is allowed.

Horses, pets, and other domestic animals are not permitted.

Fires are allowed by permit only in existing fire rings.

Do not collect or remove plants or animals.

Camp only in designated campsites. No reservations or fees required.

Camping at any one site is limited to a two week maximum stay.

Please use the latrines installed at campsites.

Carry water for washing at least 200 feet away from streams or lakes.

Leave your campsite looking better than when you arrived.

Remove all trash. Pack it in, pack it out!

IC-2 Trail Rock – Ice Cave Trail – Debsconeag Wilderness, ME

IC-1: N45° 47' 22.10" W68° 58' 42.10" (Boulder Field) *WOW-7*
The trail near the beginning with wind through, near or over small boulders, nothing tedious, but can be slippery with pine needle or leafs.

IC-2: N45° 47' 12.40" W68° 58' 33.20"(Trail Rock) *WOW-7*
Approaching the half-way mark the trail will pass between a small 14-foot boulder and a larger 16-foot boulder.

IC-3 – Split Rock – Ice Cave Trail – Debsconeag Wilderness, ME

IC-3: N45° 46' 53.00" W68° 58' 24.20" (Split Rock) *WOW-8*
Large 18-foot Split Rock located just 75-feet off trail. Located short distance before spur trail to scenic vista

IC-4 Bow Rock – Ice Cave Trail – Debsconeag Wilderness, ME

IC-4: N45° 46' 48.90" W68° 58' 27.40" (Bow Rock) *WOW-8*
Large wedge shape 16-foot boulder. Located just off trail slightly before the Ice Cave Trail turn-off.

IC-5 – Ice Cave Entry – Debsconeag Wilderness, ME

IC-5: N45° 46' 50.00" W68° 58' 30.10" (Ice Cave) *WOW-8*
There is a bottom! Unlike a Shelter or Indian Cave made from surface rock leaning upon rock, the Ice Cave chambers lie beneath earth level. The interior can have a very surreal or bizarre environment, icicles and ice flows survive longer being hidden from sunlight most of the year.

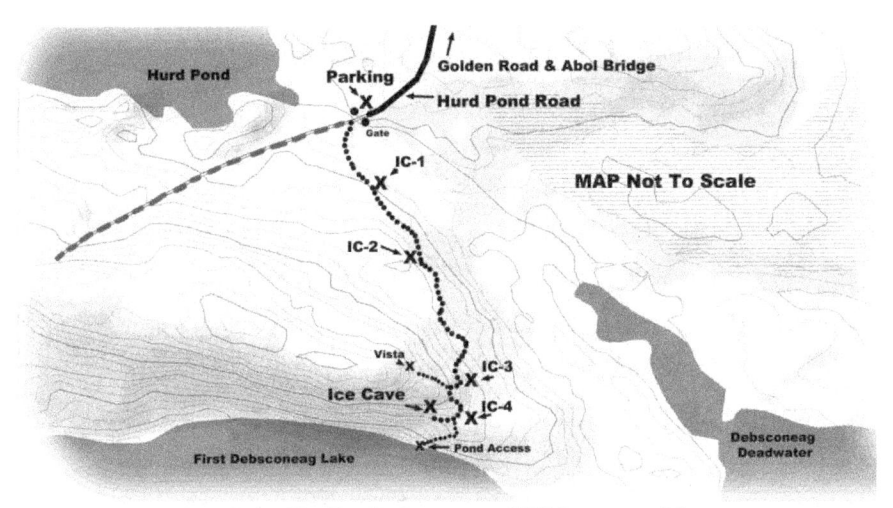

Ice Cave Trail – Debsconeag Wilderness - Map

Directions: In Medway, from Interstate I-95 use Exit-244 and travel west on Route-157, in 0.7 mile, Route-11 joins, together follow both Routes for 10.0 miles into downtown Millinocket: here Route-11 will turn left and heads south; you will turn right, heading north for 8.3 miles towards Spencer's Cove. Continue north on Katardin Avenue, as it becomes Bates Street, then Millinocket Road until you reach Spencer's Cove on Millinocket Lake.

Baxter State Park Road is paved and the Golden Road is dirt with potholes, washboard and logging trucks. For the Ice Caves in the Debsoneag Wilderness use Golden Road, you to turn left via access roads at the Dam and Campground. From the Spencer Cove Dam, follow the Golden Road westerly for 10.0 miles to Abol Bridge. The Bridge is a single lane only, use caution. Directly across the bridge turns left onto an unnamed road and follow south along the West Branch of the Prenobscott River for 1.75 miles; as the road turns away from the river and heads southwesterly, continue for 1.9 miles towards Hurd Pond. The road ends at a gate and small parking area for the Ice Caves and 1st Debsconeag Lake trail head. Just past the gate, across the small bridge and within 100 yards is where the Ice Cave Trail begins.

In this upstate Maine region, there is a vast network of roadways owned and regulated by North Maine Woods Inc. along with per person usage fees and other rules, contact or check on their web site for locations, current conditions, check points and other information: info@northmainewoods.org or www.northmainewoods.org

112. Devil's Den

Devil's Den – Andover, ME

Location: Andover (Oxford County)
Delorme Atlas & Gazetteer-Maine: map 18, D-4
Parking GPS: N44° 41' 44.57" W70° 44' 48.41"
Destination GPS: N44° 41' 41.60" W70° 44' 47.70"
Wow Factor: 8 Accessibility: Short easy path.

Information: Devil's Den is a large canyon approximately 200-feet long with 16-feet to 25-feet flume like walls. Except for a couple of pools of shallow water, the stream bed that eroded this gorge is essentially dry. Adjacent to this location is Silver Ripple Cascades, another gorge which basically parallel's Devil's Den, but now has Black Brook cascading over a few small falls, potholes and at its base a popular swimming hole.

Directions: From To reach Andover, take Route-5(Ellis River Road) north from Route-2 in West Rumford for 10.0 miles. In Andover center, at the terminus of Route-5, turn right onto Route-120 and head east for 0.6 miles. Turn left onto South Arm Road and travel north 4.6 miles. Turn left onto an unnamed dirt road, head west and down to a small pull-off parking area just prior to the Black Brook Bridge within 0.1 mile. Easy access is located by walking down between Devil's Den Gorge and Silver Ripple Cascades some 150 feet, turn left and locate the lower opening of the gorge and walk back up into its gulch.

113. Flag Rock

Flag Rock – Phippsburg, ME

Location: Phippsburg (Sagadahoc County)
Delorme Atlas & Gazetteer-Maine: map 6, D-4
Parking GPS: N43° 48' 20.1" W69° 50' 09.1"
Destination GPS: N43° 48' 20.1" W69° 50' 09.1"
Wow Factor: 4 **Accessibility:** Roadside

Information: Originally, this location has been titled *Painted Rock, Love Rock or Peace Rock*. However, when we visited we discovered the rock had been recently painted to display the American Flag. The painted flag is done well, however the rock is small being only 4 feet tall by 8 feet wide.

Directions: In Topsham, exit-24 from Interstate I-295, take Route-196 heading southeast 2.5 miles, until you meet the interchange of Route-1 in Brunswick just on the other side of the Androscoggin River. To Flag Rock, follow Route-1 north along the river towards Bath for 7.7 miles, exit at the junction of Route-209 (High Street.) Follow Route-209 south towards Phippsburg for 2.4 miles, High Street will veer right, you'll stay on Route-209 which is now Main Road. Continuing south on Rt-209 for 3.4 miles until you reach Stony Brook Road on your right. Follow Stony Brook Road west for 1.7 miles which will terminate at Meadowbrook Road. Turn left heading south; continue past *Wally Rock* on Meadowbrook Drive for 2 miles. The road will become an unpaved road and will junction with Basin Road shortly after. Turn left, drive 0.4 mile, *Flag Rock* will be on the northern side of the road.

114. Gnome House Rock & Bug-Eyed Rock

Gnome House Rock – Avon, ME

Location: Avon (Franklin County)
Delorme Atlas & Gazetteer-Maine: map 19, B-4
Gnome House Rock GPS: N44° 47' 55.90" W70° 19' 9.60"
Bug-Eye Rock GPS: N44° 48' 0.70" W70° 19' 27.50"
Wow Factor: 6 **Accessibility:** Roadside – Private Property

Bug-Eye Rock – Avon, ME

Directions: South of Phillips located on Route-4 heading east for 2.4 miles. Both painted rocks are within 0.2 mile of each other on the north side of Route-4. Located nearby are Daggett and Piazza Rock.

115. Jack-O-Lantern Rock

Jack-O-Lantern Rock – North Ellsworth, ME

Location: Ellsworth (Hancock County)
Delorme Atlas & Gazetteer-Maine: map 23, D-5
Parking GPS: N44° 36' 34.02" W68° 31' 12.11"
Destination GPS: N44° 36' 34.02" W68° 31' 12.11"
Wow Factor: 4 **Accessibility:** Roadside – End of private drive

Information: In the spirit of painted rocks, this Jack-O-Lantern is a unique subject matter when one considers that many painted rock become only frogs or toads. The creativity and practicality works well. First, the rock being essentially painted a bright orange and located next to the entry of this residential driveway is highly visible in fog or during snow-plowing. Secondly, no one is going to smash this pumpkin easily during Halloween! That said, I would not go out of the way, unless you're traveling nearby, a whimsical rock location for kids on a car trip.

Directions: From Ellsworth center, travel Route1A (Bangor Road) 7.0 miles north, rock is at end of driveway on your left at 1134 Bangor Road.

116. Jockey's Cap Boulders

JC-1 – Molly's Locket- Jockey's Cap, ME

Location: Fryeburg (Oxford County)
Delorme Atlas & Gazetteer-Maine: map 4, A-1
Parking GPS: N44° 1' 13.43" W70° 57' 52.26"
Destination GPS: As listed below.
Wow Factor: 8 **Accessibility:** Easy 0.2 mile to boulders,

Information: For such a short hike, Jockey's Cap is a great location for the boulders and its incredible panorama vista from the summit.
On top of Jockey Cap is a monument erected to honor Admiral Robert E. Peary who discovered the North Pole. Peary lived in Fryeburg (1878 to 1979) and made drawings of the area from the top of Jockey Cap. In the 1930's Jockey Cap was a ski area and had the state's first rope tow. It's has appeal for rock climbers and bouldering, with Molly's Locket having an impressive shelter cave to explore at its base.

JC-1: N44° 1' 18.20" W70° 57' 48.00" Molly's Locket *(WOW-8)*
A small cluster of rocks with a peak of 14-feet and a shelter cave. The cave is reported to have been utilized by the last of the Pequawket Indians for shelter.

JC-2: N44° 1' 17.50" W70° 57' 46.90" Spiritual Rock *(WOW-7)*
Large 12-feet high with tilted facing, nothing over significant.

JC-3: N44° 1' 17.30" W70 °57' 46.70" Peary's Boulder *(WOW-8)*
Large Hi-Lo, 16-feet to 18-feet boulder, small cap boulder on top. Appears to have favor among bouldering enthusiasts with lots of talc hand prints.

Jockey's Cap Summit: N44° 1' 19.70" W70° 57' 45.40"*(WOW-9)*
Awesome summit vista with Admiral Peary's Memorial that indicates direction and labels of landmarks or mountains on the horizon.

JC-3 – Peary's Boulder – Jockey's Cap, ME

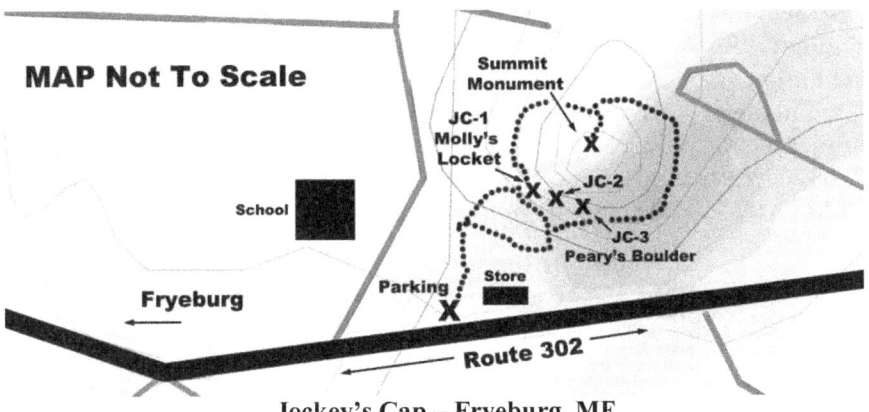

Jockey's Cap – Fryeburg, ME

Directions: In Fryeburg, at the junction of Route-5 and Route-302, travel 0.5 miles east on US-302 (Bridgton Road.) Turn left into the parking lot of the Jockey Cap Country Store just before the Dollar General. Parking for the trailhead is located on the far left in the lot, near the trailhead kiosk. From the Kiosk, a dirt trail will wind through the forest where you'll come to Molly Locket's Cave located in the front and at the base of Jockey's Cap. From these boulders access to the summit can be found in either direction within 0.2 mile. Clock-wise seems to be the popular direction with easy approach onto the summit from the back.

117. Kenyon Hill Preserve

KH-2 – Tri-Split Rock – South Berwick, ME

Location: South Berwick (York County)
Delorme Atlas & Gazetteer-Maine: map 2, E-4
Parking GPS: N43° 15' 43.74" W70° 40' 43.67" (Ogunquit Road)
Destination GPS: As listed below
Wow Factor: 7 **Accessibility:** Easy 1.0 mile blazed loop trail.
Contact: Great Works Regional Land Trust, PO Box 151, South Berwick, ME 03908 <u>Office Location</u>: Beach Plum Farm 610 Main St, Ogunquit ME 207-646-3604 email : info@gwrlt.org

Information: In South Berwick, with the transfer of ownership of 100 acres from the Maine Turnpike Authority to the Great Works Regional Land Trust, the Kenyon Hill Preserve was established in October of 2002. The property protects and consists of several acres of wetlands, 1,000 feet of frontage on the Ogunquit River, and a mixture of evergreen and hardwood forest. The main entry along with a basic dirt parking area is located near the corner of Bennett Lot Road and Ogunquit Road. **KH-6 (Fractured Ledge)** From the parking area, a painted blue blazed 1.0 mile, loop trail readily allows a hike which will pass by some classic

New England stone walls, remarkable stone ledges and between some massive glacial erratic boulders. Considering this is New England, the over-all exertion is relatively easy with only a few short and moderate small hills. Hiking boots, trekking poles and insect repellent are often good accessories even for this location.

KH-3 – High Rock – South Berwick, ME

KH-1: N43° 15' 41.60" W70° 40' 44.20" (Low Split Rock) *WOW-4*
Small and low split rock in (3) directions, not very significant.

KH-2: N43° 15' 36.79" W70° 40' 47.05" (Tri-Split Rock) *WOW-8*
Split and cleaved into thirds, photo is taken from atop of one segment.

KH-3: N43° 15' 36.50" W70° 40' 47.70" (High Rock) *WOW-7*
Large and tall mass of stone, 20-feet in height. Trail runs between KH-2 & KH-3

KH-4: N43° 15' 33.60" W70° 40' 58.40" (Rock Wall) *WOW-3*
Rocky out-cropping on the loop trail.

KH-5: N43° 15' 35.10" W70° 40' 59.00" (Rock Cobble) *WOW-5*
Large and massive out-cropping with embedded boulder,

KH-6: N43° 15' 37.30" W70° 40' 55.30" (Fractured Ledge) *WOW-6*
Tall and long cobble with extensive fractured and cracked stone work.

Directions: Heading north on Route-1and just past the center in Ogunquit, take a left onto Berwick Road. Head west on Berwick Road for 1.3 miles, you will cross over Interstate I-95, Ogunquit Road will start on the other side . Continue west 0.5 miles and at the next intersection continue right staying on Ogunquit Road. In 2.5 miles, the Kenyon Hill parking area will be on your left; if you see *Bennett Lot Road* sign you went too far, go back 100-yards for the parking area.

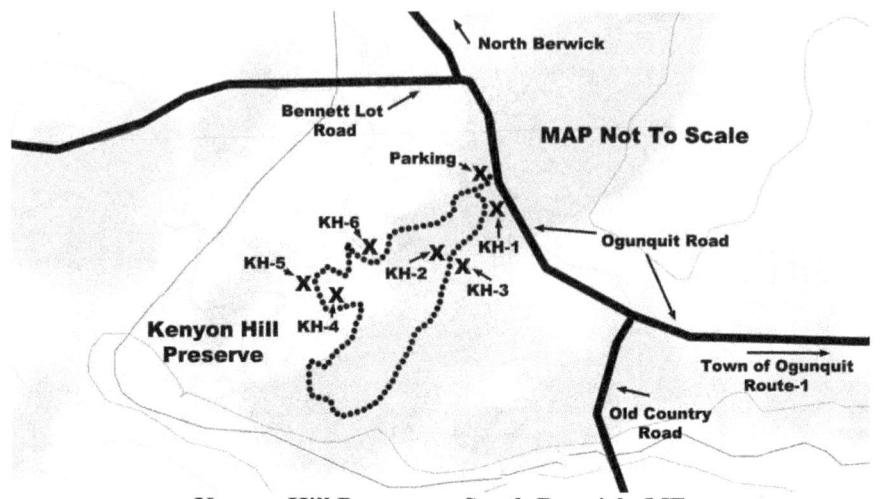

Kenyon Hill Preserve – South Berwick, ME

118. Piazza Rock

Piazza Rock – Sandy River Plantation, ME

Location: Sandy River Plantation (Franklin County)
Delorme Atlas & Gazetteer-Maine: map 19, A-1
Parking GPS: N44° 53' 31.60" W70° 32' 4.00" (Beech Hill Road)
Parking GPS: N44° 53' 12.54" W70° 32' 25.95" (AT-Trailhead Rt-4)
Spur Trail GPS: N44° 54' 15.60" W70° 31' 51.50" (Turn off AT Trail.)
Destination GPS: N44° 54' 17.30" W70° 31' 52.80" (Piazza Rock)
Wow Factor: 10 **Accessibility:** Moderate 3.5 mile round-trip to boulder.
Contact: Maine: Appalachian Trail Club P.O. Box 283 Augusta, ME 04332-0283   Email: info@matc.org or webmaster@matc.org

Information: Piazza Rock is astonishing and memorable for it juts horizontally some 60-feet from the mountain side resting solely upon a lower boulder at its base. I would be interested to learn why it has been titled "Piazza." Origin of this word is Greek and typically refers to a center of public activity, a covered marketplace or square. In New England, a *piazza* is defined more as a large covered porch or veranda. My knee-jerk-reaction upon viewing the rock, why isn't called Snake Head Rock, Lizard or Alien Head? Otherwise, its lateral extension out and beyond of any visual or additional supports is striking and phenomenal.

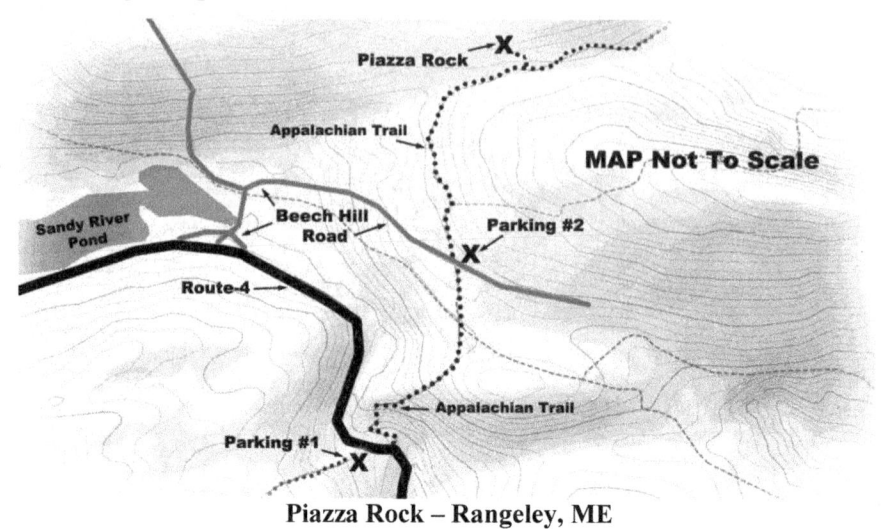

Piazza Rock – Rangeley, ME

Access to this isolated location is relatively easy. Hiking north on the Appalachian Trail from the Route-4, Appalachian Trail parking area #1, the Piazza Rock is 1.7 miles away. From the Beech Hill Road paring area #2, Piazza Rock is only 1.2 miles and a moderate trek until the spur trail which is short and steep for 0.1 mile ending at Piazza Rock.

Directions: From Rangeley center, follow Route-4 south for 9.5 miles. The Appalachian Trail parking area #1 will be on your right. Caution when crossing Route-4 as you cross over to head north on the AT Trail.

Parking #2: Head south of Route-4 for 8.5 miles, Beech Hill Road is an unofficial parking area located just past where the AT trail crosses. No signs or posting were noted here. Beech Hill Road is not paved, could be muddy or unplowed preventing access during various seasonal changes. Not recommended as an overnight parking location due to security concerns.

119. Pockwockamus Rock

Pockwockamus Rock – Baxter State Park South Entry, ME

Location: Baxter State Park Southern Entry (Piscataquis County)
Delorme Atlas & Gazetteer-Maine: map 51, E-1
Parking GPS: N45° 47' 55.80" W68° 53' 39.60"
Destination GPS: N45° 47' 55.80" W68° 53' 39.60"
Wow Factor: 8 Accessibility: Easy-Road Side

Information: Headed toward Baxter State Park through its southern entry, the often photographed Pockwockamus Rock (A.K.A Baxter Entry Boulder) has become an established iconic painted rock created and maintained by Abbott and Nancy Meader.) First painted in 1979, the rock has received restoration in 1990, 1998, and 2007, this year 2017 was to be their last. With pride, the couple has enjoyed their volunteer work, but wants to retire. *"The painting of the boulder in the Maine's wilderness can be taxing. I found out what Pockwockamus means, It's Penobscot Indian, of course, and it stands for all the mosquitoes in the world"* said Abbott Meader.

Directions: In Medway, from Interstate I-95 use Exit-244 and travel west on Route-157, in 0.7 mile, Route-11 joins, together follow both Routes for 10 miles into downtown Millinocket: here Route-11 will turn left; you will turn right, heading north for 8.3 miles towards Spencer's Cove. Continue north on Katardin Avenue, as it becomes Bates Street, then Millinocket Road until Spencer's Cove. Follow towards Baxter State Park Road from Spencer's Cove for 6.0 miles.

120. Snapper Rock - Sanders Hill

Snapper Rock – Rome, ME

Location: Rome (Kennebec County)
Delorme Atlas & Gazetteer-Maine: map 20, E-3
Parking GPS: N44° 33' 58.70" W69° 55' 18.60"
Destination GPS: N44° 33' 42.90" W69° 55' 46.70"
Wow Factor: 6 **Accessibility:** Easy 1.4 mile round trip to boulder.
Contact: Belgrade Regional Conservation Alliance
137 Main Street. PO Box 250 Belgrade Lakes, ME 04918 (207) 495-6039
e-mail: brca@belgradelakes.org   www. belgradelakes.org

Information: Marked with blue blazes, the Sanders Hill Trail is approximately 2.9 miles in total length. For our destination of *Snapper Rock* follow the old road trail from behind the parking lot kiosk for 0.2 miles. The Sanders Hill loop Trail will turn left becoming more of a path, while the old road will continue straight.
Depending upon your desire or time you can reach Snapper Rock within a 0.5 mile by either route. By turning left, you can't miss finding *Snapper Rock* by staying with the blue blazes. Eventually after hiking the twists and turn of this forested approach, the trail will cross the old road again; Snapper Rock is located at this junction. The rock is unique with a definite snout appearance of a snapping turtle head uplifted. You can return to the parking area from here by, returning on the trail you came in on, follow the unmarked and over grown road back or continue following the loop trail over Sanders Hill until it returns back to the parking area.

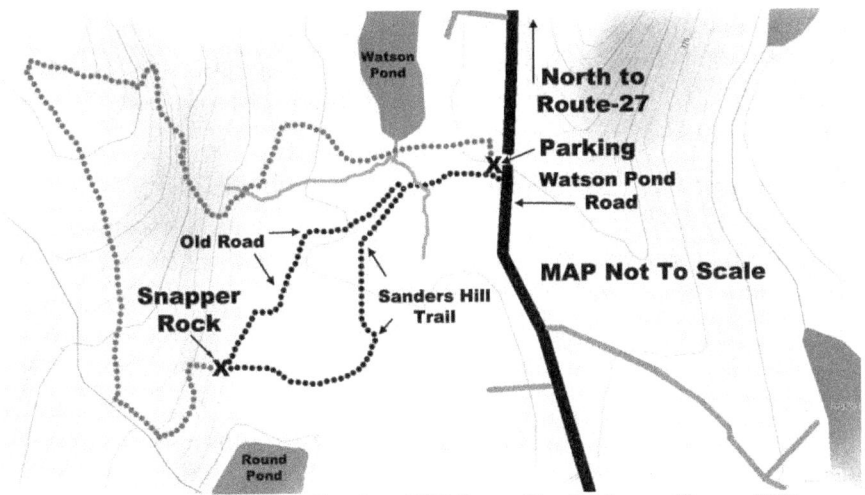

Snapper Rock on the Sanders Hill Loop Trail Map. – Rome, ME

Directions: A small parking area for a dozen cars is located on the west side of Watson Pond Road, 1.3 miles south of Watson Pond Road's junction with Route-27.

121. The Beehive - Acadia National Park

The Bee Hive – Acadia National Park - Bar Harbor, ME

Location: Bar Harbor (Hancock County)
Delorme Atlas & Gazetteer-Maine: map 16, B-4
Parking GPS: N44° 19' 49.30" W68° 11' 3.90" (Sand Beach)
Trail Head GPS: N44° 19' 53.44" W68° 11' 6.90" (Park Loop Road)
Trail Junction: N44° 19' 53.90" W68° 11' 15.46" (Ascent Trail)
Destination GPS: N44° 20' 1.50" W68° 11' 16.91" (Summit)
Wow Factor: 9 Accessibility: Prepared trail-moderate to strenuous.

Contact: Fees, maps, passes and other pertinent information, visit the National Park Service web site: www.nps.gov/acad/index.htm or Acadia National Park, 25 Visitor Center Rd, P.O. Box 177, Bar Harbor, ME 04609 **Phone:** (207) 288-3338

Information: On the east side of Mt Desert Island, *The Beehive* with an elevation of 525-feet over-looks Sand Beach. Standing from a distance this steep and rocky crag can be intimidating with visions of a fearsome or daunting ascent. Fortunately, this rocky outcrop provides you with two options to reach its summit. First, is to follow the Bowl Trail westward, circle behind and access the summit from the backside. This way is a more moderate approach and still allows stunning views of Sand Beach and the surrounding seascape. In addition, this rear approach is possibly a better choice for families with young children or themselves not as agile or well-balanced.

The hike up the Beehive Trail (a.k.a. the Beehive Cliff Trail) is a novel, exhilarating and probably will become your most memorable experience in Acadia. While it is a moderate to strenuous climb, the people who blazed this trail utilized the natural ledges, ingeniously embedded iron-rod hand-railings, and ladders to assist you during your ascent. There will be a few areas of exposed rock where you can easily scamper over. You need no special training or equipment to scale the rock. This frontal ascent is not recommended if: you have a fear of heights, young children, stormy, wet, windy or icy conditions. In addition, proper footwear is encouraged with sandals or flip-flops left on the beach. Dogs are also prohibited. As in the first approach, you start at the trailhead of the Bowl Trail off the park loop road and head west. You will quickly come upon the Beehive Trail junction where you will turn right and in a short distance you will begin your ascent up the upright granite escarpment following the blue blaze trail. Do not falter, many find once they continue to move up their fears subside and begin to savor the views or experience. In reality, the trail zigzag's up for about 0.2 mile to where you will have conquered the Beehive! On a summer weekend or vacation, this can be a busy, very busy trail, so busy the first access option might be a better suggestion if time constraints are a consideration. Probably the most difficult aspect of this hike could be finding parking in this area of Sand Beach. It is also not recommended to return down this sort of one-way trail either. It is best to continue north, over the summit, returning on the Bowl Trail. Lastly, remember to carry some water to hydrate yourself or others for you will be in the sun bearing down upon you.

There are 10 climbers in this small telephoto segment of the Beehive.

The Beehive as seen from Sand Beach. - Acadia National Park, ME

FYI: Just north of the Beehive on Champlain Mountain, is The *Precipice Trail* another cliff trail with rungs and ladders, This trail is higher, longer, steeper and more strenuous. It is often closed due to nesting Peregrine Falcons and maintenance.

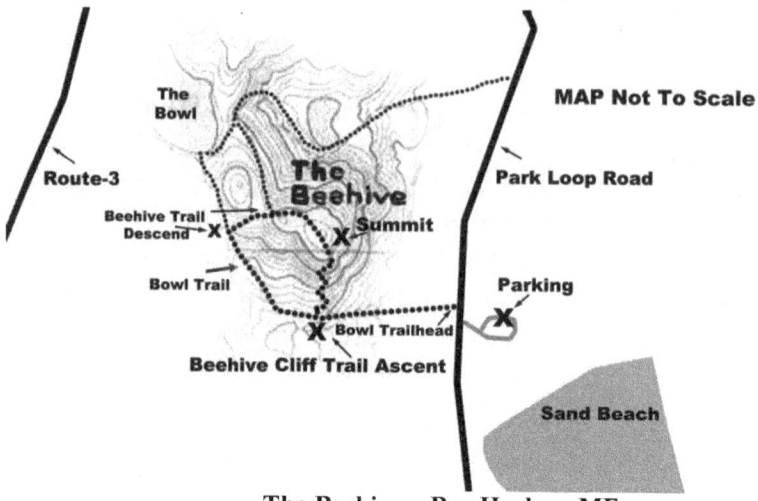

The Beehive – Bar Harbor, ME

Directions: Starting from Route-3, turn off at the Hulls Cove Entry into the Acadia National Park requires you to pay a fee (From May to October) you can have a senior or annual pass to enter the park to access to the Park Loop Road. Follow the Park Loop road 3.0 miles before turning left onto the one-way section towards Sand Beach. Sand Beach is very popular and parking is often difficult to find. The Bowl Trail begins on the right just before Sand Beach.

The Beehive looms over *Sand Beach*. – Bar Harbor, ME

122. The Pebble:

The Pebble – Harpswell, ME

Location: Harpswell (Sagadahoc County)
Delorme Atlas & Gazetteer-Maine: map 6, D-2
Parking GPS: N43° 45' 41.82" W70° 0' 49.67"
Destination GPS: N43° 45' 38.4" W70° 00' 54.6"
Wow Factor: 6 **Accessibility:** Easy, short walk 0.2 mile, on marked trail.
Contact: Harpswell Heritage Land Trust P.O. Box 359 Harpswell, ME 04079 www.hhltmaine.org outreach@hhltmaine.org (207) 721-1121

Information: Cutis Farm Preserve is located within the Harpswell Heritage Trust. Highlights of this preserve is the public access to 2,000 feet of shoreline from two different seaside coves, its glacial erratic *The Pebble* and 1.25 miles of hiking trails through woodland habitats. .

Directions: In Topsham, Exit-24 from Interstate I-295, take Route-196 heading southeast 2.5 miles, until you meet the interchange of Route-1 in Brunswick just on the other side of the Androscoggin River. For *the Pebble;* Follow Route-1 south towards Brunswick center for 0.5 mile, turning left onto Route-24 (Maine Street) for 0.6 mile, veering left staying on Route-4, then in 0.2 mile veer right onto Route-123 (Sills Drive turns into Harpswell Road.) Continue to

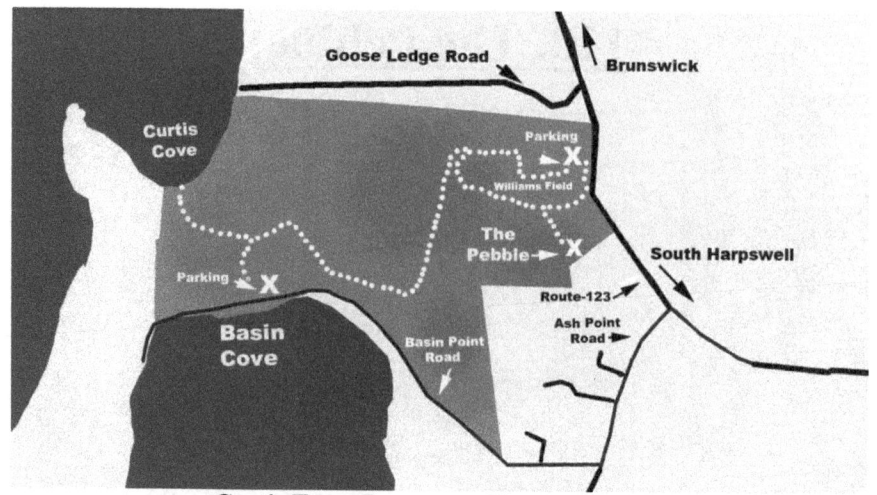

Curtis Farm Preserve – Harpswell, ME

follow Route-123 down for 7.5 miles until reaching the Curtis Farms Preserve on your right in Harpswell. There is parking in this grassy parking area for roughly 12 to 18 vehicles. From the roadside end of the parking area, follow the mowed and worn trail that skirts the perimeter of the Williams field southerly for 0.1 mile. Take the first left which is a side trail only to *The Pebble* within 100 yards.

To reach another parking area closer to the shoreline, continue on Route-123 south 0.2 mile and turn right onto Ash Point Road; take your third right onto Basin Point Road and drive 0.5 mile to the parking lot on the right, which is across from Basin Cove shoreline.

123. Wally Rock:

Wally Rock – Phippsburg, ME

Location: Phippsburg (Sagadahoc County)
Delorme Atlas & Gazetteer-Maine: map 6, D-4
Parking GPS: N43° 49' 27.3" W69° 50' 51.3"
Destination GPS: N43° 49' 27.3" W69° 50' 51.3"
Wow Factor: 6 Accessibility: Roadside

Information: Officially titled *"Wally the Frog Wizard"* (painted on backside of rock) and also referred to as *"Wally."* This 8 foot tall roadside boulder while whimsical really has insignificant features geologically speaking. Other than the painted title in the rear and a painted red line suggesting a tongue splatting a fly, the rock in reality does not resemble a frog. Obviously, someone in the town loves this rock for it has fresh paint and visitors paste the image on the web. Other than that I have not found much information on who, when or how long Wally has been around.

Directions: In Topsham, Exit-24 from Interstate I-295, take Route-196 heading southeast 2.5 miles, until you meet the interchange of Route-1 in Brunswick just on the other side of the Androscoggin River. To Wally Rock, follow Route-1 north along the river towards Bath for 7.7 miles, exit at the junction of Route-209 (High Street.) Follow Route-209 south towards Phippsburg for 2.4 miles, High Street will veer right, you'll stay on Route-209 Street which is now

Main Road. Continuing south on Rt-209 for 3.4 miles until you reach Stony Brook Road on your right. Follow Stony Brook Road west for 1.7 miles which will terminate at Meadowbrook Road. Turn left heading south 0.6 miles where Wally Rock waits on the roadside.

Acknowledgements

This book *Erratic Wandering an Explorer's Guide* would not be in existence if not for the assistance and help from acquaintances from hikers, volunteers, climbers and boulderer's, Town Clerks, National and State Parks personnel etc. Many thanks to all who assisted and never hindered my progress! Good Karma to all!

Special thanks to: Bonnie & Timothy Day. Gilsum, NH for their permission to include *Vessel Rock*. To Paul F. Welch, Goffstown, NH for access and allowing us to include *Tippin Rocks* on Shirley Hill. To the family of the late George Fillian and Bea Hobbs (his daughter), we are grateful for allowing us to include *Revolutionary Rock* in Richmond, NH. To the *Chris Miller Studio* for his awesome *Permanent Stone Pick-up Truck*. Calais, VT. The William Thayer Family for allowing usage of the *Balance Rock of Jamaica* photographed by *Porter Charlie Thayer 1882-1972* Jamaica, VT.

On the way to Glen Ellis Boulder. – Pinkham Notch, NH

About the Author.

Christy Butler is a visual artist with an Associate Degree in Liberal Studies-Majoring in Design, and a Bachelor of Arts in Business Administration majoring in Marketing and Management. Other related studies include Mass Communications, Filmmaking and Photography. After being published in variety of Literary and Specialty Magazines, along with other Audio-Visual endeavors, Butler a Vietnam Veteran, created and directed a grant-funded and web-based archive of veteran's personal photos from their military experiences: **www.shoeboxphotos.net**. This was followed by a series of New England State Waterfall posters created with Jan Butler: **www.berkshirephotos.com**. Collaborations with author Russell Dunn, began with the publication of *Berkshire Region Waterfall* Guide and later *Connecticut Waterfalls*: A Guide. *Rockachusetts* is their latest collaboration: **www.rockachusetts.com**

Christy Butler taken by Francis I. Butler at Thompson Boulders, NH.